CHILTON'S

Motorcycle Troubleshooting Guide ILLUSTRATED

STATE BOARD FOR TECHNICAL AND COMPREHENSIVE EDUCATION

Prepared by the

Automotive Editorial Department

Chilton Book Company
Chilton Way
Radnor, Pa. 19089
215—687-8200

managing editor **JOHN D. KELLY;** assistant managing editor **PETER J. MEYER;** senior editor, motorcycles **MICHAEL S. YAMPOLSKY;** editors **JAMES H. JOHNSON, JOSEPH F. PELLICCIOTI**

Member

Motorcycle Industry Council

CHILTON BOOK COMPANY   RADNOR, PENNSYLVANIA

Library of Congress Cataloging in Publication Data

Chilton Book Company.   Automotive Editorial Dept.
   Chilton's new motorcycle troubleshooting guide.

   1. Motorcycles—Maintenance and repair.
I. Title.   II. Title: New motorcycle troubleshooting guide.
TL440.C457   629.28'7'75   73-5753
ISBN 0-8019-5819-9
ISBN 0-8019-6081-9 (paper)

ACKNOWLEDGMENTS

AMERICAN HONDA MOTOR COMPANY, INC.

Gardena, California

BAYERISCHE MOTOREN WERKE AG

Munich, Germany

BERLINER MOTOR CORP.

Hasbrouck Heights, New Jersey

BSA MOTORCYCLE CORP.

Baltimore, Maryland

BUTLER AND SMITH INC.

Norwood, New Jersey

HARLEY-DAVIDSON MOTOR COMPANY, INC.

Milwaukee, Wisconsin

KAWASAKI MOTORS CORP.

Santa Ana, California

THE TRIUMPH CORP.

Baltimore, Maryland

U.S. SUZUKI CORP.

Santa Fe Springs, California

YAMAHA INTERNATIONAL CORP.

Buena Park, California

YAMAHA OF BRYN MAWR

Bryn Mawr, Pennsylvania

Although information in this guide is based on industry sources
and is as complete as possible at the time of publication, the
possibility exists that manufacturers made later changes which
could not be included here. While striving for total accuracy,
Chilton Book Company can not assume responsibility for any
errors, changes, or omissions that may occur in the compilation
of this data.

Contents

Chapter 1   Introduction to Troubleshooting 1

Approach to Troubleshooting, 1
Necessary Tools, 4
Operational Descriptions, 6
Piston Port Two-Stroke Engines, 6

Rotary-Valve Two-Stroke Engines, 8
Pushrod Four-Stroke Engines, 8
Overhead Cam Four-Stroke Engines, 8

Chapter 2   Two-Stroke Engine Troubleshooting 12

Starting the Engine, 12
Engine Does Not Start, 13
Checking the Electrical System, 13
Checking the Fuel System, 13
Compression Check, 15
Poor Engine Performance, 16
Hard Starting or Erratic Performance, 16
Engine Dies When Throttle is Opened, 17
Low Speed Misfiring, 18
RPM Related Misfire, 18
Throttle Opening Related Misfire, 18
Inconsistent Misfire on Acceleration, 18
Engine Misfires Under Load, 18
High Speed Misfiring, 19
Poor Low Speed Performance, 19

Poor Mid-Range or High Speed Performance, 20
Poor General Performance, 20
Engine Overheating and Seizure, 20
Engine Vibration, 21
Engine Noises, 21
Tune-Up, 22
Contact Breaker Points and Ignition Timing, 22
Spark Plugs, 24
Carburetor Adjustment, 25
Tune-Up Analysis, 26
Between Tune-Up Checks, 27
Oil Injection Systems, 27
Operational Description, 27
Oil Pump Troubleshooting, 31
Engine Troubleshooting, 34

Chapter 3   Four-Stroke Troubleshooting 37

Starting the Engine, 37
Engine Does Not Start, 38
Checking the Electrical System, 39
Checking the Fuel System, 44
Checking the Mechanical System, 46
Poor Engine Performance, 46
Hard Starting or Erratic Performance, 46
Engine Dies When Throttle is Opened, 49
Engine Misfires, 50
Poor General Performance, 52
Engine Vibration, 52

Excessive Oil Consumption, 52
Engine Overheating and Seizure, 54
Engine Noises, 56
Tune-Up, 57
Cam Chain Adjustment, 57
Valve Tappet Adjustment, 57
Spark Plug Service and Tune-Up Analysis, 58
Contact Breaker Point Service, 60
Ignition Timing, 60
Carburetor Adjustment, 61
Engine Troubleshooting, 61
Carburetor Troubleshooting, 65

Chapter 4   Fuel System Troubleshooting. 68

Description and Operation, 68
Direct-Control Type Carburetion, 68
Constant Velocity Carburetor, 70
Carburetor Troubleshooting, 76
Indications of a Rich Mixture, 76
Indications of a Lean Mixture, 76
Excessive Fuel Consumption, 76
Backfiring Through the Intake Manifold, 76

Backfiring Through the Exhaust System, 76
Carburetor Flooding, 76
Fuel Feed, 77
Cable Controls, 77
Effect of Altitude on Carburetion, 77
Carburetor Tuning, 77
Air Filters, 77

Chapter 5   Electrical System Troubleshooting 78

Operational Descriptions, 78
Magneto Generator, 78
DC Generator, 78
Starter Generator, 78
Alternator, 80
Capacitor Discharge Ignition (CDI), 84
Constant Loss Ignition, 84
Troubleshooting the Charging System, 85

Troubleshooting the Ignition System, 91
Troubleshooting the Starting System, 92
Component Testing, 93
Japanese Machines, 93
British Machines, 94
Coils, 96
Battery, 97

Chapter 6   Clutch and Transmission Troubleshooting 100

Automatic Centrifugal Clutch, 100
Manual Clutch, 101
Constant Mesh Transmissions, 102
Shifter Mechanism, 104
Kickstarters, 107
Troubleshooting the Clutch, 109
Clutch Drags, 110
Clutch Slips, 112
Clutch Chatters, 113

Troubleshooting the Gearbox, 114
Gears Grind When Shifting, 115
Shifter Pops Out of Gear, 116
Shifter Does Not Return, 118
Kickstarter Jams, 119
Kickstarter Slips, 120
Clutch and Transmission Troubleshooting, 121

Chapter 7   Chassis Troubleshooting 124

Operational Descriptions, 124
Front Forks, 124
Steering Damper, 130
Rear Swing Arm, 131
Rear Shock Absorbers, 132
Drum Brakes, 135
Disc Brakes, 137
Final Drive, 138
Troubleshooting the Front Forks, 138
Leaking Fork Seals, 138
Excessive Vibration, 140
Poor Damping Action, 141
Poor Rebound Action, 141
Excessive Steering Head Play, 141

Heavy of Stiff Steering, 142
Troubleshooting the Shock Absorbers, 142
Troubleshooting the Swing Arm and Frame, 143
Troubleshooting the Final Drive, 146
Chain Drive, 146
Shaft Drive, 147
Sprockets, 148
Troubleshooting the Brakes, 148
Drum Brakes, 148
Disc Brakes, 150
Troubleshooting the Wheels, 153
Chassis Troubleshooting, 155

Appendix 161

Metric Conversion Charts, 161

Degree Wheel for Valve Timing, 166

1 · Introduction to Troubleshooting

Have you ever optimistically donned helmet, jacket, and gloves, wheeled out the old beastie, and then kicked away at it for half an hour until reduced to a quivering, sweating mass of flesh? And what did you do next? Tear blindly away at it in hopes of stumbling on a solution, or maybe call the shop and watch forlornly as they load your disabled steed into a van. Take heart America, Chilton's *Motorcycle Troubleshooting Guide* is here to save the day.

There are certain steps which, if followed, can transform the task of troubleshooting into an exact science. Random efforts often prove confusing, so a logical method should be adopted. Consider the whole as being made up of three component systems, each of which must be thoroughly checked out until the malfunction has been located and eliminated. The first system to approach, and the one which is most often at fault, unless of course your motor has expired with a metal rending bang, is the electrical system. There are so many subtle things which can go wrong here, and which sooner or later probably will go wrong, that a very systematic approach must be adopted. The next most common area of trouble is the fuel system. A partially blocked fuel line, for instance, can cause some misleading symptoms. Third is the mechanical system, and failures of this sort will probably require a little help from your friends in getting the bike home or to a shop.

What it all amounts to is that you need spark to the plugs, fuel to the combustion chamber, and the compression necessary to cause the fuel to explode. If any one of these factors is missing the machine won't run; or at least it won't run properly. Your job is to determine what's missing and why, and then correct it. In most cases you'll soon be back on the road if you remain composed and work logically. It is essential that you record, mentally at least, the results obtained from each experiment, otherwise you run the risk of merely adding to the confusion instead of alleviating it, or possibly even interfering with the proper operation of a system which was functioning normally. Restore things to their original condition if what you tried failed, unless of course you know for sure that whatever you are working with is badly out of kilter. Each test performed provides certain data, so all you have to do is work to reduce the number of possible variables until the problem presents itself. Isolate the problem within its system and the struggle is half over.

Approach to Troubleshooting

Before you start, try to determine if this is a new problem, one that's been there since you've had the bike, or one that's

1

been coming on gradually. If you are an aware rider you will know whether or not performance has been diminishing, and consulting the appropriate section may provide an immediate answer. Intermittent malfunctions are usually related to the electrical system and can be difficult to track down. Sudden losses of power, unless accompanied by a big bang, are usually due to a problem with the primary ignition circuit, and gradual losses of power are usually traceable to a mechanical problem (except where maintenance has been neglected). Keep in mind that no one is infallible, yourself included, so whenever the bike starts acting up after it has been worked on, look first to those areas that were involved regardless of the nature of the work.

Let's say that your engine won't start one morning, but it was fine the night before. The most obvious thing to check first, but one which is often overlooked, is the fuel supply. Even if there is gas in the tank, a low supply can sometimes make starting difficult. Check to see if you have fuel at the carburetor by unscrewing the float bowl plug (if applicable), or by removing the float bowl. If there is no fuel you've already isolated the problem, or at least one problem, and you can begin to work on that.

There are only a few conditions that will cause a sudden loss of compression, and they will normally only occur when the engine is running. You should be able to tell if you have sufficient compression simply by the way the engine sounds and feels as it cranks over, or if you have the spark plug out, by covering the plug hole with your finger and kicking the engine through. If the pressure forces your finger off the hole, there should be enough compression for the engine to start. (Of course, the most accurate way to check compression is by using a compression gauge.)

Running a compression check

The final area, and the one which is most likely to cause you to pull your hair out, is the electrical system. The first thing to do is check to see if you are getting spark to the cylinders by removing the plug lead and inserting a metal object such as a nail into it. Then, *using a piece of rubber for insulation*, hold the nail about 1/8 in. away from the engine and

Checking for fuel at the float bowl

Checking for spark at the plug lead

crank it over with the ignition on. If you have a fat healthy spark at the plug lead, remove and check the spark plug for a fouled condition. A plug may look good but it can still be defective (and may even come from the factory with hidden defects) so it's a good idea to check things out with a new plug. Ground the plug, in its connector, against the cylinder and crank over the engine while watching the plug tip for a spark. If there is no juice at

Making sure the plug is good

the plug lead, trace the ignition system back with a test light. Start by checking for electricity at the points while they are open. If you have juice there the problem lies in the coil, spark plug wires, or in the wires between the coil and points. If you

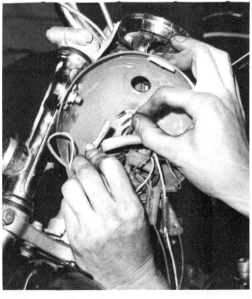

Make sure the snap connectors are clean and tight

find that there is no supply of electricity to the coil, look for loose connectors in the wiring between the coil and the ignition switch. Speaking of connectors—whenever you have a problem these should be given close scrutiny as the little devils have a habit of vibrating and pulling loose for no particular reason, causing far more trouble and aggravation than any other part of the electrical system.

All of this can be considered troubleshooting the engine to get it running, not troubleshooting to cure running faults. Once you have found the general location of the trouble it is usually quite simple to make pinpoint checks or temporarily substitute new or improvised parts to determine exactly where the problem lies. The most important thing to remember is to try to remain rational and approach the troubleshooting procedures logically. If you do this, chances are that you'll find the source of unpleasantness and save yourself time, money, aggravation, and embarrassment (when the mechanic tells you that you pushed the bike four miles and paid him five dollars to replace a fuse).

Troubleshooting an engine that is running poorly is often a bit trickier than trying to determine why an engine won't start. You will still be involved with the compression, fuel system, and electrical system of your engine but the problems will be more subtle and harder to detect. It pays here, if you are making adjustments or are fine tuning, to make one adjustment at a time, thoroughly check the results, and record the findings. Otherwise you will confuse yourself, ruin the results of one adjustment with another, and accomplish nothing.

When trying to diagnose a running fault, remember to check all the parts related to the component you are examining. For example, if you are carefully inspecting a carburetor, don't forget to check the intake tube clamps, the air filter, and the fuel filter to make sure that the carburetor is not being sabotaged in one way or another by those components (too much air, or too little air and fuel). If you are checking for sufficient spark, don't forget to make sure that the plug connector is tightly attached to the wire and that the insulation is not worn or cracked, etc. Look for the little things, and do it systematically and thoroughly. In many cases a qualified mechanic may be able to help you with a specific problem without even having to look at the bike. He's seen it all before, so don't hesitate to ask. The worst it can get you is a service appointment for next week.

Necessary Tools

There are certain special tools which are necessary to do a thorough job, and without these little gems solutions will probably be a long time coming. It isn't necessary to purchase all of them since your dealer and most gas stations will have them, but none are so expensive that the cost of owning your own would be prohibitive. First, you must have a complete set of hand tools that fit your bike. If you use standard American tools on a Japanese bike you will round off the nuts and bolts. This might be necessary in a tight spot but the next time you have to work with them you will have a lot of trouble. One special hand tool that is invaluable for working on Japanese machines is an impact driver. Properly used, this tool can mean salvation for torqued on screws.

A test light is another tool which you must have if you are going to work effectively with the electrical system. Finding a short in a wiring harness is a miserable job at best, but if you expect to go after it without a test light it will be all but impossible. Most lights work off of the machine's own power supply and are cheap to buy or easy to make. All these consist of are a bulb and two leads. You can make one by soldering one lead to the bulb's base contact and another to the side of the metal casing. Attach an alligator clip to the end of each lead and you have a first rate test light. Make sure you use a bulb with the same power rating as the machine's electrical system; a tail light bulb is just perfect for this purpose. One drawback with a tester like this is that if the battery is dead or if the machine isn't equipped with one, the light will be of no use to you, so the best type of light is one with a self-contained power source. These, though slightly more expensive, are well worth it. Of course, you can easily make your own by wiring a regular 1½ volt battery in se-

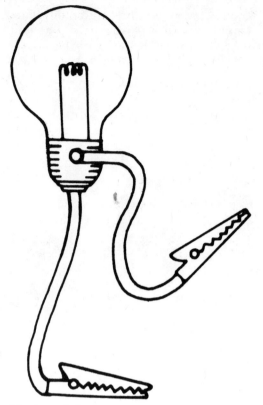

A basic test light

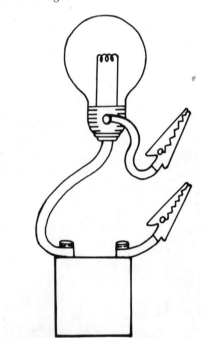

A test light with a self-contained power source

ries with your bulb. Make sure when using this type of test light that you keep the machine's own power turned off or you will blow your tester bulb.

Some other tools and gauges which you may want, such as compression, vacuum, and oil pressure gauges, and feeler gauges, dial indicators, and a torque wrench, can

A vacuum gauge

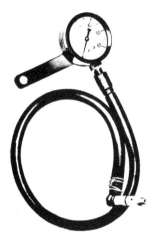

An oil pressure gauge

Using a dial indicator to check a fork leg for bending

serve dual purposes. A compression gauge is almost a necessity for keeping track of what's happening behind those cylinder walls. If you check your compression every second tune-up, you'll know when the rings or valves need attention, or when carbon has built up to a dangerous level. If you have a vacuum gauge you will be able to determine if your carburetor is

sucking air through a manifold leak or if the crankcase on your two-stroke is leaking compression and robbing the machine of power, and you will be able to balance

Checking for leakage of the inlet needle

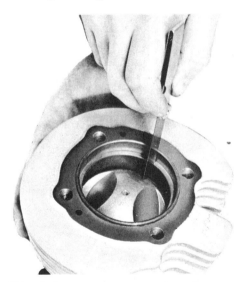

Using feeler gauges to measure piston ring gap

the manifold vacuum on multicylinder bikes. A dial indicator is very useful but rates somewhat lower on the priority list of tools specifically for troubleshooting. But for locating piston position or for measuring runout or endplay when rebuilding an engine, it can't be beat. The feeler gauge is one tool which no bike owner should be without. Of course, you can always use a folded matchbook cover to set breaker point and spark plug gap if necessary, but just wait until those valves speak up and demand adjustment.

Operational Descriptions

PISTON PORT TWO-STROKE ENGINES

Before you try to determine what's wrong with your engine you should know how it works when everything is right. The simplest type is the piston port two-stroke single which only has three main moving parts. The ports are located in the cylinder wall and are opened and closed by the piston's movement. Their functions are:

Intake port—admits fresh fuel mixture from the carburetor into the crankcase.

Transfer ports—provide passages for the mixture between the crankcase and combustion chamber. These are also known as scavenging ports.

Exhaust port—releases burned gases from the combustion chamber into the exhaust pipe.

Basically, this is what happens during a 360° rotation of the crankshaft, beginning with the piston at top dead center (TDC):

Downstroke—the piston descends from the previous cycle and exposes the exhaust port, letting out the expanding burned

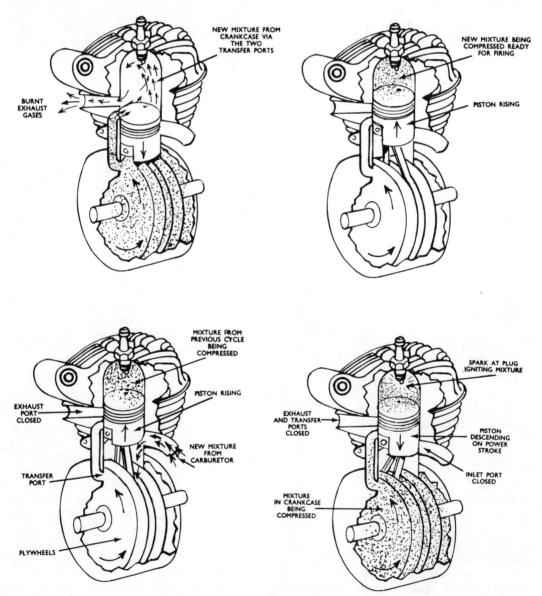

Two-cycle engine operation.

gases. Simultaneously, the piston's downward movement compresses the fuel mixture from the previous cycle in the airtight crankcase.

As the piston continues to descend, it also exposes the transfer ports. The compressed mixture waiting in the crankcase now rushes through the ports and fills the combustion chamber, while at the same time sweeping any remaining burned gases out the exhaust port.

Upstroke—after reaching its lowest point of travel, the piston begins to ascend and closes off the transfer ports. At the same time, the piston's upward movement creates a partial vacuum in the crankcase.

As the piston continues to ascend, it closes off the exhaust port and begins to compress the mixture in the combustion chamber. Meanwhile, the bottom of the piston exposes the intake port and a fresh fuel mixture is sucked into the crankcase. When the piston approaches top dead center, ignition occurs and the piston once again descends to begin another cycle.

As described, ignition occurs once every 360° or, more appropriately, once every two strokes of the piston (one down and one up). Hence, the term two-stroke engine.

A recent improvement in piston port design is the five-port cylinder, and the main difference between it and the conventional type lies in the five-port cylinder's more efficient exhaust sweep.

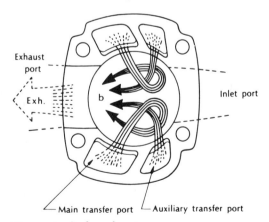

Five-port cylinder exhaust sweep

The earlier Schnuerle loop scavenging system has two transfer ports that aim streams of fresh mixture toward the back of the cylinder; this sweeps out most of the remaining exhaust gases, but leaves one

area untouched in the middle of the combustion chamber. The five-port system, on the other hand, has two additional auxiliary transfer ports. These extra ports direct a small charge of fresh mixture right at the dead spot and force it out the exhaust port. This complete exhaust sweep creates more space for the incoming mixture, and,

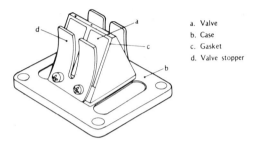

a. Valve
b. Case
c. Gasket
d. Valve stopper

Three-port cylinder exhaust sweep reed valve assembly

as a result, the engine has more low and mid-range power, runs cooler, and consumes less fuel.

The newest development in two-stroke engineering is the seven-port cylinder used in conjunction with a reed valve. The valve consists of a die-cast aluminum block with flexible stainless steel reeds that open and close the intake port. The reeds

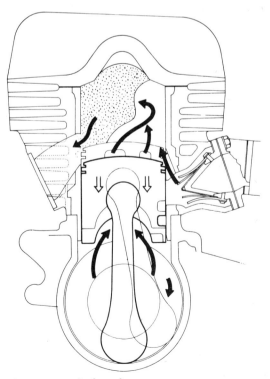

Seven-port cylinder exhaust sweep

are actuated by crankcase vacuum and, therefore, admit only the necessary amount of fuel. When combined with the improved scavenging ability of the seven-port cylinder, the valve helps reduce fuel consumption, increase low-end pulling power, and flatten out the horsepower and torque curves.

ROTARY-VALVE TWO-STROKE ENGINES

The rotary-valve two-stroke operates on the same basic principles as the piston-port type, but is constructed differently and offers some distinct advantages.

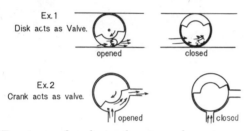

Two means of employing the rotary valve system

The valve itself is a resin hardened fiber disc with a cutaway section along its circumference. The disc is mounted directly to the end of the crankshaft and is enclosed within a narrow sealed chamber located between the crankcase and the carburetor. As the valve rotates, the cutaway section exposes the port and allows the fresh fuel mixture to be sucked into the crankcase. Then, when the cutaway section ends, the port is sealed by the disc and no more mixture can enter.

What is the advantage? In the piston port system the intake port is located in the cylinder wall along with the transfer and exhaust ports. Therefore, intake timing (when the port opens and closes) is dictated by the piston skirt and limited by the size and position of the other ports. In the rotary-valve type, on the other hand, the intake port is located in the side of the crankcase, and intake timing is determined by the position (on the disc) and duration of the valve cutaway.

This independence from piston control and cylinder design complications allows intake timing to be set, and easily adjusted, for optimum engine breathing. As a result, the engine has greater flexibility and delivers more power throughout a wider range.

PUSHROD FOUR-STROKE ENGINES

The four-stroke engine requires four complete strokes of the piston to complete one power cycle. During the intake stroke the intake valve opens and the fuel mixture is drawn into the cylinder as a result of the sudden vacuum created in the combustion chamber. As the piston moves toward the top of its travel on the compression stroke, both valves are closed and the fuel/air mixture is compressed. When the breaker points are opened by the action of the breaker cam, the spark plug fires and ignites the charge. The resulting combustion forces the piston down in the power stroke. As the piston moves down toward its lowest point of travel, the exhaust valve opens, and as the action of the flywheel sends the piston back up on the exhaust stroke, the remains of the previous charge are forced out past the exhaust valve. Just before the piston reaches the top of its travel, the intake valve opens and the exhaust flow induces the intake flow which continues while the exhaust valve closes. The process then repeats itself since each of the four cycles has been completed.

The basic valve train of four-stroke engines consists of camshaft driven pushrods which actuate rocker arms, which in turn operate the valves. Usually, the camshaft is gear driven directly by the crankshaft through gears which reduce the rate of rotation to ½ the engine speed.

OVERHEAD CAM FOUR-STROKE ENGINES

Many of today's high performance engines, notably Hondas and Ducatis, incorporate an overhead camshaft. Some models, such as the Honda 750, have rocker arms which are actuated by the camshaft, and some very exotic designs, such as the Kawasaki 900, have twin cams that operate the valves directly. These twin cam designs have the advantage of being able to operate the valves directly, without the need for rocker arms. Keeping down the noise of chain operation is a problem with some overhead cam designs but it has been effectively reduced by the use of automatic or manual cam chain tensioners. The chain rides on light rollers on both sides of the cam drive gear, and usually one of these rollers is spring

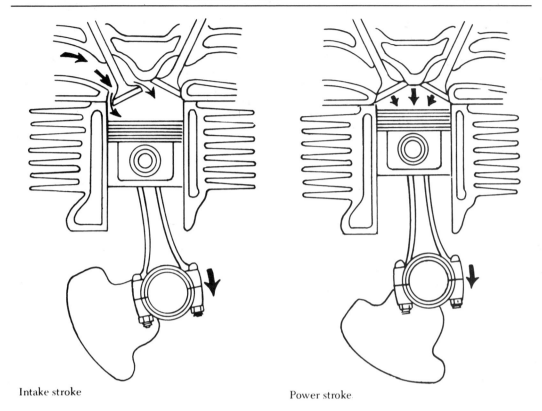

Intake stroke

Power stroke

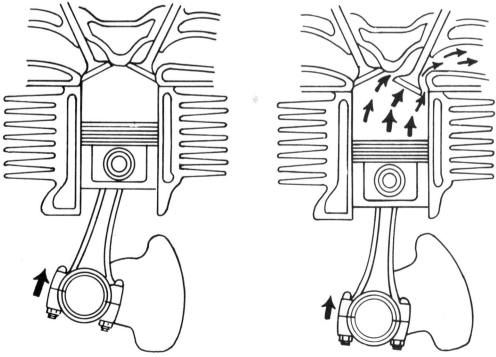

Exhaust stroke

Exhaust stroke

Four-cycle engine operation

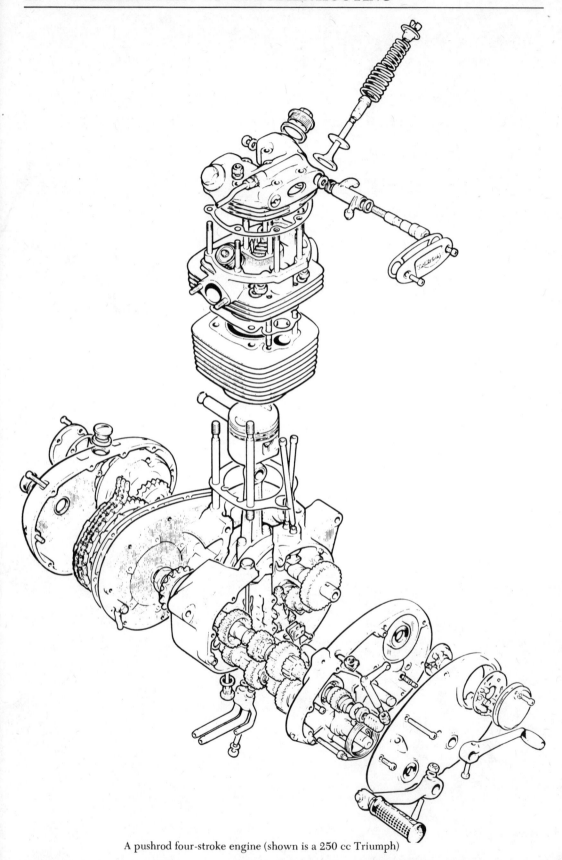

A pushrod four-stroke engine (shown is a 250 cc Triumph)

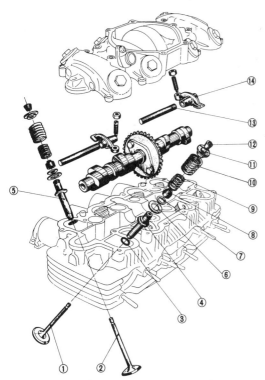

An overhead cam design (shown is a Honda 500)

1. Exhaust valve
2. Intake valve
3. O-ring
4. Exhaust valve guide
5. Intake valve guide
6. Valve spring seat (outer)
7. Valve spring seat (inner)
8. Valve seal
9. Inner valve spring
10. Outer valve spring
11. Retainer
12. Split collar
13. Rocker arm shaft
14. Rocker arm

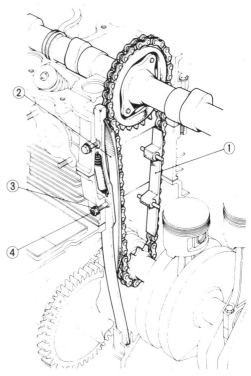

Cam chain tensioner design (shown is a Honda 500)

1. Cam chain guide
2. Cam chain tensioner
3. Lock nut
4. Adjusting screw

loaded to take up slack as the chain wears and stretches.

The advantage of an overhead cam design is that the reduced weight of the valve train allows the engine to turn higher rpm. In addition to this, overhead cam engines have much less valve floating problems than pushrod engines where the engine can begin to turn faster than the valves can operate. The only disadvantage of an overhead cam design is that it necessitates a tall engine which raises the center of balance and makes designing a handling frame more difficult.

2 · Two-Stroke Engine Troubleshooting

Starting the Engine

Normally, an engine will not decide, overnight and of its own accord, not to start the next morning. Unless a machine has been recently worked on or has been in storage for some time, a flat refusal to fire up will have usually been preceded by hard starting and a noticeable loss of performance. If this is the case, and you want to get the bike running without a hassle, run through the following starting procedure, regardless of the technique you normally use. Don't forget that your way has failed dismally this time.

Most modern two-strokes do not use a choke, as such, to aid cold weather starting. Instead, a mixture enrichening device is utilized, and it is very important, with a cold engine, to keep the throttle completely closed while operating the starter. Try starting your engine using this method:

1. Turn on the fuel tap. (You didn't forget, did you?)
2. Switch on the ignition and apply full "choke."
3. Kick the engine over briskly four or five times (or operate the electric starter for five full seconds.).

If your engine has not started and you have been at it for some time, take a minute to remove the spark plug(s). With the plugs out, kick the engine through a few times with the ignition off and the throttle closed to clear the combustion chambers. The plugs should then be dried and cleaned as thoroughly as possible and reinstalled. If the engine still will not start, walk to a distance not less than ten feet away from your machine, sit down, light a cigarette (or whatever you smoke), and relax.

If you are late for something or in a bad mood, pull the key out of the ignition and go away—at this point you are likely to do more harm than good. If, however, you are able to get hold of yourself, and if you have a few minutes to spare, read on. Pay particular attention to these simple points:

1. Chances are that there is nothing seriously wrong with your engine. It is most important that you remain calm and analytical in your approach.
2. Take care to perform all the operations described, and don't close your mind to problems that you may not want to see.
3. If necessary, mark down results as you go along. If nothing else, this may help you locate the problem next time you have trouble.

Engine Does Not Start

For an engine to start, three basic conditions must be met: there must be compression, there must be a reasonably correct fuel/air mixture, and there must be a good spark arriving at the right time at the spark plug. Any engine starting problem can be attributed to one of these three things.

If your engine has not been serviced for a while, don't waste a lot of time trying to figure out why it won't start. The wisest thing to do in this case is perform a complete tune-up. It just could be that all of your engine systems are slightly out of adjustment and are conspiring together to keep the engine from starting. If the engine has been properly serviced, check for improper adjustment or faulty operation of components in the systems.

First, it can be assumed that if your engine was running yesterday, it still has good compression today. Compression may gradually disappear over many miles of use, but, over a short period of time, it will rarely decrease enough to cause hard starting—unless accompanied by unusual noises and a dramatic decrease in performance. If it takes the normal amount of effort to kick the engine over using the kickstart lever, you can be reasonably sure that there is sufficient compression present for the engine to fire. If in doubt, remove the spark plugs and place your thumb over each plug hole, using enough force to seal it, while turning the engine over. If there is enough compression to break the seal, there is enough compression for the engine to start.

To check for positive fuel flow, simply remove the fuel line at the carburetor and observe the amount of fuel that issues from it. If anything more than a restricted dribble comes out, the carburetor is receiving enough fuel for the engine to start. It would be a good idea here to check the tightness of the carburetor intake tube clamps. If these are loose, an air leak might be creating a fuel mixture lean enough to be sabotaging all your efforts.

Once you are satisfied that fuel is present, it is time to move on to the ignition system. The most effective and reliable way to check the sparking system is to observe the spark at the spark plug. Remove the plug and replace it in its connector cap. Switch on the ignition and, while holding the base of the plug against the crankcase or cylinder, crank the engine over briskly. A fat, hot spark should be seen (and heard) across the plug electrodes. If the spark is weak, or there is no spark at all, elminate the plug and stick a nail or other metal object into the connector cap and rerun the test holding the nail about $1/4$ in. from the engine. If you have spark now, install a new set of plugs and your engine should start. If there is still no spark, the fault lies with some other ignition system component, which will be covered in the next section.

You should, by now, be aware of the problem area. Refer to the following sections for more detailed checks of each system.

CHECKING THE ELECTRICAL SYSTEM

A lack of spark at the spark plug high tension wire spells out problems in some other area of the ignition system. When checking ignition components, start with the most basic and obvious areas, and work from there. Don't overlook the obvious and the simple. In many cases you will find that your problem is so basic and uncomplicated that you'll feel like a fool after discovering it. Some of the obvious faults to look for are:

1. Kill switch in the OFF position. (Don't laugh, it has happened.)

2. Undercharged battery or loose or dirty battery terminals. On many machines, it is absolutely essential that the battery be producing nearly full voltage for the engine to start.

3. Faulty ignition switch. If the lights don't work or the horn doesn't blow, you can be pretty sure that this is your problem, unless . . .

4. The main electrical fuse has blown out. On most machines, the fuse is located near the battery in a plastic in-line holder. If the fuse is blown, an emergency replacement can be made using any type of metal foil such as found on a cigarette pack or chewing gum wrapper. Remember, though, that the fuse may have blown due to a short circuit, and, if this is the case, you may be taking a chance on burning up the

wiring harness by eliminating the fuse from the system.

5. Loose or dirty connections in the wiring. Check all the connections you can get to for tightness. If loose or dirty, correct the condition and try starting the engine again.

6. On magneto equipped bikes, a blown bulb can shut down all or part of the electrical system. Don't overlook this as your source of trouble.

If you haven't found your albatross in any of these obvious areas, it's time to look a little more closely at the spark generating components of the ignition system. At this point you will need a test light. If your bike has a battery, the test light need only consist of a small 6 or 12 volt light bulb (whichever is applicable) with two wires attached so that it will light when connected to a power source. If your machine doesn't incorporate a battery, a test light with a self-contained power source is necessary. The test light is used to determine where the flow of electricity has been interrupted. Start at the point where you should have juice but don't, and work back toward the power source. If, for example, you find that you have power at the coil but none at the points, check the wire connections and then check the continuity of the low tension wire using the test light. In this manner you can discover faults that are invisible and otherwise detectable only by trial and error replacement. Faults that should be checked for include:

1. Frayed or internally broken wiring.
2. Faulty or weak ignition coil.
3. Improperly grounded points base plate, due to looseness, oil or, on some machines, a broken ground strap or "pigtail."
4. Points shorted due to foreign matter on the contacts or grounding of the "hot" lead.

Once you have isolated the specific area of the trouble, refer to Chapter 4 for more detailed tests. Refer also to Chapter 4 for complete operational descriptions and information on CDI systems.

CHECKING THE FUEL SYSTEM

As mentioned earlier, delivery of fuel to the carburetor is the first thing to check for when hard starting is experienced and the fuel system is suspected. Discon-nect the fuel line at the carburetor and check flow at this point while taking care not to dump gasoline all over the engine. Lack of flow can be caused by any of these conditions:

1. Empty gas tank (you'd better look).
2. Clogged fuel line.
3. Fuel tap not functioning properly or in OFF position.
4. Gas tank cap vent plugged.
5. Fuel strainer (in fuel tap or tank) clogged.
6. Fuel line kinked.

If your machine has been in storage, it is possible that the carburetor has gummed up from the fuel evaporating and leaving a residue. In this case the best thing to do is disassemble and clean the carburetor be-

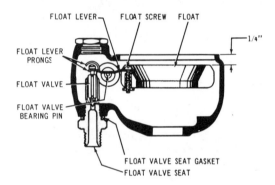

CROSS SECTION OF CARBURETOR
BOWL SHOWING FLOAT MECHANISM
AND FLOAT SETTING

fore going any further. In doing so, you can ensure that the jets are clear, that the float needle and seat are not sticking and causing flooding, and that all passages are clear. Flooding can also be caused by a hole in the float, which will allow the float to fill with gas and sink. To check for this condition, simply remove and shake the float. If there is any indication of fuel inside the float, it should be replaced with a new one.

Some machines are quite sensitive to the float level setting; however, the float level will rarely vary from the correct setting unless the float arm or tang has been bent. If any doubt exists here, consult a repair manual applicable to your model for the correct setting specifications. Note also that on Mikuni carburetors equipped with an O-ring around the needle and seat unit, it is very important that the O-ring be in good condition.

As a final measure, make sure that the

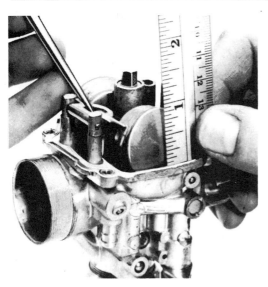

Measuring and adjusting float height (Hodaka shown)

carburetor mounting screws are tight and that the throttle cables and starter jet cables (if applicable) are properly adjusted and not binding.

COMPRESSION CHECK

A compression check will tell you quickly and simply what condition the top end components of your engine are in. A quick test can be made by placing your finger over the spark plug hole, but the use of a compression gauge will give you far more accurate and convincing results. Be sure to hold the throttle wide open when using the gauge, and crank the engine over long enough to be sure that you are getting a maximum reading. Look for a minimum compression of about 110–120 psi, and a maximum deviation between cylinders of 10–15 psi. Low or varying compression readings mean either worn

Measuring compression pressure with a compression gauge (1).

rings or cylinder bore, or a leak between the head and cylinder barrel. In either case, the head and barrel should be pulled for inspection. This is one area where the two-stroke has it all over the four-stroke. With fewer moving parts and generally less bulk, performing a top end overhaul on the usual two-stroke is quite straightforward and simple.

It should be noted here that after many miles of use, sometimes carbon buildup in the head and on the piston crown can increase compression to the point where the engine will "ping" even on quite moderate throttle openings, and have a tendency to run much hotter than normal. If this is the case, which a compression test can bear out, the head should be pulled for decarbonization and a look at the rings and bore.

Unlike the four-stroke engine, which does not have a pressurized crankcase and can tolerate leaks around the crankcase area, the two-stroke depends on crankcase pressure for the filling of the combustion chamber with fuel. In this way the two-stroke engine acts like a pump; as the piston travels downward it decreases the volume of space inside the crankcase and forces the fuel up through the transfer ports. Therefore, any crankcase leaks are disastrous for the performance of the two-stroke engine. In addition to this, the crankshaft throws in two and three cylinder two-stroke engines are spaced either 180 or 120 degrees apart (the pistons do not move up and down at the same time), and therefore, the individual crankchambers must be sealed off from each other. This poses the additional problem of possible internal leakage, not to mention the possibility of a leak into the transmission case area. Fortunately, the quality of the seals and the standards of machinework on the crankcase mating surfaces are excellent, which greatly reduces the chances of case leakage. Also, the labyrinth (metal spiral) seals used by some manufacturers last virtually forever.

If a crankcase leak is suspected, remove the carburetor and seal the intake port with your hand. Rotate the engine to position the piston at bottom dead center (BDC), and blow into the exhaust port with a steady pressure. If you don't pass out, you should be able to tell whether air is escaping from the crankcase. If it is, a piece of rolled up paper can help you to locate any leaks around the crankcase joint area. A leak into the transmission can be detected by listening at the transmission breather. An internal seal leak in a twin or triple will show up through the carburetor or exhaust of the adjacent cylinder. In any case, the engine will have to be removed and torn down for repair.

Poor Engine Performance

HARD STARTING OR ERRATIC PERFORMANCE

This section has been designed to help any unfortunate whose engine has suddenly decided to worry him into a bleeding ulcer. If you haven't laid a wrench on your bike for 20,000 miles, or the odometer just turned around to zero again, or your faithful machine has carried you all of 11,521 miles, not counting the time the speedometer was broken, or your three-year-old has never been cruised at less than 9,000 rpm, our humble suggestion is that your time would be better spent servicing, tuning, and/or rebuilding, rather than troubleshooting. Take the time to repair known faults first, and your specific problem might just disappear in the process.

The first items to check for, as always, are the obvious ones. Is the gas tank at least ¼ full? Sometimes a machine will be hard to start if the fuel supply is very low. Is the battery at or near full charge? An easy way to check is to observe the intensity of the headlight. If it is dim when the engine isn't running, have it recharged before doing anything else. Make sure that all electrical connections are clean and tight, and that the battery ground strap or cable is secured properly. Check to see if the ignition switch is playing tricks on you by applying the brake while jiggling the key (ignition on) and watching to see if the brake light flickers. Ensure that you have a sufficient flow of fuel to the carburetor by pulling off the line at the carb and observing the flow.

If you've gotten this far and still not discovered the problem, remove and examine the spark plugs. Although not the problem

Spark plug condition

Electrode coated with carbon deposit

Electrode fouled with oil

Electrode overheated or burnt

that it has been in the past, spark plug fouling is still common in many two-stroke engines. Electrodes that are wet and black (gas fouled), or covered with a thick, soft deposit (oil fouled) should be cleaned or replaced. A gas fouled plug means that your engine is flooded or running rich, or that the plug heat range is too cold. An oil fouled plug indicates (unless the plug has been in use for some time) that either the engine is being over-oiled or, again, the plug is too cold for conditions. It may pay off, if your plugs become oil fouled often, to check and adjust the oil pump setting or be more careful when mixing your fuel.

The next area to investigate is the ignition timing. The timing can be off for one of three reasons: the contact breaker plate has come loose and allowed the timing to slip; the rubbing block that rides on the breaker cam has worn, altering the points gap and changing the timing; or the points have been gapped or replaced without also checking and adjusting the timing. All

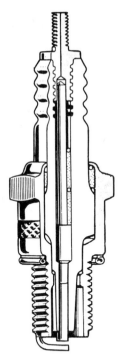

Spark plug construction

modern two-strokes are very sensitive to timing variations, and considerable care must be used to adjust the timing exactly to specification. If the engine kicks back when you are trying to start it or backfires at low rpm, suspect the ignition advance mechanism. Although it rarely happens, you may find that the advance unit has weak or broken springs, or that the unit has frozen. Check the condition of the points, and replace or clean and gap them if necessary. If they are badly pitted, do not hesitate to replace the condenser at

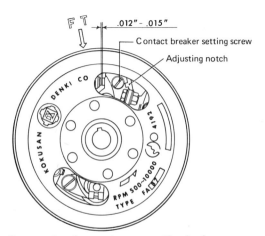

Contact breaker points gap (flywheel magneto type shown)

the same time. If oily, examine the distributor drive seal and replace it if any oil is leaking past.

If you can't remember the last time your air filter was serviced you should be given twenty lashes with a wet reed valve. A dirty filter can cause hard starting, rich running, overheating, lousy performance, plug fouling and rotten gas mileage. This

Removing an air filter for cleaning (a good thing to do once in a while)

especially applies to dirt and desert driving. Even though you installed a Filtron, it still has to be cleaned now and again.

Finally, if you've just taken your bike out of storage and it was running well before you put it away, your carburetor is probably gummed up with residue from evaporated fuel and oil. This can usually be remedied by spraying one of the aerosol carburetor cleaners directly into the carburetor while the engine is running, eliminating the need for disassembly and cleaning.

ENGINE DIES WHEN THROTTLE IS OPENED

Most cases of engine lag can be attributed to an extremely twitchy throttle hand. It must be understood that two-stroke engines nowadays produce lots and lots of power for their size, and that the carburetor throat size compared to the engine displacement is equally huge. This means that you can't crack the throttle wide open from low engine speeds without experiencing a slight lag, even with a finely tuned engine.

If the lag is exaggerated or overly obtrusive, chances are that the carburetor is at fault. Problems to look for are:

1. Clogged air filter.
2. Carburetors badly out of synchronization on twins and triples.
3. Starting jets not returning to fully closed position.

4. Idle speed set too low.

5. Air leak around carburetor intake tube flanges.

LOW SPEED MISFIRING

If your engine misfires on acceleration from low speed, the chances are, again, that carburetion is at fault. An overly rich mixture is generally the culprit and should be checked as follows:

1. Make sure that the air filter is not clogged.

2. Reset the idle adjustment screws to be certain that the idle circuit is as close to perfect adjustment as possible.

3. Remove the float bowl and examine the float needle and seat valve. If it is dirty or worn it could be hanging up and allowing the float bowl to overfill.

4. Make sure that the starting jets are returning to the fully closed position.

If none of this solves your problem and your machine can't exactly be considered a youngster, it may be time to rebuild the carburetors. One thing that you might try first, however, is to replace the plugs with new ones. Sometimes spark plugs can be awfully weird, not firing at low voltages or short circuiting at high voltages, and it wouldn't hurt to see if new ones help.

RPM RELATED MISFIRE

In most cases, if your engine misfires at a certain rpm regardless of the gear you are in or the throttle opening used, it can be put down to a timing problem. Check and adjust the timing, and if this doesn't clear up the trouble, the ignition advance unit should be examined. If in doubt, replace the complete unit or, at the very least, the springs.

THROTTLE OPENING RELATED MISFIRE

If a misfire occurs at a certain throttle opening, regardless of the gear you are in or the revs the engine is turning, the problem is caused by the mechanical parts of the carburetor. Carefully examine the needle and needle jet for wear and damage, and make sure that the slide is not worn and can move up and down freely.

INCONSISTENT MISFIRE ON ACCELERATION

An inconsistent misfire, throughout the rpm range at various throttle openings,

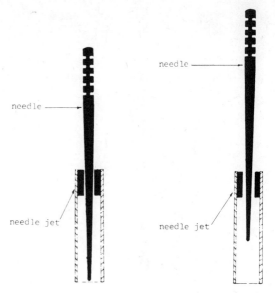

Needle jet and jet needle operation

can usually be attributed to the ignition system. If your machine is about due for a tune-up anyway, now would be a good time to take care of it. At the same time, go over the whole electrical system, checking for loose connections, condition of the battery, deteriorated high tension wires, etc. Normally, you will find that it is something simple, like a loose condenser wire, that is causing your headaches. Take care to check everything in your search.

ENGINE MISFIRES UNDER LOAD

A load can be placed on an engine in many ways, such as running up a steep hill in high gear, riding at high speeds against a head wind, using maximum acceleration constantly, etc. All of these cases involve large throttle openings, and in each of them the misfire can usually be stopped by reducing the amount of throttle.

The first symptom to look for in this instance is overheating. Remove and examine the spark plugs, looking for a lighter than normal color and eroded electrodes.

An overheated, burned spark plug

If overheating is occurring, investigate the following possible causes:

1. Excessive carbon build-up in the combustion chamber and on the piston crown.

2. Improper timing or a faulty ignition advance unit. Note that timing becomes more critical at high engine load and rpm.

3. Air leak at the intake tube flanges between the carburetor and cylinder.

4. Too "hot" a spark plug. In many cases it is necessary to go to plugs that are one or two steps colder in heat range when cruising at high speeds or running in hot weather.

Rich running can also be considered when you encounter misfiring under load. Check first for a clogged air filter, and then check to make sure that the main jet is the right size. Although most two-strokes will run well even on a cheap regular grade of gas, it would be a good idea to check for contamination of the fuel. To do this, simply remove the float bowl (taking care not to dump the gas out) and smell the fuel in it. If it smells like kerosene or separates as if it had water in it, drain the entire fuel system and buy your gas somewhere else.

HIGH SPEED MISFIRING

A high speed misfire is, in many cases, simply the first indication that a tune-up is necessary. If you need a tune-up do it, and if one was recently performed go back and check it because somebody probably fouled up.

If this isn't the case, rich running, as indicated by a black, sooty spark plug, could be causing the misfiring. Check again for a clogged air filter, and, if you've been fooling around with the main jet size, you have probably selected one that is too large.

If you experience spark plug electrode erosion which indicates overheating, check for lean running. You may have an air leak at the intake tube flanges (again), or the float level may be set too low causing fuel starvation at high speeds. Look also for leaking cylinder head and cylinder-to-crankcase gaskets or a leaking crankshaft oil seal (see "Compression Check" section), any of which can cause a lean running condition.

Finally, check the high tension components of the ignition system. The coil

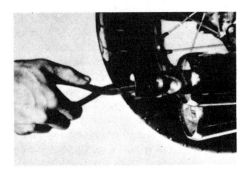

Removing the exhaust baffle (H1)

Burning baffle carbon deposits off with a torch

should be capable of producing a fat, hot spark, and the high tension (spark plug) wires must be clean and free of breaks or deterioration of the insulation.

One more thing: very often, clogging of the muffler baffles can lead to high speed misfiring in addition to fouled plugs, even when everything else is in perfect condition. The baffles should be removed and cleaned without fail at the manufacturer's specified intervals.

POOR LOW SPEED PERFORMANCE

Normal service items are usually at fault if you are experiencing poor or erratic performance in the lower third of the rpm range. Do not mistake a few seconds of unsteady or rough running, after long periods of slow running or idling, for poor low speed performance, because this is the quite normal result of combustion chambers being loaded with partially burnt fuel and oil due to slow running. If necessary, perform a complete tune-up first, then begin checking the following areas:

1. Make sure that the fuel tank vent is not clogged.

2. Make sure that the starter jet cables

are correctly adjusted, and that the jets open and close fully.

3. Check and adjust, if necessary, the float level.

4. Disassemble and clean the carburetors, paying particular attention to the low speed circuit.

5. Check the ignition advance unit for free operation, and replace the springs if weak or broken.

POOR MID-RANGE OR HIGH SPEED PERFORMANCE

Again, after normal tune-up items have been attended to, look for the following:

1. Frozen ignition advance pivots or weak or broken springs.

2. Restricted fuel lines, clogged fuel tap or tank vent, or improper float level adjustment.

3. Incorrect carburetor alignment on twins and threes. (Loosen the carb clamps and rotate them so that their tops are level, using a small steel ruler to check.)

4. Incorrect main jet size.

5. Worn or broken piston rings or a leaking head gasket. A compression check will reveal any top-end mechanical problems.

6. Weak battery. Don't be fooled into thinking that because the battery is strong enough for the engine to start, it is strong enough for the engine to fire properly at high speeds. With some machines the battery must be at or near full charge in order for the ignition system to work strongly at high rpm.

POOR GENERAL PERFORMANCE

A tune-up, spark plug check, and compression check will tell you just about everything you'd ever want to know about the condition of your engine. If one of these checks indicates that something bad is going on inside the engine, don't waste your time looking for trouble elsewhere. Wishful thinking won't help. If the engine checks out OK, however, and you're still not satisfied that performance is as good as it should be, look for dumb things like dragging brakes, a tight chain, a slipping clutch, etc. And if you do happen to locate a problem of this type, shame on you for not knowing sooner.

ENGINE OVERHEATING AND SEIZURE

Overheating to the point of seizure is much less common today than it was even ten years ago, thanks to the advent of oil injection systems and advances in metallurgy. However, mostly due to the fact that motorcycle engines require a stream of air passing through the fins for cooling, partial seizure still happens once in a while. Slow trail riding in hot weather, overloading a small bike, and extended periods of idling can all contribute to overheating which could cause a partial piston seizure. A brand new or rebuilt engine is particularly prone to overheating, and care should be taken in the first few hundred miles to use small amounts of throttle and a moderate rev range. If a mild seizure does occur, just letting the engine cool off for a few minutes will generally free it again, probably without any damage. Strange noises and a loss of performance, however, mean that you'd better pull the head and cylinder to have a look at the piston and bore.

If your bike is overheating (noticeable as a drop in performance and an inordinate amount of heat radiating from the cooling fins), look for these causes:

1. Insufficient amount of oil, due to incorrect mixing or an out of adjustment oil pump.

2. Incorrect (lean) fuel/air mixture, caused by an intake air leak or incorrect carburetor jetting.

3. Improperly adjusted ignition timing or a faulty ignition advance unit. Two-strokes are very sensitive to timing variations, and overheating can easily result from a careless setting.

4. Carbon buildup in the combustion chamber. Excessive carbon buildup can cause an increase in the compression ratio, which will increase the amount of heat produced by the engine. In addition, the carbon tends to remain very hot, causing pre-ignition and adding to the overheating problem.

5. Clogged exhaust port and muffler baffles. This causes an increase in back pressure, which in turn increases the amount of heat retained by the engine, as well as the throttle opening necessary to maintain the same level of performance. (Engine heat produced is directly related to the amount of throttle opening being used.)

6. Too "hot" a spark plug, which can ultimately cause a holed piston. The heat range of a spark plug refers to the heat dissipating ability of a plug. Therefore, a hot plug retains (not produces) more heat than a colder plug will, causing more heat buildup in the cylinder head.

7. Oily or dirty cooling fins, which are prevented from performing their job of dissipating heat as quickly and over as large an area as possible.

ENGINE VIBRATION

Nearly all abnormal engine vibration can be attributed to two causes: loose or broken engine mounts, or incorrect ignition timing. If broken mounts are suspected, be sure to check the mounts under the bolt heads and nuts, where hidden fractures can occur. Although it happens only with high mileage engines, it is possible that worn crankshaft bearings can cause excessive vibration, which of course would show up more gradually than the other causes would.

ENGINE NOISES

Engine noises are often the first indication of component malfunction or excessive wear. It is important, however, that you don't confuse normal noises with those indicating a problem. Nearly all motorcycles produced today are air-cooled, and use a great deal of aluminum alloy in their engines. Both of these factors contribute to the transmission of normal noises and should not be cause for alarm.

Two-stroke engine noises are the most suceptible to misinterpretation because of the varying levels. An engine that has been run under load in extreme heat, for example, can emit some very frightening sounds but run quietly the next morning. This is not to say that you shouldn't be concerned when you hear these noises, but rather that you should learn the difference between the expensive thump of bad main bearings and the harmless piston slap of a cold off-road single.

Inconsistent Noises

A clicking or clattering under moderate acceleration is usually the result of carbon buildup on the rings which reduces the end gap, or it could be excessive side clearance of the rings.

A heavier clicking, sometimes heard as a double click in quick succession, is most often a sign of excessive clearance between the wrist pin and its bearing.

A definite knock heard under acceleration generally means that the connecting rod bearing is worn.

Pinging under hard acceleration is caused by incorrect ignition timing, cheap or contaminated fuel, excessive carbon buildup, or overheating.

A low rpm rattle, especially when the engine is cold, is normally attributable to piston slap. This is nothing serious, and is characteristic of some models, even when new.

Consistent Noises

A grating rattle, noticeable when the engine is idling in neutral, is clutch and primary drive noise. This is quite normal with some models, and not very serious in any case. The noise may be audible when running under a light load at low speed, and should disappear almost completely when the clutch is disengaged.

A sharp knock at all engine speeds could be the piston rings hanging up as they pass the ports, and is very serious.

A heavy thump throughout the rpm range is descriptive of worn main bearings. Worn mains are also sometimes noticeable as loud whirring or screeching from the bottom end.

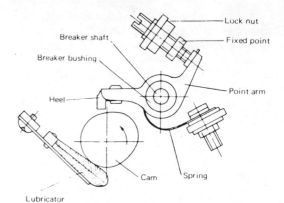

Typical breaker point arrangement on magneto models

Tune-Up

When performing a tune-up, you are restoring to peak efficiency certain engine components that are subject to changes in operating efficiency during use. A tune-up is nothing more than a series of adjustments that are performed in logical order, one at a time, to predetermined specifications. There is no guesswork involved. There are no complicated disassembly procedures and it is not necessary for you to have years of experience in diagnosing engine problems. All tune-up operations are quite straightforward.

A two-stroke tune-up involves the following procedures, in the order given below:

1. Contact breaker point cleaning and gapping (if so equipped);
2. Ignition timing adjustment;
3. Spark plug cleaning and gapping or replacement;
4. Carburetor idle speed and mixture adjustment;
5. Multi-carburetor synchronization (if so equipped);
6. Throttle cable adjustment.

Keep in mind, however, that while the procedures are both quick and simple, two-stroke engine design inherently makes each adjustment critical.

Items not covered in this chapter, such as air filter servicing, cleaning and checking of the battery, etc., can affect the results of the tune-up. It is assumed that you have maintained your bike at least passably well. If not, it is recommended that you spend a little time on routine service before beginning these procedures.

CONTACT BREAKER POINTS AND IGNITION TIMING

Flywheel Magneto Ignition

On machines equipped with flywheel magneto ignition, contact breaker adjustment and ignition timing are accomplished in one operation.

1. Remove the ignition access cover, then separate the points and check their condition. Blueing and slight pitting are signs of normal wear; built up mounds and matching depressions require point set replacement. It is also a good idea to replace the points if you can't remember exactly when you installed the present set.

2. If you are going to reuse the same points, clean them up by running a point file or piece of fine sandpaper between them. Remove any deposits and smooth out the pitted surfaces, then apply a non-oily solvent to the contact surfaces.

NOTE: *Apply solvent to a new set of points as well, since many of them are coated with a protective film.*

3. Snap the points shut on a white business card (or piece of heavy paper) to remove the filings and cleaning fluid. Repeat this step until the points leave a clean imprint.

4. Rotate the engine by putting it in gear and turning the rear wheel. Observe the points as they open and close. If they do not meet squarely, replace the set.

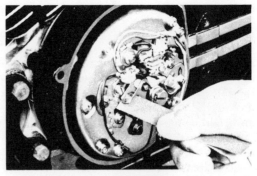

Cleaning the breaker points

5. Rotate the engine until the marks on the flywheel and crankcase are aligned. Loosen the point breaker plate just enough to allow it to be turned, and adjust the position of the points so that they are just opening. Retighten the breaker plate.

6. Check the adjustment by rotating the engine and observing the points. They should just begin to open when the flywheel and crankcase marks fall into alignment.

NOTE: *If a test light with a self-contained power source is not available, the precise moment that the points open can be determined by placing a piece of cellophane between them and pulling gently. When the cellophane is freed, the points have begun to open.*

7. Finally, check and adjust the point gap as per the manufacturer's specifications and lubricate the breaker cam with a high melting-point grease.

Checking breaker point gap

Timing pointer and mark (C and D). Lockscrews (E and A) shown also

Flywheel and crankcase marks (A and C)

DC Generator Ignition

On models with DC generator ignition (usually in combination with an electric starter), the contact breaker point gap and ignition timing are set separately.

1. Inspect and clean the breaker points as previously described for the flywheel magneto models.

2. Rotate the engine until the points are at their widest gap.

3. Loosen the points securing screw(s) slightly and adjust the points gap to between 0.012–0.016 in. (0.3–0.4 mm). Retighten the screws, making certain that the points gap is not disturbed as the screws are tightened.

4. Align the timing pointer with the mark on the breaker cam and loosen the breaker plate adjusting screws. Shift the plate up or down until the points just begin to open. A test light can be used to determine the exact moment that the points break. Retighten the screws, making certain that the plate does not move when the screws are tightened.

5. Finally, recheck the adjustment, and lightly lubricate the breaker cam with a high melting-point grease.

AC (Alternator) Ignition

1. Clean and inspect the breaker points as previously described for the flywheel magneto models.

2. Turn the crankshaft until each set of points are at their maximum gap (one at a time). If the gap is not within 0.012–0.016 in., loosen the points securing screws and adjust the points base plate until the gap is within specification. Retighten the screws, taking care not to disturb the gap.

NOTE: *The following steps outline the procedure for setting the timing using a dial gauge. Some bikes are provided with timing index marks, making use of the dial gauge unnecessary unless the accuracy of the marks is in question. If your machine is so equipped, simply align the pointer with the mark for each cylinder, in turn, and proceed as outlined below, eliminating operations involving the dial gauge.*

3. Remove the spark plug from the left cylinder and install a dial gauge in its place. Position the crankshaft so that the left piston is set at the manufacturer's specified distance before top dead center for setting the timing on your model.

Dial gauge in place

4. Connect a test light to ground and to the left cylinder points wire. Loosen the points mounting plate screw (allowing the entire points assembly to be shifted) and adjust the left cylinder points until they are just opening, as indicated by the test light. Retighten the screw, taking care not to disturb the setting.

5. If an adjustment screw is provided on the timing pointer (on models so equipped), loosen the pointer and align it with the left cylinder timing mark on the breaker cam. *Do not turn the rotor.* Since

you have determined the exact piston position with the dial gauge, checking and adjusting the accuracy of the pointer in this manner allows you to use the pointer with the mark for the remaining cylinder(s) without having to use the dial gauge on them.

6. Adjust the remaining cylinder(s) in the same manner as the left one, rotating the engine to bring the piston to the correct position using either the dial gauge or pointer, as before. Upon completion, lightly lubricate the breaker cam with a high melting point grease.

Capacitor Discharge Ignition (CDI)

Models equipped with capacitor discharge ignition do not use contact breaker points. Instead, a signal generator is used which does not emit a pulse unless the engine is running. Therefore, ignition timing cannot be set statically as is the case with the other systems. It can only be observed with a stroboscopic timing light.

Since this system does not employ contact breaker points, it is not subject to their wear. As a result, once initial timing has been set (as it is at the factory), it very rarely requires adjustment.

SPARK PLUGS

Cleaning and Gapping

Sandblasting is the best method of cleaning plugs provided you get all the sand particles off. It is very quick, very thorough, and your local gas station may be equipped to do the job. Carefully scraping deposits off the plugs with a wire brush or knife blade will also work just fine, and is a lot more practical if you foul them anywhere other than right in front of a gas station equipped with a sandblaster.

Check and set the spark plug gap with a wire feeler gauge. Most gauges are equipped with a little notch in the handle for bending the ground electrode to achieve the proper gap.

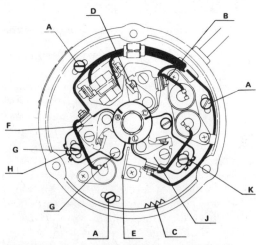

Ignition breaker points arrangement of the Kawasaki three, showing the timing pointer (E)

Gap measurement is made between the ground and positive electrodes

NOTE: *It's a good idea to install new spark plugs at tune-up intervals and keep the most recent ones (if they are in good condition) as spares. In the long run, new plugs every 2,000 miles will prove economical (better gas mileage, lower oil consumption, etc.)*

Replacement

There are several important points to keep in mind when replacing plugs:

1. Do not experiment unnecessarily with different spark plug heat ranges. The plug supplied with your bike should perform well in almost all situations. Spark plug heat range refers to the ability of a plug to dissipate heat relative to another type of plug, *not* to the amount of heat or quality of spark that it produces. If you do find it necessary to try a different heat range because of fouling or erosion of the electrodes, follow this rule of thumb: use the coldest heat range possible that will not foul and cause misfiring in the conditions that you normally ride.

2. Make certain that you get the correct reach plug. Most models use either a ½ or ¾ in. reach; installing the wrong one will bring about either plug fouling or eventual (if not immediate) engine damage. Too short a reach causes rapid carbon buildup; too long a reach causes excessive heat concentration on the piston crown or, in some cases, causes the piston to hit the plug electrode on each stroke (of which there wouldn't be very many).

CARBURETOR ADJUSTMENT

Idle Speed and Mixture

1. Turn the idle mixture (air) screw(s) in until it seats *lightly*.

CAUTION: *Too much pressure when turning in the adjustment screw will damage the seat.*

Throttle stop and air screw location on late piston port engines

2. Back out the idle mixture (air) screw(s) the recommended number of turns.

3. Start and warm up the engine. Then, with the throttle grip completely closed, turn the idle speed (throttle stop) screw(s) in or out until the engine idles at the specified rpm.

NOTE: *On multis, you can check idle speed synchronization by holding one hand behind each muffler and noting the exhaust pulse frequency. Reset the idle*

Spark plug
Cylinder head

(Too long)
Overheating

(Proper)

(Too short)
Carbon build-up
results in a sooty
spark plug

Make sure you install the correct reach spark plug

3. When installing either new or used plugs, make certain to use a plug wrench *only* and remember to torque the plug to specifications. Using any tool other than a plug wrench can easily strip the threads in an aluminum head, and failing to torque the plug properly will inhibit its ability to dissipate heat. If a torque wrench is not available, screw the plug down finger tight, then turn it an additional ¾ turn.

Throttle stop adjustment on rotary valve engines

speed screws until the cylinders are firing alternately and at the same rate. If one cylinder is backfiring or its pulses are erratic, stop the engine, turn all idle speed screws in until lightly seated, then turn them back out equally a couple of turns (enough to prevent stalling). Start the engine and turn one cylinder's idle speed screw in, then out, and note any increase or decrease in engine speed. At the position where ½–1 turn does not cause a variation in rpm, the cylinders should be firing smoothly and at the same rate. The idle rpm may be higher than specified, but by equally backing out the idle mixture screws, you can lower it to normal.

Multi-Carburetor Synchronization

After setting ignition timing, points, plugs, idle speed, and mixture, you also must synchronize the carburetor throttle slides on multi-cylinder engines.

1. Make certain that the carburetor bodies are level and parallel to each other by viewing the float bowl joining gaskets from the side and rear, or by using the edge of a small steel ruler across the carb tops.

2. If the bodies are misaligned, loosen the carb mounts. Reposition the bodies correctly and tighten the mounting clamp screws, then check the starter jet cables to make certain that some free-play exists and that all jets will close fully.

3. Remove the carburetor/air cleaner elbow(s).

4. Twist the throttle grip fully open to lift up the slides.

5. Slowly open and close the throttle grip and watch or feel the slides as they are being lowered; they should hit bottom (audible as a single click) simultaneously.

6. If the slide positions are unequal, raise or lower one to match the other by turning the cable end adjuster at the top of the carburetor.

Throttle Cable Adjustment

Proper adjustment is an important factor in extending cable life, ensuring proper actuation and reducing the possibility of a failure. On most models, a cable runs from the twist grip to a junction block and, from the junction block, one or more cables are routed to the carburetor(s). One end of each cable is fitted with an adjust-

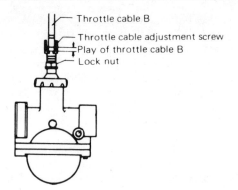

Typical throttle cable arrangement at the carburetor top

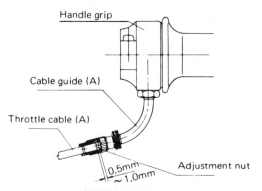

Typical throttle cable arrangement at the twist grip

Starter cable adjustment at the carburetor

ment nut, located at the twist grip cable guide and at the carburetor top(s).

After setting the specified free-play at each cable separately, start and warm up the engine, then turn the handlebars from side to side and note any change in idle rpm. If a variation occurs, one of the cables is either adjusted incorrectly (not enough free-play) or is binding somewhere along its route. On most models, there should be about ⅛ in. free-play in the cables.

TUNE-UP ANALYSIS

The factories equip each model with standard spark plugs and carburetor jets.

The values of these items, however, are not necessarily the best for every machine. Ignition, spark, and carburetion requirements vary with atmospheric conditions and riding habits. In some cases, the engine runs poorly with the standard plugs and jets. The easiest method of determining what changes (if any) should be made involves removing the spark plugs and reading their appearance and condition.

To enable you to make accurate interpretations, the engine must first be in perfect tune and mustn't be suffering from any internal mechanical ills. Bad rings or leaking carburetors, seals, etc., will cause erroneous readings.

Spark Plug Readings

1. After a complete tune-up and after installing new plugs, take the machine out and ride it as you normally would.

NOTE: *If this isn't feasible, set the bike up on its center stand or some boxes and run the engine at approximately your normal throttle opening (most often used).*

2. After a few minutes of highway cruising, riding around the block, rock bashing, or standing in the driveway holding the throttle open, shut the engine off *immediately*. Don't let it idle or turn over under compression.

3. Remove the spark plugs and inspect the insulating porcelain around the positive electrode:

a. White in color—plug is too hot or fuel mixture is too lean.

b. Blistered—plug is too hot or fuel mixture is too lean.

c. Tan in color—this indicates *correct* plug heat range and mixture.

d. Dark brown in color—plug is too cold or fuel mixture is too rich.

e. Oily—plug is too cold or oil mixture is too rich.

f. Black in color—plug is too cold, fuel mixture is too rich, or carbon buildup is excessive.

g. Plug condition should be almost identical on multis.

If your plug readings were only slightly abnormal, changing to a one step hotter or one step colder spark plug should be all that is necessary. When one step is insufficient, some carburetor mixture changes should also be made.

Carburetor Mixture Adjustment

The fuel/air mixture can be altered at the needle jet and the main jet. The jet needle is adjusted by repositioning its clip in a different groove, and the main jet is adjusted by replacing it with a different size.

If the plug reading indicated too rich a mixture, install a one step smaller main jet; if it indicated too lean a mixture, install a one step larger main jet. Should more than a one size main jet change be needed, you should also reposition the jet needle clip one groove higher (reading was rich) or lower (reading was lean) to balance out the system.

IMPORTANT: *Make mixture changes gradually and carefully. Too lean a mixture, especially in two-strokes, can easily cause engine damage. In general, these engines should be set up to run as rich as possible without fouling plugs.*

BETWEEN TUNE-UP CHECKS

Remove and inspect the spark plugs occasionally between tune-ups; any sudden changes will give you ample notice of an engine problem before it causes too much damage. For example, if one plug on a twin starts blistering, you know that the mixture must be too lean, since the plug was normal at the last inspection. Therefore, you can immediately suspect some kind of air leak and check the possible sources before the lean mixture causes overheating and possibly piston seizure.

Oil Injection Systems

OPERATIONAL DESCRIPTION

Kawasaki—Superlube and Injectolube

Both the Superlube and Injectolube systems include an oil reservoir, oil feed line, oil pump, and oil delivery lines. The pumps are of the plunger type and are driven by the end of the crankshaft through reduction gears. The amount of oil fed to the induction passage delivery line and crankcase drillway (Injectolube) is determined by two variables: the speed of plunger operation and the length of plunger stroke. These variables are set by

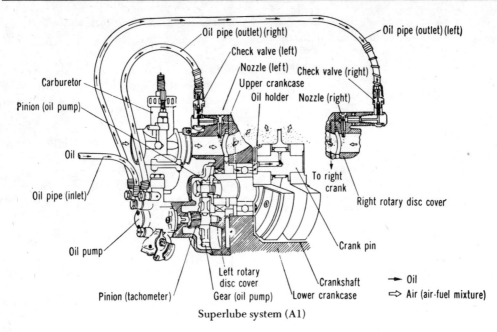

Superlube system (A1)

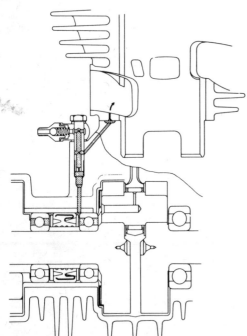

Interjectolube oil nozzle arrangement (H Series)

The essential difference between the Superlube and Injectolube systems is the extra lubrication to the crankshaft main bearings provided by the Injectolube type. An additional output port in the oil pump leads to a drillway in the crankcase, which in turn leads to smaller passages to these critical points.

Suzuki—Posi-Force and C.C.I.

Called originally "Posi-Force Lubrication," later changed to "C.C.I.," this system is now used on all Suzuki products from the 50 cc bikes up to the new 750 cc three.

Direct oil injection has distinct advantages over the old oil-mist method, and indeed over other less sophisticated oil injection systems. Outstanding features include decreased engine wear at high rpm (particularly with the new C.C.I. modifications), less accumulation of carbon in the exhaust system and on the piston, much reduced exhaust smoke, and elimination of the chore of mixing the oil and gas.

Although variations in engine design require slightly different oil routing, accommodating direct port, reed valve and rotary valve configurations, the system works in basically the same manner for all machines.

On all twins, except the T-125, a plunger-type oil pump, operated by the crankshaft, supplies oil through tubes to both the right and left crankshaft bearings at a predetermined pressure. The volume of the pump is directly controlled by engine rpm

the engine rpm and the degree of throttle opening, respectively. The pump effectively meters the amount of oil according to engine speed and load and, as a result, no more and no less than the required amount is consumed. The pump also houses a check valve that keeps the oil output pressure constant and seals the delivery line when the engine is not operating.

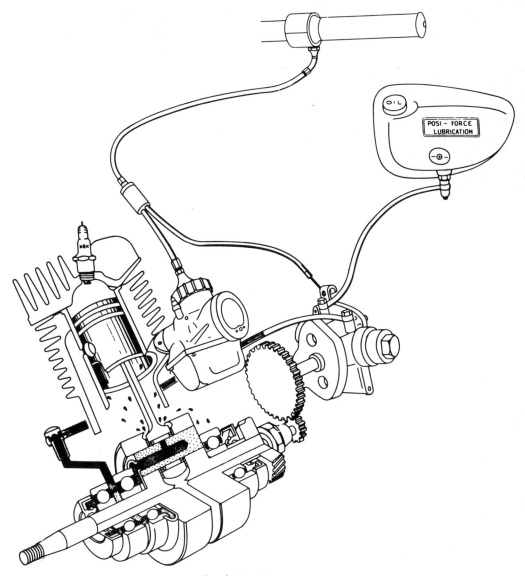

Suzuki Posi-Force system

and throttle slide opening so that just the right amount of oil is metered to lubricate without waste. The oil passes from the bearings through the crankpins and there lubricates the connecting rod needle bearings. From there, the oil is thrown off the crankpins by centrifugal force, atomized and blown up on the cylinder walls and connecting rod small end bearings. The C.C.I. system is almost identical to this, except that separate tubes spray oil directly onto the cylinder walls to add to the oil mist supplied from the crankpins. With both Posi-Force and C.C.I., the center crankshaft bearing is lubricated by the transmission oil, the drippings from which

flow back into the transmission via a return hole in the crankcase.

On the T-125 twin, oil from two of the four injection tubes lubricates the left and center bearings and crankpins and is sprayed as a mist on the cylinder walls. The other two tubes inject oil into the carburetor inlet ports from where it is then drawn into the crankcase to lubricate the connecting rod small end and cylinder walls. On this model, the right crankshaft bearing is lubricated by the transmission oil.

The Posi-Force system used on singles is similar to that used on twins. A plunger-type pump, controlled by engine rpm and

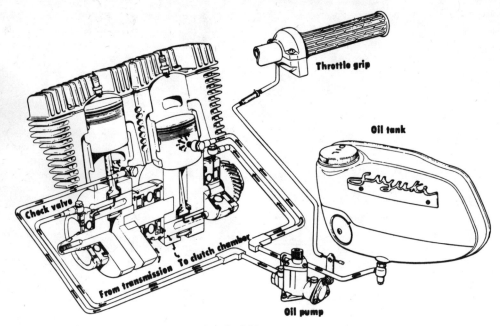

Suzuki CCI system

throttle opening, meters oil through one or two tubes to the engine. The left-side (or single if it has only one) tube supplies oil directly to the left crankshaft bearing, from where it passes through the crankshaft to the hollow crankpin to lubricate the connecting rod needle bearings. The oil is thrown off the crankpin, and is blown as a mist up over the lower cylinder walls and connecting rod small end bearing. Models having only one injection tube, such as the K-10P, K-11P, and B-100 P, have their right crankshaft bearing lubricated by oil mist from the crankshaft chamber.

On models with two tubes, the oil that is

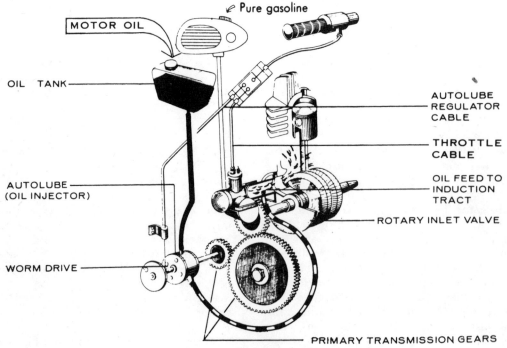

Yamaha Autolube system

injected from the right-side tube enters the intake port (or the cylinder directly) and is sucked into the crankcase to help lubricate the cylinder walls. With this sytem, the right crankshaft bearing is lubricated by the transmission oil in the same manner as the center bearing on twins.

A variation of this system is used on models with rotary disc valves, such as the A-100, AS-100, TC-90, and TS-90. One tube supplies oil to the left crankshaft bearing, through the crankpin and is sprayed on the cylinder walls and connecting rod small end bearing. The other tube supplies oil to the rotary disc valve and the right crankshaft bearing.

Yamaha—Autolube

Yamaha was the first major manufacturer to offer an effective and reliable oil injection system. The Autolube system, introduced in the early 1960's, pioneered the throttle and rpm related injection of oil directly into the intake port. The Autolube pump is a plunger type and is driven by the crankshaft or clutch (early models) through reduction gears. The amount of oil fed to the crankcase delivery line is determined by two variables—the speed of plunger operation and the length of plunger stroke. These variables are set by the engine rpm and the degree of throttle opening, respectively. The pump effectively meters the amount of oil according to engine speed and load and, as a result, the precise amount of oil needed is delivered. The pump also houses a check valve that keeps the oil output pressure constant and seals the delivery line when the engine is not operating.

OIL PUMP TROUBLESHOOTING

It is inadvisable to attempt disassembly and repair of the oil pump. The internal parts are machined to very exacting tolerances and it is highly unlikely that the pump can be reassembled to factory specifications. In addition to this, oil pump failure rarely occurs due to internal malfunction.

Spark Plug Comparison Chart

THREAD SIZE	HEAT RANGE	NGK STANDARD TYPE	NGK PROJECTED TYPE	CHAMPION Y—Projected Type	AC S—Projected Type	AUTO-LITE	BOSCH	KLG P—Projected Type	LODGE Y—Projected Type
14 mm	hot	B—4E	BP—4E	{N21, N16Y	47XL	AG9	W95T2, W125T2	FE20	BLN, BL14
				{N18	46XLS	AG7, AG52		FE30	CLNY
				N8, N84, 88, 14Y	46N, 46XL	AG5	W145T30, W160T2	FE50, FE45P	CLNH, CC14
		B—6ES	BP—6ES	N6, N12Y, UN12Y	45N, 45XL, C45XL	AG4, AG42	W175T2, W175T30	FE70, FE55P	HLNY
					44N, 44XL, 45XLS, 44XLS				
				N11Y, N10Y, N5		AG3, AG32	W200T27, W200T30	FE75	*HBLN
					44XLS, 43XLS, 43XL				
¾ in.		B—7E, B—7ES	BP—7E	N9Y, N8Y	43N, 43XL	AG2, AG23	W225T2, W230T30	FE80, FE65P	HLN
		B—7EC °		N4	C42N		W240T2, W240T28	FE100	2HLN
		B—77EC °		N62R			W250P21, WG250T28	FE220	
		B—8E, B—8ES	BP—8ES	N3, N6Y, N7Y	42XL, 42XLS		W260T28, W265P21	FE250	HLNP, 3HLN
		B—9E		N60R	41XLS				
Reach	cold	B—10E		N57R					

° Competition type with short side electrode.

Spark Plug Size and
Heat Range Chart

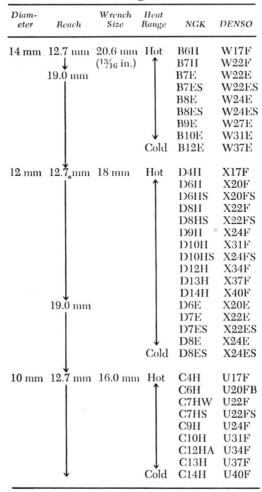

Diam-eter	Reach	Wrench Size	Heat Range	NGK	DENSO
14 mm	12.7 mm ↓ 19.0 mm	20.6 mm (1¾₁₆ in.)	Hot ↑	B6H	W17F
				B7H	W22F
				B7E	W22E
				B7ES	W22ES
				B8E	W24E
				B8ES	W24ES
				B9E	W27E
			↓	B10E	W31E
			Cold	B12E	W37E
12 mm	12.7 mm ↓ 19.0 mm	18 mm	Hot ↑	D4H	X17F
				D6H	X20F
				D6HS	X20FS
				D8H	X22F
				D8HS	X22FS
				D9H	X24F
				D10H	X31F
				D10HS	X24FS
				D12H	X34F
				D13H	X37F
				D14H	X40F
				D6E	X20E
				D7E	X22E
				D7ES	X22ES
			↓	D8E	X24E
			Cold	D8ES	X24ES
10 mm	12.7 mm ↓	16.0 mm	Hot ↑	C4H	U17F
				C6H	U20FB
				C7HW	U22F
				C7HS	U22FS
				C9H	U24F
				C10H	U31F
				C12HA	U34F
			↓	C13H	U37F
			Cold	C14H	U40F

Engine Troubleshooting

Difficult or No Starting

Possible Causes	Inspection and/or Remedy
1. Ignition System	
a. Weak or dead battery	Check for a bright blue spark by shorting the spark plug against the cylinder cooling fins and kicking the engine over. If there is no spark, or it is very weak, check battery output, then clean and tighten terminal connections.
b. Bridged, fouled, or dirty spark plug	Clean or replace. Make sure the plug is of the correct heat range.
c. Incorrect spark plug gap	Reset.
d. Burned, dirty, or incorrectly gapped ignition points	Clean or replace. Set correct gap.
e. Incorrect ignition timing	Reset.
f. Faulty condenser	Test condenser capacity and replace if necessary.
g. Faulty magneto, generator, or alternator	Test voltage output and isolate trouble source as described in "Electrical Systems."
h. Faulty wiring harness	Check for short circuits, poor grounds, etc., and repair as necessary.
2. Fuel System	
a. No fuel delivery	Check the fuel level and switch to reserve. Disconnect the delivery line at the carburetor and make sure there is free fuel flow. If not, look for a clogged gas tank vent, fuel petcock, or delivery line.
b. Stuck carburetor float	Dissassemble the float bowl and make sure that the float operates freely and that the float needle seat is free from obstruction.
c. Poor quality fuel	Inspect the spark plugs and if yellow-brown sulphur deposits are evident, flush and refill the fuel tank with fresh, good quality fuel.
3. Loss of Compression	Check cylinder compression as described in "Tune-Up Analysis."
a. Loose spark plug	Usually caused by overtorquing the plug and stripping the cylinder head threads. Either a HeliCoil insert or a new cylinder head will be required.
b. Loose cylinder head	Make sure the head is correctly fitted and torqued.
c. Broken head gasket	Replace.
d. Worn piston rings	Replace.
e. Excessive piston-to-cylinder wall clearance	Replace the piston and rings; rebore or replace the cylinder.
f. Leaking crankcase seal	Replace.
g. Warped or sheared rotary valve disc	Replace.
4. Fuel Mixture (Hard Starting)	See "Tune-Up Analysis" and determine if the carburetion is lean or rich. Make sure that all adjustments are correct and the air cleaner isn't dirty.
a. Lean mixture	Check the intake manifold and inspect the throttle stop screw(s), starter jet(s), and pilot jet.
b. Rich mixture	Inspect the air screw, air jet, needle jet, and air cleaner element.

Hard Starting or Irregular Idle

1. Ignition System	
a. Weak battery output	Check battery voltage and make sure that all connections are tight and clean.
b. Dirty or incorrect spark plug	Check plug condition, heat range, and electrode gap.
c. Incorrect ignition timing	Reset.
d. Dirty or worn out points	Replace the points and check for any signs of oil leakage around the breaker cam. Wet points usually indicate a faulty oil seal.
e. Faulty condenser	If the points were badly burned or discolored, it's very likely that a bad condenser is the cause. Replace it and be safe.
f. Faulty automatic advance	If the engine backfires when starting, inspect the advance mechanism and make sure it is functioning properly.
g. Faulty magneto	Check the slip ring and pick-up for grease, dirt, etc., and clean as necessary.

Engine Troubleshooting

Hard Starting or Irregular Idle

Possible Causes	Inspection and/or Remedy
2. Fuel System	
a. Incorrectly adjusted carburetor idle circuit	Check all parts associated with the idle circuit (see "Fuel Systems"). Clean and readjust as necessary.
b. Clogged carburetor fuel jets	If the bike has been stored or left sitting for some time, there is the possibility of sediment or oil residue obstructing fuel flow through the main and needle jets. Clean all the jets in solvent and blow them dry with compressed air.
3. Dirty Air Cleaner	Clean or replace.
4. Excessive Carbon Buildup	Decarbonize the engine.

Misfire During Acceleration from Idle

1. Incorrect Idle Mixture	A misfire while accelerating from a standstill is often caused by too rich an idle mixture. Readjust the idle mixture and, if necessary, remove and clean the jets.
2. Water in Carburetor Float Bowl or Fuel Petcock	Drain and flush with fresh gasoline.
3. Faulty Spark Plug	Look for signs of bridging, tracking, or flashover (see "Tune-Up Analysis"). Sandblast or replace the plug.

Misfire at a Given Throttle Opening Only

1. Faulty Carburetor	Disassemble and inspect all carburetor parts for nicks, scratches, etc. Pay particular attention to the needle jet and jet needle.

Misfire at a Given RPM Only

1. Faulty Automatic Advance	This type of misfire is usually caused by the automatic advance unit getting hung up. Inspect the mechanism and make sure it operates properly and smoothly.

Intermittent Misfire

1. Ignition System	Check all items in the ignition/electrical system: points, plugs, high-tension wires, grounds, and wiring harness connections.

Misfire Under Load

1. Faulty Spark Plug	Inspect the plug for signs of overheating. Install a cooler plug, if necessary.
2. Incorrect Ignition Timing	Make sure that the timing is right on because it becomes more critical as load increases.
3. Dirty Air Cleaner	Clean or replace.
4. Incorrect Fuel Mixture	Make sure that the fuel mixture is not too rich. Check main jet size.
5. Poor Quality Fuel	Check plug condition and, if necessary, drain and replace the fuel.

Engine Troubleshooting

High-Speed Misfire

Possible Causes	Inspection and/or Remedy
1. Ignition System	
a. Faulty spark plug	Check plug condition and heat range.
b. Incorrect spark plug gap	Reset.
c. Faulty condenser	Test and, if necessary, replace.
d. Faulty ignition coil	Inspect the leads for signs of corona discharge: soft rubber.
e. Faulty high-tension leads	Test and, if necessary, replace.
2. Fuel System	
a. Incorrect fuel mixture	Inspect the main and needle jet for any nicks, etc. Also make sure the jet needle clip is properly positioned and the needle is not damaged.
b. Incorrect float level	Reset.
c. Air leak	Inspect the fuel induction passage and make sure there is no place for air to enter other than the carburetor throat.
3. Loss of Compression	Measure cylinder compression as described in "Tune-Up Analysis."
a. Broken head gasket	Replace.
b. Broken cylinder base gasket	Replace.
c. Leaking crankcase oil seal	Replace.
4. Dirty Air Cleaner	Clean or replace.
5. Carbon Buildup in Head and/or Exhaust Passage	Decarbonize.

3 · Four-Stroke Troubleshooting

Since you're reading this the chances are pretty good that you are already plenty annoyed, so the first thing to do is sit down and cool off. Your bike wants to tell you what's wrong, but unless you're feeling receptive you might not understand what it's saying.

Starting the Engine

If you aren't familiar with the machine it may just be that you are doing something wrong. It's amazing how much trouble, for example, a big single can give to someone who's only used to riding twins. A bike is a lot like a woman; sometimes it takes patience to turn them on.

Make sure you are going through the starting drill correctly. Turn the fuel tap to the ON position, provided you know that there is enough fuel in the tank, or to the reserve position. If you aren't sure which is correct, disconnect the fuel line and check for fuel flow. If the machine is equipped with Amal type carbs that have "ticklers," depress the button until gas begins to run out, then close the choke or air slide, or do what ever is necessary to enrich the mixture. Kick the engine through a couple of times with the key off and the throttle opened, or use the electric starter button

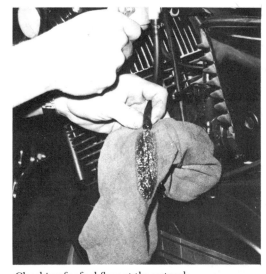

Checking for fuel flow at the petcock

Priming an Amal type carburetor

37

(with the key on and the kill switch in the OFF position) to spin the engine through and loosen everything up. Now turn on the key, open the throttle ⅛ of its full travel and the spark advance (if applicable) about half-way, and get ready to do some kicking. Use all your weight on the lever, and straighten your kicking leg out on the way down. If you have a single with a compression release, depress the kick starter until the piston is felt to be approaching its strongest point of compression; then operate the release, while slowly moving the starter lever a couple of inches, until the piston is past compression. This should be done each time before you kick over a single, but don't worry, it will become like second nature in no time at all.

A lot of riders tend to yank open the throttle the first time the engine sounds like it may start, and they wind up with a flooded engine. To clear it out, just open the throttle wide and spin the engine through a couple times, or let it sit for a while; it will dry out faster if you remove the spark plugs. If the bike still won't start try to bump start it. Get a good run going, with the clutch pulled in and the transmission in the lowest gear that won't lock up the rear wheel; then hop on and pop the clutch as you hit the seat. If, after doing this for a while, you can't get it started, you better start troubleshooting.

Engine Does Not Start

Systematically make sure that all the necessary systems are working, and do a tune-up if you are uncertain of the machine's state of tune. Is turning the key on completing the circuit and getting juice to the primary ignition circuit? If the bike is battery operated, the lights and horn should work; however, if the battery is discharged it may make starting difficult. If the machine doesn't have a battery you can ground a spark plug, while still in its cap, against the cylinder head and kick the bike over. Doing this isn't a bad idea with battery equipped machines as it removes all doubt. If you are getting juice you should be able to see a spark. If everything checks out and you are sure you are

Checking for spark at the plug

getting spark go on and check the fuel system.

If your machine has Amal type carbs equipped with ticklers you can be fairly certain the carburetor is doing its job if tickling produces a gas flow. If the carb has no provision such as this, remove the float bowl drain plug, or the whole float bowl, and see if there is gas there. If so, the chances are good that the carbs are alright, so the only remaining system is the mechanical.

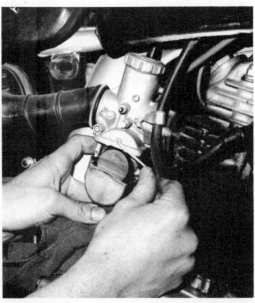

Checking for fuel in the float bowl

Provided the machine has compression, and that the clutch is working so the engine turns over, the bike should start. If the clutch isn't working you should be able to tell just by kicking the bike over. To make sure, put the bike in gear and roll it to check the clutch. You should be able to hear the engine turn over when the clutch is engaged. The next thing to check is the compression. You should be able to tell if it has reasonable compression by kicking the engine through, or by putting your finger over the spark plug hole and seeing if there is enough compression to push your finger away, but of course using a compression gauge eliminates much of

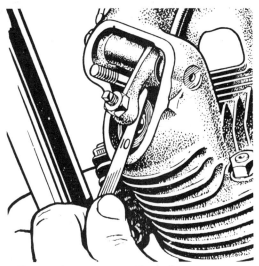

Adjusting the tappets on a Triumph

Compression tests provide a glimpse behind the cylinder walls

the guesswork. A compression check will tell you whether or not you have trouble in the top end. Compression pressure in the cylinder should be about 140 psi. To obtain an accurate reading, make sure the compression gauge is properly seated in the spark plug hole and hold the throttle open all the way while cranking the engine until the needle on the gauge stops advancing. Low readings can indicate a leaking head gasket, valves that are too tightly adjusted, stuck, or burnt, or worn piston rings.

If you obtain a low reading, squirt oil into the spark plug hole and recheck the compression. If the pressure increases significantly, this indicates that the rings are worn. If it does not increase and there is evidence of a cylinder head gasket leak, the chances are that the head gasket is blown and must be replaced. If there is no evidence of a bad head gasket or worn rings, the process of elimination points to the valves. To make certain that it is not merely insufficient valve clearance that is

doing you in, back out the valve adjusters a couple of turns and recheck the compression. Do this even if you have adjusted the valves because you may have been mistaken. If you still don't have good compression, button it up and get ready for a top end overhaul.

By now you hopefully know which system is sabotaging your attempt to go riding, so now it's time to concentrate on finding exactly what is wrong.

CHECKING THE ELECTRICAL SYSTEM

Electrical problems are usually very subtle, and unless you get lucky and find something blatant like an electrical connector that's worked itself loose, you'll have to carefully check over every inch of

Snap connectors, such as on these coils, can work loose leaving you with no spark

wiring. You should have an appropriate wiring diagram and a test light that's suited to your needs. If your bike has a magneto ignition, or if it's stone dead (and of course you already checked the fuses now didn't you?) you'll need a light with a

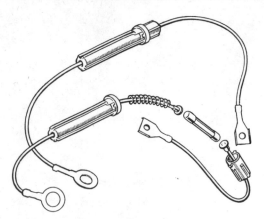

The fuse is usually located near the battery

Testing wiring harness for continuity

self-contained power source that can check for continuity. If you've got a battery ignition model you can get by with a simple test light since it will tell you where the current stops.

Always start at the point where you don't have juice and work toward the power source. Some of the things to look for are dirty, corroded, or loose connections; burn marks that may indicate a short; heavily pitted or burnt points (which probably mean a bad condenser); frayed wires at rubbing points (i.e. at the steering head and at the alternator or magneto); bad brushes (generator equipped machines); poor grounding (many English bikes have the lighting circuit grounded to the frame); or bad bulbs (on magneto equipped machines a bad bulb can short out the whole system). There may be hidden damage, such as a wire that has broken in the middle of the wiring harness. If something like this is suspected use a test light with a self-contained power source to test for continuity through the wire. Jiggle the wire to make sure it isn't an intermittent short that only occurs when the bike is vibrating. A word about switches—on many Japanese machines the switch assemblies are very delicate, and repeated removal and installation can loosen up the leads just enough to cause an intermittent short. If you get power sometimes, and then sometimes it cuts out (like after you start the machine) suspect the kill switch. On multicylinder bikes like the Honda fours, such a situation can make it possible to have two cylinders firing normally, and the other two firing intermittently or not at all. In fact, whenever you have an ignition problem

The carbon contact on this magneto's kill button disintegrated

keep the ignition switch and kill button in mind.

To get an idea of how the electrical system operates, let's break it down. The ignition circuit runs from the power source to the spark plug and is the one which has failed when there is no juice anywhere on the machine. The lighting circuit feeds off the ignition circuit and directs the current to all of the accessories. On most battery equipped models this system can fail without affecting the ignition circuit, but on magneto equipped machines they are all tied in together (although they still are two separate systems) so if part of the complete circuit breaks down, even if it's

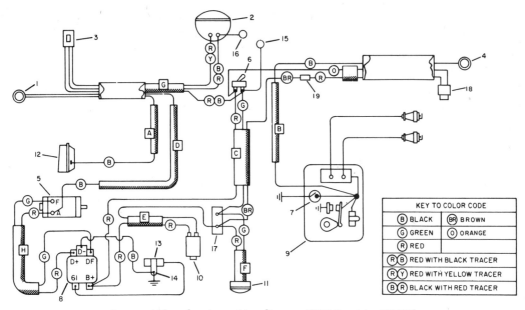

A magneto based system wiring diagram (1969 Sportster XLCH)

KEY TO COLOR CODE	
(B) BLACK	(BR) BROWN
(G) GREEN	(O) ORANGE
(R) RED	
(R)(B) RED WITH BLACK TRACER	
(R)(Y) RED WITH YELLOW TRACER	
(B)(R) BLACK WITH RED TRACER	

A. Conduit (one wire)—black
B. Conduit (one wire)—black
C. Conduit (two wires)—red and green
D. Conduit (one wire)—black
E. Conduit (two wires)—red
F. Conduit (two wires)—red and green
G. Conduit (three wires)—red wire with black tracer, red wire with yellow tracer, black wire with red tracer
H. Conduit (two wires)—green and red

1. Horn switch—two black wires
2. Headlamp—black wire with red tracer and red wire with yellow tracer
3. Headlamp dimmer switch—red wire with black tracer, red wire with yellow tracer, black wire with red tracer
4. Ignition cut-out switch—black wire
5. Generator
    F terminal—green wire
    A terminal—black wire
6. Light switch—red, green and red with black tracer wires
7. Ignition ground switch lock
8. Voltage regulator—
    DF terminal—green wire
    D+ terminal—red wire and condenser wire
    B+ terminal—two red wires
    D— terminal—black wire
9. Magneto—black wire
10. Stoplight rear switch—two red wires
11. Tail and stop lamp—red and green wires
12. Horn—black wire
13. Capacitor—black wire connected to regulator D— terminal
14. Grounding screw—black wire
15. Speedometer lamp
16. High beam indicator lamp
17. Terminal strip
18. Stoplamp front switch (late 1969)
19. Connector (late 1969)

just a blown bulb, the whole system is knocked out.

The ignition circuit can be further broken down into the high and low tension systems. The high tension system consists of the coil, the spark plug's high tension lead, and the spark plug, and is called the high tension system because the coil boosts the relatively low voltage produced by the alternator, generator, magneto, or whatever to the very high voltage necessary for a spark to jump the gap at the electrode. The low tension system starts at the battery, on battery equipped models, or at the magneto and runs to the coil. In

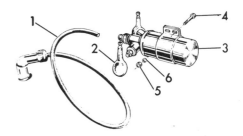

A H-D Sprint high tension system

1. Spark plug cable
2. Terminal cover (2)
3. Spark coil
4. Mounting screw
5. Nut
6. Washer

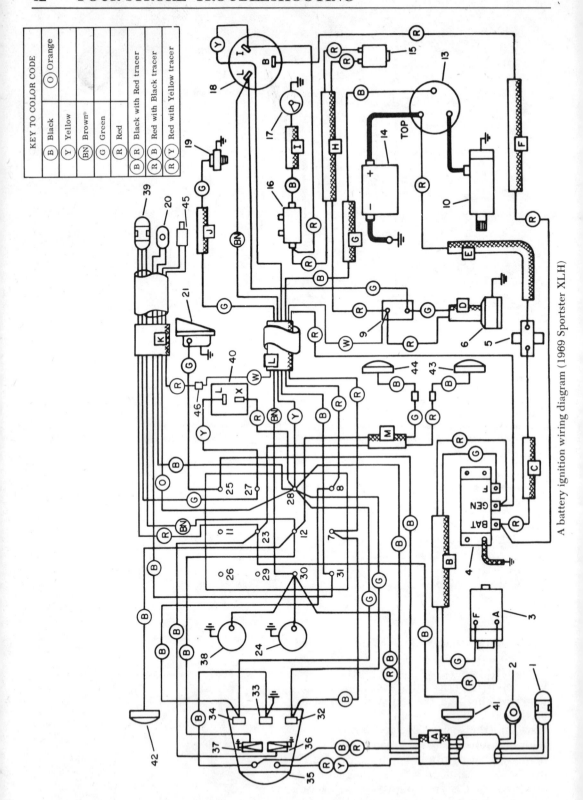

KEY TO COLOR CODE	
B	Black
Y	Yellow
BN	Brown
G	Green
R	Red
B R	Black with Red tracer
R B	Red with Black tracer
R Y	Red with Yellow tracer
O	Orange

A battery ignition wiring diagram (1969 Sportster XLH)

A. Handlebar (five wires)—red wire with black tracer, black wire with red tracer, red wire with yellow tracer, and 2 black wires

B. Conduit (two wires)—green and red

C. Conduit (one wire)—red

D. Conduit (two wires)—red and green

E. Conduit (one wire)—red

F. Conduit (one wire)—red

G. Conduit (one wire)—black
H. Conduit (two wires)—red
I. Conduit (one wire)—green
J. Conduit (one wire)—green
K. Handlebar (5 wires)—red, brown, green and 2 black wires
L. Conduit (five wires)—brown, yellow, black, red and green
M. Conduit (2 wires)—red and green

1. Headlamp dimmer switch
2. Horn switch
3. Generator F and A terminals
4. Regulator
   BAT terminal
   GEN terminal
   F terminal
5. Overload circuit breaker
6. Tail lamp
7. Terminal
8. Terminal
9. Junction terminal board
10. Starter motor
11. Terminal—not used with standard wiring
12. Terminal
13. Starter solenoid
14. Battery
15. Stoplight rear switch
16. Ignition coil
17. Circuit breaker

18. Ignition-light switch
19. Oil signal light switch
20. Starter button
21. Horn
22. Terminal plate
23. Terminal
24. Speedometer light
25. Terminal
26. Terminal—not used with standard wiring
27. Terminal—not used with standard wiring
28. Terminal
29. Terminal—not used with standard wiring
30. Terminal
31. Terminal
32. Oil signal light
33. High beam indicator light
34. Generator indicator light
35. Headlamp
36. Left direction signal pilot lamp
37. Right direction signal pilot lamp
38. Tachometer light
39. Direction signal switch
40. Direction signal flasher
41. Left front direction lamp
42. Right front direction lamp
43. Left rear direction lamp
44. Right rear direction lamp
45. Stoplamp front switch (late 1969)
46. Connector (late 1969)

between there may be an alternator or generator to recharge the battery (if applicable) and provide the current demanded by the engine's speed, and there may be other options such as an ignition switch, a kill switch or button, or an electric starter.

Somewhere along the line provision must be made to interrupt the flow of juice so the spark plug will fire at the correct time. Traditionally this is accomplished through use of a contact breaker and condenser. The condenser stores up juice while the points are closed, and then when the breaker cam opens the points, the current is free to flow and the charge which has been building up in the condenser is released. When a condenser goes bad it leaks current and then the charge isn't strong enough to jump the point gap effectively. It is this leaking current which burns and pits points because it is never cut off as it should be.

Try and localize the problem before you start tearing things apart. If you can, for example, determine that the problem is at the point plate you may find that it's just a bad ground or something cheap like that. If you work with a wiring diagram you should be able to figure out which component leads to attach the test light for testing continuity. If you can find out for sure

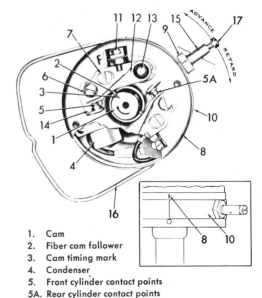

1.   Cam
2.   Fiber cam follower
3.   Cam timing mark
4.   Condenser
5.   Front cylinder contact points
5A. Rear cylinder contact points
6.   Lock screw
7.   Adjusting screw
8.   Timing mark
9.   Adjusting stud lock nut
10. Timing adjusting plate
11. Wire stud screw
12. Circuit breaker lever
13. Pivot stud
14. Contact point and support
15. Timing adjusting stud
16. Cover retainer
17. Control wire lock screw

A contact breaker in use on Harley-Davidson Twins

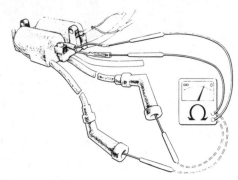

Testing coils for continuity

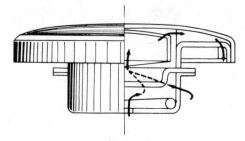

Air flow through a Honda gas cap

which part is the troublemaker you can replace the part and see if the problem is resolved. Be sure before you start swapping parts though, because most parts men won't take back an electrical part once its been on the bike. Consult Chapter 5 for more detailed information on the subject.

CHECKING THE FUEL SYSTEM

As mentioned previously, the first thing to check for here is fuel delivery. Blockage of a fuel line or carburetor jet may come on suddenly if loose matter lodges in a passageway. If the bike is running when the problem comes on it will almost always begin to sputter and wheeze before it cuts out, but if the machine has been in storage for a while it may have become blocked by deposits and consequently will fail to deliver enough fuel for combustion. Two items which often go unnoticed are the air cleaner and the gas cap vent. A clogged or oil soaked air cleaner will cause so excessively rich a mixture that the engine can't breathe well enough for combustion to occur, and if the vent is

plugged, air can't get in to replace the gas which is used, and a partial vacuum is created which prevents the fuel from flowing.

The first thing to determine in instances of fuel starvation is at what point the fuel flow is blocked. Disconnect the fuel line at the petcock and turn on the tap. If the fuel won't flow at this time, remove and inspect the petcock. Many models have a fuel filter located on top of the petcock which

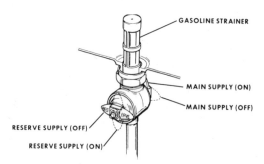

GASOLINE STRAINER

MAIN SUPPLY (ON)

MAIN SUPPLY (OFF)

RESERVE SUPPLY (OFF)

RESERVE SUPPLY (ON)

A diaphragm type petcock with fuel strainer

can become clogged by impurities in the gas or by rust particles from inside the tank. The petcock should also be cleaned out with a suitable solvent or replaced if defective. Another possibility, although somewhat remote, is that the fuel line itself

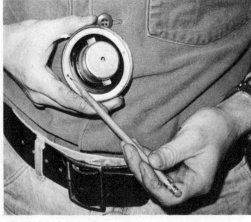

Check for a clogged gas cap vent

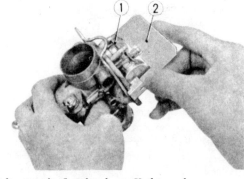

Adjusting the float level on a Keihin carb

1. Float
2. Float level gauge

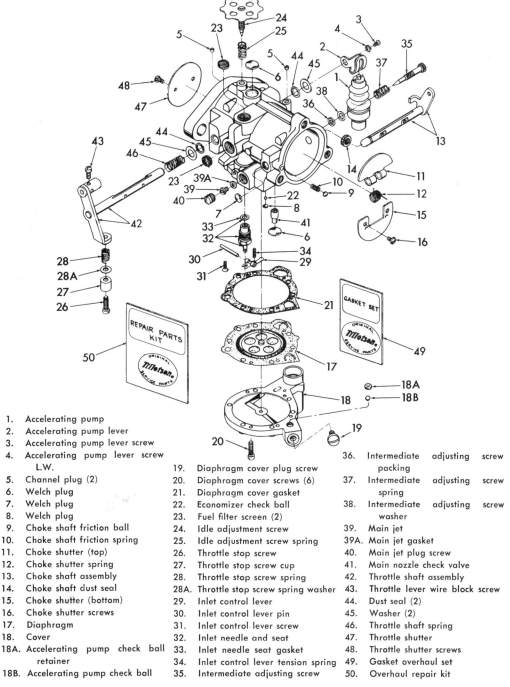

A Harley-Davidson model HD diaphragm type carburetor

1. Accelerating pump
2. Accelerating pump lever
3. Accelerating pump lever screw
4. Accelerating pump lever screw L.W.
5. Channel plug (2)
6. Welch plug
7. Welch plug
8. Welch plug
9. Choke shaft friction ball
10. Choke shaft friction spring
11. Choke shutter (top)
12. Choke shutter spring
13. Choke shaft assembly
14. Choke shaft dust seal
15. Choke shutter (bottom)
16. Choke shutter screws
17. Diaphragm
18. Cover
18A. Accelerating pump check ball retainer
18B. Accelerating pump check ball

19. Diaphragm cover plug screw
20. Diaphragm cover screws (6)
21. Diaphragm cover gasket
22. Economizer check ball
23. Fuel filter screen (2)
24. Idle adjustment screw
25. Idle adjustment screw spring
26. Throttle stop screw
27. Throttle stop screw cup
28. Throttle stop screw spring
28A. Throttle stop screw spring washer
29. Inlet control lever
30. Inlet control lever pin
31. Inlet control lever screw
32. Inlet needle and seat
33. Inlet needle seat gasket
34. Inlet control lever tension spring
35. Intermediate adjusting screw

36. Intermediate adjusting screw packing
37. Intermediate adjusting screw spring
38. Intermediate adjusting screw washer
39. Main jet
39A. Main jet gasket
40. Main jet plug screw
41. Main nozzle check valve
42. Throttle shaft assembly
43. Throttle lever wire block screw
44. Dust seal (2)
45. Washer (2)
46. Throttle shaft spring
47. Throttle shutter
48. Throttle shutter screws
49. Gasket overhaul set
50. Overhaul repair kit

may be clogged. This of course can be easily remedied by poking something through it.

If the problem still eludes you it's time to pull apart the carburetor. Try tapping on the float bowl with a wrench before tearing into the carb because it may just be a hung-up float, and make certain the choke is working correctly. It helps to have an exploded diagram or a step-by-step list of procedures (such as is found in the individual Chilton *Repair and Tune-Up Guides*), but if you take your time and are attentive to how it came apart you shouldn't have any trouble. Use a light hand on the wrenches, especially on Japanese carbs, and avoid scoring, gouging, or in any way deforming the parts. Clean it out carefully with a suitable solvent and then put it back together using all the parts which come in a carb rebuilding kit. Take special care in adjusting the float level, and make sure the float and valve move freely. It's not necessary to install a kit, but once the gaskets are used they may leak and cause an excessively lean mixture. Consult Chapter 4 for additional information.

CHECKING THE MECHANICAL SYSTEM

Mechanical problems generally come on slowly, and assuming your engine hasn't expired with the proverbial big bang, it probably indicated something was going wrong before it stopped running. An engine can't break down due to mechanical difficulties overnight if it was running the day before, unless it breaks while you're kicking it over, so try to remember if it was making any unusual noises when last run.

It should be very easy to localize the problem to one of the following areas; top end, bottom end, clutch, or transmission. Running a compression check, as described previously, should tell you what's happening in the top end, and cranking the bike over will let you know if the bottom end is free. Kicking the bike will let you know right away if the kick starter mechanism is damaged, and whether or not the engine turns over will say something about the state of the clutch. The gearbox, unless totally wiped out, shouldn't keep a machine from starting.

Poor Engine Performance

HARD STARTING OR ERRATIC PERFORMANCE

If you've got an old machine that has never run quite right, or if your machine is equipped with high performance parts this section is not for you. No amount of tuning can smooth out a rough idle caused by a worn carburetor slide, or make a machine

with a hot cam idle well. What we're dealing with here is the machine that has been getting progressively worse, or one that suddenly becomes difficult to start, and consequently also probably runs erratically.

If your machine has a battery assisted ignition and the battery is weak or poorly grounded you'll have trouble getting it started because the battery is supposed to provide the impetus to get things rolling. A quick trip to the gas station, and a subsequent check with a hydrometer, will indicate whether or not the battery is sufficiently charged. If the reading of any cell is below 1.200 at 68° F, the battery should

Keep an eye on the battery's specific gravity

be recharged using a low-output charger, such as a trickle charger, according to the manufacturer's directions. A good battery should read between 1.260–1.280 at 68° F. Make sure the terminals are clean and secure.

Next, take a close look at the spark plug's condition and heat range. Maybe it's too cold a plug for the engine or climate, or possibly it wasn't even designed for use in your particular kind of engine. Consult the "Tune-Up Analysis" section for additional information, and for hints on how to read engine condition by looking at the plug.

How is the carburetor idle mixture screw (if applicable) adjusted? It is possible that the adjustment may have been

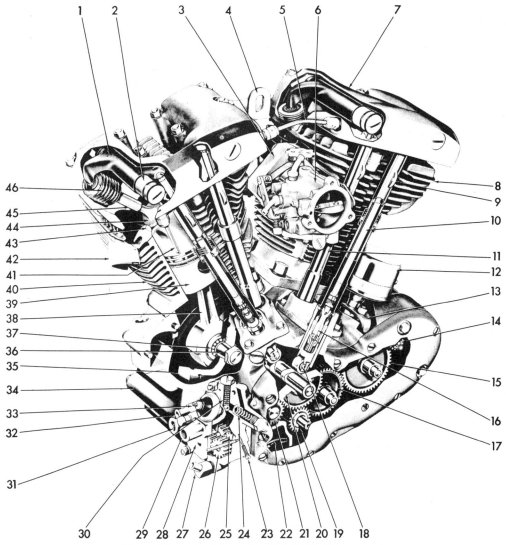

The visible engine (shown is a 1967 H-D Glide engine)

1. Rocker arm	17. Intermediate gear	33. Oil pressure switch
2. Rocker arm shaft	18. Tappet and roller assembly	34. Crankcase
3. Carburetor insulator	19. Pinion gear	35. Flywheel
4. Engine mounting bracket	20. Cam gear	36. Crankpin
5. Oil line	21. Breather gear	37. Connecting rod roller bearing
6. Carburetor	22. Breather screen	38. Connecting rod
7. Rocker arm cover	23. Chain oiler screw	39. Piston
8. Cylinder head	24. By-pass valve	40. Cylinder
9. Push rod cover keeper	25. Oil feed pump drive gears	41. Overhead oil line
10. Push rod	26. Oil scavenger drive gears	42. Exhaust port
11. Push rod cover	27. Oil feed nipple	43. Exhaust valve seat
12. Circuit breaker (timer)	28. Oil pump cover	44. Exhaust valve
13. Clamp	29. Oil return nipple	45. Exhaust valve guide
14. Generator drive gear	30. Check valve	46. Valve spring
15. Idler gear	31. Breather outlet	
16. Hydraulic lifter	32. Chain oil return	

changed by engine vibration, or the needle's seat may have been beveled by a heavy handed mechanic somewhere along the way. If the machine has a preset idle circuit it may be partially blocked by gum residues or foreign particles, and in this case an overhaul, or at least a thorough cleaning may be in order.

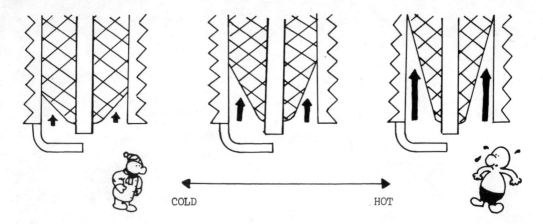

COLD   HOT

The next thing to check is the ignition timing which normally changes with wear of the points and the cam fiber rubbing block. Dirt or oil, or perhaps a cracked rubbing block may cause an intermittent miss so make sure the point plate is well grounded and clean. While you are at it take a look at the automatic advance unit (if applicable) and the cam itself. The springs on the advance mechanism may be worn or damaged, or the cam may be scored from many miles of use without sufficient lubrication. Even though the advance unit looks fine it may be slightly off, so you should first static-time the engine and then check the advanced timing with a strobe light. If the bike kicks back at you when you try to start it, look immediately to the spark advancer.

While you're checking out the timing, how about the points? If they are burned, worn or pitted, they should be dressed up or replaced. If they are badly pitted or

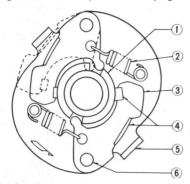

Spark advance mechanism

1. Breaker cam
2. Governor spring
3. Governor weight
4. Rubber bushing
5. Stopper
6. Governor weight support

burned they should be replaced as a matter of course, and the condenser should be held suspect. You probably won't have access to a factory tester, so if you think the condenser is faulty you should replace it

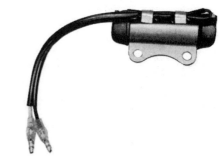

Condenser

and note whether there is a difference in performance. If the points are oily it is necessary to locate the source of the oil leak and repair it, or the points are just going to act up again soon. All of the above information also pertains to magneto equipped machines, and in addition you should also pay attention to the condition of the slip ring. It too, like the points, must remain clean in order to properly perform its function.

By now you've hit on all tune-up points except the valves. Valves work themselves loose, not tight, so if the bike has begun to run progressively worse it's not valves. The valves could be slowly burning, or their seats or guides could be in need of attention; this should show up during a compression check. However, if you just tuned the bike and it has become hard to start, and it won't run at high revs, the valves may be adjusted too tight, so adjust them carefully and see what happens.

Another thing a compression check may indicate is that the rings are worn, the head gasket leaks, or the piston has a hole in it. Any one of these indicates that it soon will be time to do a top end job. If the rings are worn you'll know it by the voluminous blue smoke, and if the gasket leaks, the spark plugs will look burnt.

Overheated spark plugs may also indicate a leak at the intake manifold. An easy

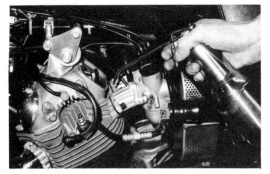

Checking for air leaks at the intake manifold

way to determine if this is the case, and to locate the leak, is to squirt some solvent on the manifold while the bike is running. If the idle smooths out it was leaking, and the bubbles will reveal the leak.

Two more remote possibilities which would most likely only pertain to poorly maintained older machines are a clogged air cleaner or exhaust baffle. If the air filter element becomes oil soaked or filled

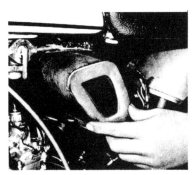

A dirty air cleaner can rob your machine of horsepower

with dirt it can restrict intake air flow so much that the machine becomes a hard starter and a poor performer. A clogged muffler can also cause hard starting because it creates excessive back pressure. The solution in either case is to remove the offending item and clean it thoroughly or replace it.

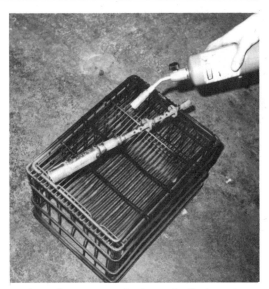

Carbon deposits can be burned off the exhaust baffle

Lastly, if the machine has been stored for a while and then is put into service without being properly serviced, there may be gum deposits in the jets, or the float may hang up. The solution here is a thorough cleaning or an overhaul.

ENGINE DIES WHEN THROTTLE IS OPENED

Theoretically, you should be able to crack open the throttle of a well tuned machine as fast as you'd like without causing the engine to bog, but in practice this is not usually the case. On many machines, someone with an exceptionally fast throttle hand is going to have problems regardless of how well the machine is tuned, so these hints are more for the rider who notices that throttle response has become slower than normal.

The first thing to check is the state of tune of the machine. Although the problem is probably related to the carburetor, bogging or stumbling may be caused by retarded ignition timing. This would cause a decrease in performance, but still allow the engine to start easily. While you are tuning, take special care to get the carburetor settings as close as possible to factory specifications, because this symptom is often caused by too rich a mixture. Also, the idle speed of the engine is very important for fast throttle response. If you are trying to impress your riding buddies by having a machine that ticks over at 600 rpm, the carburetor can't handle the sudden increase in venturi size and the subsequent pressure demands of the main jet.

Next, check the choke assembly for proper operation. If the linkage is improperly adjusted it may cause the engine to be partially choked at all times. Also, make sure nothing is holding the choke linkage in a partially choked position. This was found to be a problem on some Sportsters on which the air cleaner was keeping the lever from reaching its seat fully.

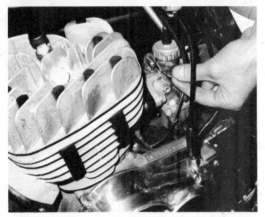

Make sure the choke is operating correctly

If you still haven't found the problem it's time to overhaul the carburetor. Maybe the idle jet is partially clogged or the needle is in the wrong position. It is possible that an air leak at the intake manifold has been compensated for by installing the wrong size jets, and therefore the vacuum is reduced too much to immediately provide enough fuel.

ENGINE MISFIRES

If your engine misses off the line, but runs fine the rest of the time, funny carburetion is probably the reason. Most likely the reason is too rich a low speed mixture which is indicated by a rough idle, black exhaust smoke, and misfiring upon application of the throttle. It is necessary to lean out the mixture to relieve this situation. If this problem presents itself only during the early stages of the day's ride it may be due to water in the float bowl or fuel strainer. What happens is that water is drawn into the carb before the gas, and this causes the engine to misfire since water won't burn. Misfiring at the low end can also be caused by a clogged air cleaner or a dirty spark plug, but in most cases this will result in poor performance throughout the engine's range.

If you have a miss that occurs at a certain rpm regardless of what gear you are in, the first thing to suspect is a defective automatic advance mechanism (if applicable) that operates correctly up to a certain point. Examine the springs of the advance mechanism carefully, and replace them, or

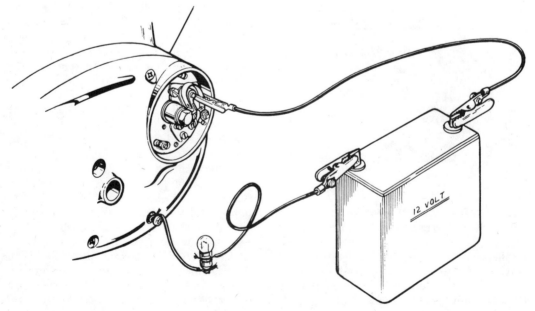

A simple static timing arrangement

Checking the advanced timing

the unit, if they appear stretched or damaged. If the machine is equipped with a battery ignition the problem may be improper timing. A simple adjustment will indicate if this was the problem. Static timing doesn't tell you anything about how the engine is timed once the automatic advance comes into play, so static time the engine, then strobe time it and compare results.

One other possibility is that an excessively rich mixture is causing "eight cycling," but this is unlikely. In any event your spark plug should tell you if the mixture is so rich that such a condition could exist.

Completely erratic misfiring is most likely due to an electrical problem somewhere. On machines with a battery ignition, look at the ignition system from the battery to the plugs, but don't overlook the ignition and kill switches, and on a magneto system check everything including the ammeter, turn signals, stop light switch, etc.

If you start dropping shots while running uphill, it may be caused by several things. First, check the plug; it may be breaking down from overheating because the gap is set wrong or because it has the wrong heat range. Improper mixture caused by too large a main jet, or by a clogged air cleaner may be the reason, or the engine just may be really out of time. A more obscure possibility may lie in the octane rating of the gas you are using. High compression engines need high octane fuel to really get it on, so don't sell out your engine's performance for mere pennies.

High rpm misses, and by this we mean on the left side of the red line, are difficult to cure because there are so many possible contributing factors. In many cases the culprit will be a component that is losing its edge, and therefore only begins to act up when pushed to its limits. Plugs, condensers, coils, or leaking high tension leads are some of the more common causes, but the possibility of damaged parts shouldn't be overlooked.

One of the first things to check is the carburetion. The main jet controls mixture at high speeds, so if you've got the wrong size jet, or if the jet is damaged, you're going to have problems. Other carburetor related problems are a dirty air cleaner, improper float adjustment (probably too low), or an improperly adjusted choke. It is possible that the problem is caused by air leaks at the intake manifold or by a stopped up exhaust pipe, but these sorts of things would show up at lower revs, and might even keep the machine from ever reaching high rpms.

If it is an electrical problem, arriving at a solution may be more difficult. A spark plug that has fouled before may never get it on at high revs again. Check the plugs and replace them if they are worn out or fouled. Is the heat range correct for the conditions? Is the gap too large for the spark to make the jump at high speeds?

If the problem is caused by a bad condenser, the points ought to tell you because they will probably pit quickly. The only way to determine if this is the case is to replace the condenser and see what happens. The same applies for a coil. Unless your dealer has a factory tester you'll probably have to substitute a new part and check the results. If the high tension lead is leaking, or if the plug cap isn't on tight, there might not be enough juice getting to the plug at high speeds. Run your fingers along the high tension lead while the engine is running. If your fingers tingle replace the lead and/or cap.

If you haven't found the solution yet it's got to be mechanical. A burnt or bent valve, a tired advance mechanism, or an air leak at the exhaust pipe could cause a high speed miss. If all else fails tune it up carefully again and make sure the valves aren't too tight.

One of the most annoying misses occurs when the engine is backing down from high revs. This sounds more like a pop in the pipes than a miss, and can be very difficult to solve. A slightly overrich mixture or unbalanced manifold vacuum (on the multi-cylindered super bikes) are the most common causes, but it also may be caused by a pinhole in the exhaust system or by a chipped valve seat. In any case, the plugs will probably look normal and it isn't dangerous—just a nuisance.

POOR GENERAL PERFORMANCE

Any machine which is left at idle too long, or which is run very slowly in traffic, will build up surpluses of fuel and carbon that will cause low speed stumbling. This can usually be cleared up by a couple of high rpm shifts, unless of course the plugs have become irrevocably fouled in which case they will have to be pulled and cleaned or replaced.

If your machine always runs poorly at low speeds, but runs fine once you open it up, look to the carburetor for the solution. A proper tune-up according to the manufacturer's specifications is in order, or, if the bike is loaded with high performance goodies, a little experimenting with the idle circuit may help some. Don't forget to check the needle adjustment.

If you've eliminated carburetion as the source of the troubles, check the timing. More than likely a good tuning will fix things up.

If the engine just doesn't have any punch at high speeds the first thing to do is to run through your maintenance and tune-up procedures. A machine with a clogged air cleaner, dirty points, a poor state of tune, or a weak battery is not going to give all it can, so check these things first.

If, after making sure everything is as it should be, the machine still doesn't want to get out of its own way, look for mechanical weaknesses. An older bike may have weak valve springs, worn rings or poorly seated valves that are robbing it of compression, or a clutch that slips when heavily stressed.

If all of the above checks out and you still can't get what you want out of the machine maybe you are just expecting more than the machine is able to offer. In that case it's time to get a bigger bike.

If the machine won't perform throughout the power range, and you've made certain that everything is just as it should be, look for the ridiculous like an oil pump that isn't clearing the sump, or brakes that are dragging. Other things that can slow you down are bad wheel bearings, a dry or overtightened drive chain, or something rubbing against the tires.

ENGINE VIBRATION

Vibration is a bad sign and its cause should be determined before everything falls apart. The most common cause, outside of those possibilities dealt with in Chapter 7, is loose or damaged engine mounts, so check these out carefully.

Other possible causes, and these will usually come on gradually (or immediately following some work that wasn't done right), are an incorrectly assembled clutch, improper ignition timing, a worn crankshaft, or bad main bearings. The solution should be sought immediately as all of these are serious, and will probably be shortly followed by some sort of massive failure.

EXCESSIVE OIL CONSUMPTION

It is impossible to dogmatically place a limit on when oil consumption becomes excessive because each machine has its own characteristics. Some early Nortons, for example were oil burners because they did not use valve seals, but that doesn't mean they are less of a machine than a perfectly oil tight Honda. The oil we're concerned with here is that which is used up by the engine, not that which winds up on the garage floor or the rear wheel. You are alright until you begin to get a blue smoke from the pipes, an oil soaked spark plug, and amazing deposits on the exhaust pipe and baffle.

The first thing to consider is what kind of oil you are using. If you try to run a lightweight oil in a Harley during the summer you are going to burn up more oil than necessary. If the breather pipe is clogged you are going to use up a lot also. These things don't present any problem, but if it's bad valve guides or seals, bad rings, or a bad pump check valve, it's going to mean some work.

If all of a sudden you don't have any oil pressure, it's because either the pump is jammed, the pressure check valve is clogged, or the pump drive is broken. If the pressure drops off gradually it may be due to excessive clearances in the parts which are supplied under pressure. In either case you shouldn't try to run the engine as serious damage will result.

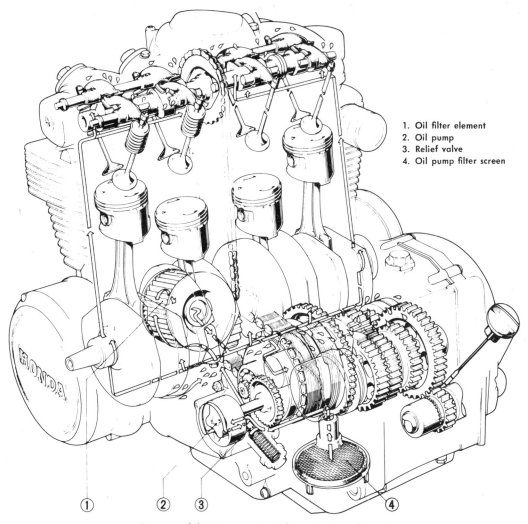

1. Oil filter element
2. Oil pump
3. Relief valve
4. Oil pump filter screen

Dry sump lubrication system (shown is a Honda 500)

A relatively common problem, especially with machines whose oil has not been changed as often as it should have been, is a lack of return to the tank. The causes of this will vary, but the symptoms, excessive consumption, heavy exhaust smoking, and a visible lack of return to the tank, are fairly universal.

Usually this is caused by a failure of the return pump, a blocked oil line, a stuck check valve, a blown gasket, or something else in the return system. Another possibility is that the feed pump has failed; this can be differentiated from a return failure because the smoking and consumption won't be present.

An intermittently stuck check valve is a

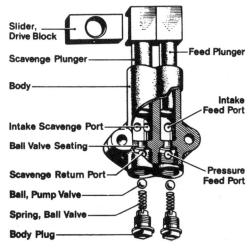

Plunger type pump (shown is a Triumph 650)

Slider, Drive Block
Scavenge Plunger
Body
Feed Plunger
Intake Feed Port
Intake Scavenge Port
Ball Valve Seating
Scavenge Return Port
Ball, Pump Valve
Spring, Ball Valve
Body Plug
Pressure Feed Port

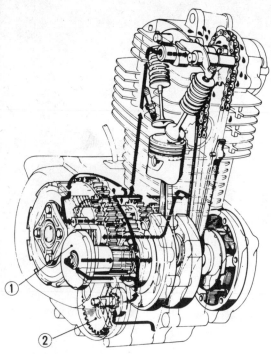

Wet sump lubrication system (shown is a Honda 100)

1. Oil filter
2. Oil pump

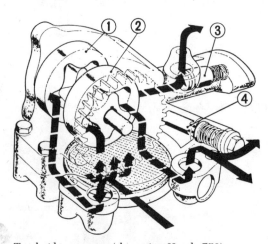

Trochoid type pump (shown is a Honda 750)

1. Delivery pump   3. Leak stopper valve
2. Scavenger pump   4. Relief valve

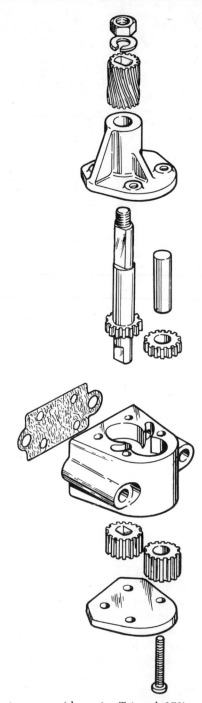

Gear type pump (shown is a Triumph 250)

fairly common problem, and can be caused by something as simple as a small piece of grit around the ball's seat. The only way to relieve a situation like this is to repeatedly flush the system. Generally this is not immediately dangerous, but may seem so because the oil trapped in the sump will be burned resulting in enough smoke to thrill the heart of any two-cycle afficionado.

ENGINE OVERHEATING AND SEIZURE

These are interrelated because overheating causes, or usually immediately precedes, seizure. A bike usually seizes after

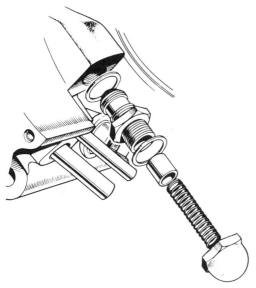

Oil pressure relief valve (shown is a Triumph Trident)

Pre-ignition holed this piston (Courtesy of Kiekhaefer Mercury, Fon du Lac, Wisconsin)

This damage was caused by detonation due to the use of poor fuel (Courtesy of Kiekhaefer Mercury, Fond du Lac, Wisconsin)

being run with an insufficient amount of oil. What happens is that the piston expands because the oil isn't present to carry away the heat and to lubricate the cylinder walls. Eventually the piston expands so much that it can no longer move freely in the cylinder and the engine stops . . . suddenly. If you should ever feel the engine start to lose power, and if it should start feeling abnormally tight, move your hand over to the clutch lever and back off on the throttle. If you should hear a very metallic screech, pull in the clutch right away and look for a way out of the traffic; your bike is going to stop very soon. If this happens let the engine cool off for as long as possible before you try starting it again. In any case, be prepared to tear it down and have the cylinders honed at the very least.

Part of the cooling process is carried out by the fuel mixture because gas absorbs a lot of heat quickly, much more so than the air it gets mixed with. A lean mixture, in which there isn't enough gas to cool off the engine, causes the engine to run hot. If the mixture is too rich it doesn't burn efficiently and fouls the plugs. Therefore, if your carburetor is set too lean, or if you have air leaks at the intake manifold, the engine will overheat, and may even seize or hole a piston.

Ignition timing is also critical in keeping an engine running cool. The engine is timed for a spark to occur at a certain number of degrees before top dead center. If the spark is retarded, by the time the plug fires, the piston has moved too far and is subjected to excessive heat; this also can cause a holed piston.

Using too hot a spark plug can also cause overheating and a holed piston. For this reason, it is always recommended that you determine why a plug fouls and correct the situation, instead of using a hotter plug in hopes that it won't foul.

As was mentioned before, probably the greatest reason for overheating and subsequent engine seizure is running with an insufficient oil supply. Overheating can also be caused by using oil with too light a viscosity for the machine and the conditions. Rather remote possibilities are an overworked or dirty engine. If you do a lot of first gear mucking about in the woods, or if you expect your 80 cc trail bike to haul your 300 lb body up a 60° grade all day,

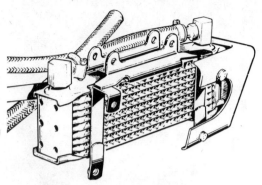

An oil cooler used on the BSA Rocket 3

well you're just doing it all wrong. Also, make sure the bike isn't being forced to overwork because of increased resistance caused by too tight a chain, bad bearings, or rubbing brakes.

Finally, the subject of cleanliness. An air-cooled engine needs to be able to bathe itself in the breezes. If your bike is covered with caked-on grease and road grime it will run hotter than necessary. A clean bike is a happy, healthy bike.

ENGINE NOISES

One of the first indications of change in the condition of your motorcycle is the sounds that emanate from it. A thoughtful rider will know something is going wrong long before it happens and may be able to rectify the situation before it leads to costly repairs. Every machine has its own sounds and these sounds will remain constant until something begins to go wrong. Pay attention to this and whenever a new sound appears consult your local mechanic because he's the one who's heard them all before.

Valve Clatter

When tappet adjustment time comes rolling around you'll know it because the valves will let you know. They always make some noise, especially when cold, but will really get noisy when in need of attention. When listening to the tappets keep in mind that as long as you can hear them they're alright. If you can't hear anything as soon as you start the bike they're too tight and will cause damage to the valve train. One good way of listening to the valves is to place the metal tip of a screwdriver against the rocker box and listen through the handle.

Pinging

Poor quality gasoline, advanced ignition timing, incorrect spark plug heat range, or a piece of metal or carbon in the combustion chamber can be the cause of pinging (or pinking if we're talking about a British bike).

Pinging sounds are generally associated with the top end, and occur at mid throttle range during acceleration. Most of the time it is caused by pre-ignition due to the use of low octane fuel in a high compression engine. The unnecessary detonation causes undue strain on piston assemblies and bearings.

If the ignition timing is advanced too far, the force of the combustion will try to force the piston down before it completes its rotation. This is another type of pre-ignition and is as harmful as the use of poor fuel. When pistons end up with holes in them it is often due to this, but may also be due to using the wrong heat range spark plug.

If the plug in use is too hot it can't dissipate heat quickly enough and begins to act like a glow plug. This also causes pre-ignition and can be corrected by using a colder plug.

Carbon or metal pieces in the combustion chamber can heat up and act like a glow plug. This is less common than the others and only occurs when the engine is running hot. The only way to quiet this type of pinging is through top end surgery.

Piston Slap

Slap occurs most often at mid throttle range during acceleration and requires a top end job to eliminate it. The noise is metallic and is caused by excessive piston-cylinder clearance. If the noise goes away after the engine warms up, the condition is not urgent but you'd better start planning on rebuilding the top end quite soon. One notable exception to this is in the case of big singles. These engines often slap even when in good condition, so perform all possible checks before tearing into things.

Knock

If you hear a mighty knocking noise coming from the bottom end while accelerating, you can be pretty sure the main bearings haven't long to go. It also may be a crankshaft problem and is remedied in either case by taking down the entire engine.

Rap

When the connecting rod bearings start to go, rap develops. This is most often heard during deceleration and increases in intensity with the speed of the engine.

Double Rap

This is caused by excessive piston/piston pin clearance and is most noticeable as a quick succession of raps at idle speeds.

Whine

In overhead cam engines an unusually loud whine often indicates a loose cam chain. It may also stem from primary or drive chains that are too tight or in need of lubrication.

Engines with ball or roller bearings in the bottom end don't thump when they go bad like plain bearings do, instead they whine and screech a lot. This rarely happens unless the machine has been run dry or really abused.

Tune-Up

When performing a tune-up you are restoring to peak efficiency certain engine components that are subject to changes in operating efficiency during use. A tune-up is nothing more than a series of adjustments performed in a logical order, one at a time, to predetermined specifications. There is no guesswork involved. There are no complicated disassembly procedures, and it is not necessary for you to have years of experience in diagnosing engine problems and speed tuning. All tune-up operations are quite straightforward.

A tune-up involves the following procedures, which should be performed in the order indicated:

1. Cam chain adjustment (if applicable);
2. Valve clearance adjustment;
3. Spark plug service and compression check;
4. Contact breaker points service;
5. Ignition timing;
6. Carburetor adjustment;
7. Any remaining maintenance operations which have been neglected such as cleaning the air and fuel filters, adjusting the drive chain, adjusting the clutch, etc.

Depending on the type of machine, the equipment necessary to perform a tune-up will vary as will the procedures and specifications. Since there are so many varieties of valve and ignition adjustments it is impossible to go into any detail on specific procedures. You should have the manufacturer's handbook, or a suitable substitute such as the individual Chilton Repair and Tune-Up Guides, a set of hand tools, a timing light or continuity tester of some sort, and any individual tools that may be necessary in the case of your particular machine (if you have a machine with a magneto, for example, it may be necessary to have a puller to remove the rotor to get at the points).

CAM CHAIN ADJUSTMENT

The basic reason for adjusting the cam chain is to reduce the noise of its operation. Some machines, such as many of the small displacement Hondas, have automatic chain adjusters that require no additional service. However, on the larger machines on which manual adjustment is necessary, it is a good idea to adjust the chain right away so its noise won't confuse you while you try to listen to the valves.

On Hondas, when the chain has stretched to the point where its noise level no longer can be adequately reduced, you can perform the adjustment in the manner adopted by the factory racing team. Place the kill switch in the OFF position, loosen the adjuster locknut, and turn the key on, then insert a thin piece of mechanic's wire or a screwdriver into the adjuster pushrod tube until seated on the pushrod. By operating the starter motor you can feel the pushrod moving in and out. When the rod is all the way in toward the engine, secure the adjuster locknut. It may take a little while to get the feel of this system, but it is without a doubt the most efficient method of adjustment. Take care not to apply any pressure on the pushrod though, as you may damage the mechanism; just let the pushrod move the screwdriver as it will.

VALVE TAPPET ADJUSTMENT

Valves should be set with the engine stone cold, except on certain machines which have accommodations for adjustment with the engine running. 450 Hondas, for example, can be adjusted either hot or cold, but great care must be exercised if it is done hot to avoid damaging the valve mechanism.

Since the clearances you will be working with are relatively small, take care to adjust the valves as closely as possible to specifications. Excessive clearance can cause unnecessary noise and accelerated cam lobe wear, and insufficient clearance can be responsible for hard starting, rough running, and ultimately, burned valves and valve seats. Take your time and make sure you've done it right. Make sure the surface of your feeler gauges is smooth and unmarred or an accurate adjustment may not be attained. After the first or second time you will develop a feel for the correct clearance and the job will go much faster.

SPARK PLUG SERVICE AND TUNE-UP ANALYSIS

The condition of the spark plug has a great deal of influence upon how an engine runs. Regardless of what it looks like, the spark plug, if it has many thousands of miles on it, should be replaced at this time as a matter of course. The spark plug high tension lead and connector should also be checked, and any component which appears to be in a less than perfect condition should be replaced.

Examine the tip of the plug and decide which plug in the illustration it most closely resembles. Check also for a cracked insulator or damaged threads. Light carbon deposits can be removed in a spark plug cleaning machine (which some garages have and will probably let you use), or by carefully scraping them away with a

small sharp instrument. Heavy carbon deposits are indicative of either a rich fuel mixture or too cold a plug heat range for the conditions in which it is being used. Be wary, however, of using a hotter plug unless actual plug fouling is occurring. Heat range does not refer to spark intensity, but to the ability of a spark plug to dissipate heat. A cold plug will dissipate heat rapidly, while a hotter plug will dissipate heat more slowly. The danger in using too hot a plug is that it will retain enough heat to cause pre-ignition and eventually severe overheating and piston failure. Generally, you should use the plug recommended by the manufacturer, or select the coldest heat range that is possible to use without fouling.

Oil fouling indicates excessive oil consumption caused by worn or sticking piston rings, worn valve stems and guides, or faulty valve stem oil seals. Do not attempt to cure oil fouling by using spark plugs of

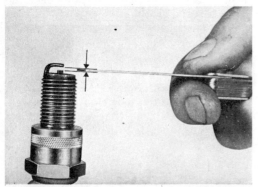

Make sure the plug is gapped according to specifications

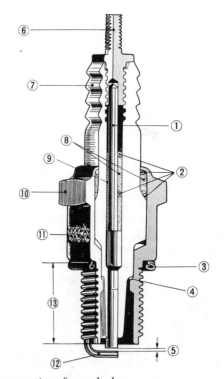

Cross section of a spark plug

1. Center electrode
2. Wire packing
3. Gasket
4. Plate packing
5. Spark clearance (gap)
6. Terminal
7. Insulation (with corrugation)
8. Filled powder
9. Bonding
10. Hex nut
11. Metallic main body
12. Ground electrode
13. Length of thread (reach)

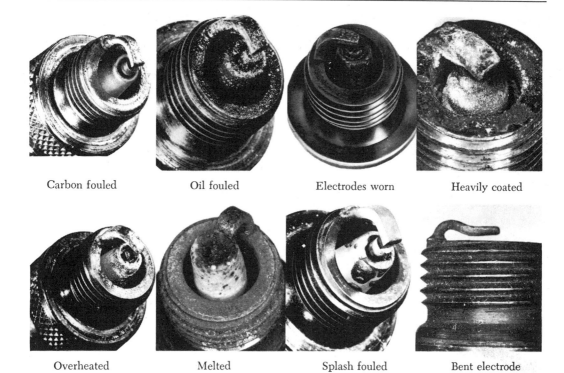

Carbon fouled	Oil fouled	Electrodes worn	Heavily coated

Overheated	Melted	Splash fouled	Bent electrode

Carbon Fouled Plugs
If only one plug is carbon fouled and others are normal, check ignition wiring for a break or loose connections. A compression check might indicate mechanical trouble in that cylinder.
If all plugs are sooted, fuel mixture might be too rich, spark gap could be too large, or the plug heat value is too high.

Oil Fouled Plugs
Plugs may have been "drowned" with fuel during cranking. If choke operates properly, fouling could be caused by poor oil control. A hotter plug is needed.

Excessive Electrode Gap
If all plugs have brown-gray deposits and electrode wear from .008" to .010" greater than original gap, they are completely worn. Replace entire set.

Heavily Coated Plugs
Heavy deposits, if easily flaked off, result from scavenger additives used in some brands of fuel. Though this accumulation creates heat buildup, its chemical nature causes only minimum electrical shorting. Replacement plugs should have same heat range.

Chipped Insulator
If one or two plugs in a set have chipped insulator tips, severe detonation was the likely cause. Bending the center electrode during gapping can also crack the insulator. Replace with new plugs of the correct gap and heat range. Check for over-advanced timing.

Normal, Usable Plugs
Plugs with evenly-colored light tan or gray deposits and moderate electrode wear (.005 gap growth) can be cleaned, regapped, and reinstalled.

All Plugs Overheated
If set has dead white insulators and badly eroded electrodes (.001" erosion per 1,000 miles), check ignition timing for over-advance. Install next colder heat range.

One Plug Badly Burned
If one plug in a set has melted electrodes, pre-ignition was likely encountered in that cylinder; check for intake manifold air leaks and possible cross fire. Be sure the one plug is not the wrong heat range.

Mechanical Damage
A broken insulator and bent electrodes result from some foreign object falling into the combustion chamber. If valves overlap, objects can travel from one cylinder to another. Always clean out cylinders to prevent recurrence.

One or Two Plugs "Splashed" Fouled
Some plugs in a relatively new set may have splashed deposits. This may occur after a long-delayed tune-up when accumulated cylinder deposits are thrown against the plugs at high engine rpm. Clean and reinstall these plugs.

Bent Side Electrodes
Improperly gapping plugs will weaken side electrode and alter electrical performance of spark plug.

a hotter heat range. The cause of oil burning should be determined and corrected. Run a compression test as described earlier in this chapter.

Burnt electrodes indicate too lean a fuel mixture or too hot a spark plug heat range. Check for air leaks at the carburetors and intake tubes, and check the fuel tap and lines for restrictions. Try using a plug whose heat range is one step colder.

Replace spark plugs that have damaged insulators or threats. If the old plug is to be reused, thoroughly clean the threads and insulator before installing it. Gap the electrode according to the manufacturer's specifications and lubricate the threads lightly with graphite or engine oil before installing either a new or used plug, then tighten the plug down about 1/4 turn past finger tight. Make sure you use a gasket on the plug, even if it's only a used one, because the plug is only intended to extend so far into the combustion chamber. Threads in an aluminum cylinder head can be easily cross threaded or stripped, therefore great care should be exercised when starting the plug into the threads. If you should strip the threads pull the head and take it to your dealer or a local machinist to have it helicoiled. Inserts are available for thread repair, but to insure that no particles fall into the cylinder, the head should be removed before attempting any repairs. If you plan to run a compression check do so before installing the plugs, but only if the engine is near normal operating temperature.

CONTACT BREAKER
POINT SERVICE

Examine the contact points for pitting, misalignment, and excessive wear of the rubbing block that rides on the breaker cam. If the points are in good condition except for a slight amount of pitting, they may be cleaned up using an ignition point file. Allow the points to spring shut on the file and move it back and forth without exerting any pressure against the point surface. Remove dirt and grit from between the points by pulling a thick piece of paper, such as a business card, through the points two or three times. Remember that the object is to restore the points to a serviceable condition, not a like-new condition. You don't want to remove too much of the point surface.

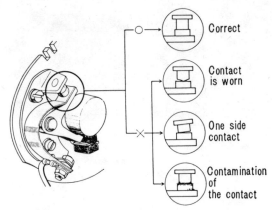

Points should be properly aligned

If the points are heavily pitted, replace the points and condenser. These can be obtained, in many cases, as a unit already mounted on a base plate, or as separate components which can be mounted in place of the worn units. Disconnect the electrical leads, taking care to note where everything goes, unscrew the components from the base plate assembly (depending of course on the type of machine you are working with and the manner of replacement you have chosen), and mount the new parts. If separate components are to be used, make sure to properly insulate the points with insulating washers which must be used in their original positions (unless your machine is supposed to have grounded points). Tighten things down firmly but avoid using excessive pressure as this may crack the insulating washers and cause unwanted grounding of the points. When the new parts are mounted reconnect the electrical leads.

Place a drop or two of some non-oily solvent on a piece of paper and pull it through the points to remove any dirt or preservative coating on the contact surfaces. Put a small daub of distributor cam lubricator or another high melting-point grease on the contact breaker cam. This will prevent the point rubbing block and the breaker cam from wearing excessively and thereby reducing the points gap.

IGNITION TIMING

Ignition timing should be carried out according to the manufacturer's instructions. Whenever possible, on machines which have both static and dynamic timing marks, the engine should be first static timed and then dynamic timed so a comparison can be made, and so the operation of the automatic advance unit (if applicable), can be checked.

CARBURETOR ADJUSTMENT

Again, because of the variations in carburetor design and manufacturer's specifications, it is impossible to give explicit instructions on carburetor adjustment within the confines of this book.

Carburetor tuning is largely a matter of patience and feel, the latter being developed with practice. Take your time and work with the procedures until you feel confident that the bike is responding properly. Do not hesitate to check and recheck your settings until you know they're right. Keep in mind that wear or abuse may necessitate an adjustment that is far removed from that recommended by the factory, so you'll have to play hit-and-miss for a while. After you have done it a few times you'll be able to tune the carburetor rapidly and accurately.

It is a good practice to check the mixture after you've set it. The best way to do this is to clean the spark plugs, install them, and then run the engine up to a high speed, pull in the clutch (if applicable) and cut the power. Do not allow the machine to come back to an idle speed, or allow it to run at low rpm before shutting it off (on centrifugal clutch models you can only check the average operating mix-ture). Remove the plugs and check their condition; if there are several plugs, even if they are fed by the same coil and/or carburetor, each plug should be checked separately because air leaks may be causing a different mixture to occur in one cylinder. If you've done a good job, providing you are using the right heat range plug, the electrode will look milky or tan. If the mixture is too lean the plug will look bleached and white. Repeat the above process, while making small ($1/4$–$1/8$ turn) adjustments, until the plug looks like it should.

If you ever see your exhaust pipe turn yellow or blue you can be sure that the mixture is way too lean and you should correct the situation immediately. If the bike blows dark smoke out of the exhaust pipe and you are fairly sure that everything is alright inside, check for too rich a mixture and correct it immediately. It's safest to have the mixture slightly rich, but if it gets too rich it will cause accelerated carbon build up, and may cause damage to the top end because the fuel cleans the protective oil coating off the cylinder walls.

If you are unable to arrive at a satisfactory adjustment, it may be because the needle is in the wrong position in its clip, or because the main jet is the wrong size. The larger the main jet, or the higher up the needle, the richer the mixture. For additional information consult Chapter 4.

Engine Troubleshooting

ENGINE FAILS TO START

Possible Causes	Remedy
Gas tank empty, petcock off, or fuel line clogged	Fill tank, open petcock, or blow out disconnected gas line
Engine flooded	Remove spark plugs and dry out
Insufficiently charged battery	Check electrolyte levels and charge battery
Corroded, loose, or broken battery terminal connections	Clean, secure, and/or replace
Fouled or improperly gapped spark plugs	Clean and gap, or replace
Spark plug cables leaking or damaged	Replace as necessary
Badly oxidized or dirty contact points	Consult section on Contact Breaker Points

Engine Troubleshooting

ENGINE FAILS TO START

Possible Causes	Remedy
Contact breaker points or ignition timing out of adjustment	Consult section on Contact Breaker Points
Loose connection in ignition circuit	Check wiring harness connections
Defective ignition coil or condenser	Replace as necessary
Clutch slipping and not turning engine over	Consult Chapter 6
Valves sticking or too tight	Consult section on Valve Tappet Adjustment
Engine and transmission oil too heavy for climatic conditions	Drain oil and replace with a lighter grade

ENGINE IS HARD TO START

Possible Causes	Remedy
Spark plugs in bad condition or partially fouled	Consult section on Spark Plugs
Contact breaker points dirty, pitted or out of adjustment	Consult section on Contact Breaker Points
Battery insufficiently charged	Check electrolyte level and charge battery
Carburetor out of adjustment	Consult section on Carburetor Adjustments
Defective ignition coil or condenser	Replace as necessary
Oil too heavy for climatic conditions	Drain oil and replace with a lighter grade
Ignition timing out of adjustment	Consult section on Contact Breaker Points
Loose or intermittently grounded wires at battery, coil or contact breaker	Check connections and consult Chapter 5
Poor compression	Consult section on Tune-Up Analysis
Contact breaker advance mechanism sticking	Consult section on Contact Breaker Points

ENGINE IDLES POORLY AND MISFIRES DURING ACCELERATION

Possible Causes	Remedy
Spark plugs dirty	Clean as described in Spark Plug section
Weak spark	Consult section on Electrical Troubleshooting and Chapter 5
Poor connection at spark plug cable	Check connection
Air leakage at carburetor manifold	Consult Chapter 4
Obstruction in carburetor main jet	Consult Chapter 4
Incorrect carburetor adjustment	Consult section on Carburetor Adjustments
Water in carburetor	Disassemble and clean
Mixture too rich (mid-throttle range misfire)	Consult section on Tune-Up Analysis

Engine Troubleshooting

ENGINE IDLES POORLY AND MISFIRES DURING ACCELERATION

Possible Causes	Remedy
Retarded ignition timing (low speed, poor performance)	Adjust ignition timing
Automatic advance unit sticking (low speed, poor performance)	Lubricate breaker cam and advance unit

SPARK PLUG FOULS REPEATEDLY

Possible Causes	Remedy
Too cold a plug for the type of service	Use a plug one step hotter (consult section on Spark Plug Service and Tune-Up Analysis)
Piston rings badly worn	Replace as necessary
Cracked ceramic portion of spark plug	Replace plug
Too rich a fuel mixture	See Tune-Up Analysis

LOSS OF COMPRESSION AND POWER

Possible Causes	Remedy
Valves sticking due to gummed valve stems	Disassemble and clean or replace as necessary
Valve tappets set too close	Consult section on Valve Tappet Adjustment
Collapsed or damaged piston	Replace as necessary
Badly worn piston rings	Replace as necessary
Damaged head gasket	Replace as necessary

ENGINE PARTIALLY SEIZES OR SLOWS AFTER SUSTAINED, HIGH-SPEED OPERATION

Possible Causes	Remedy
Spark plug too hot and causing preignition	Use a plug one step cooler
Piston seizure	Replace piston and rings as necessary
Carburetor mixture too lean causing overheating	Consult sections on Carburetor Adjustment and Tune-Up Analysis
Insufficient oil supply, oil not circulating, or pump working insufficiently	Examine pump and repair as necessary and/or clean out oil lines

ENGINE OVERHEATS

Possible Causes	Remedy
Valves or rings excessively worn	Replace as necessary
Insufficient oil supply, oil not circulating, or pump working insufficiently	Examine pump and repair as necessary and/or clean out oil lines
Heavy carbon deposits on piston crown	Disassemble and decarbonize

Engine Troubleshooting

ENGINE OVERHEATS

Possible Causes	Remedy
Retarded ignition timing	Adjust ignition timing
Automatic advance unit sticking in the retarded position	Lubricate the breaker cam and advance unit

ENGINE DETONATES OR PREIGNITES

Possible Causes	Remedy
Spark plug too hot for service application	Use a plug one step cooler
Spark excessively advanced	Adjust ignition timing
Carburetor mixture too lean	Consult section on Carburetor Adjustments
Excessive carbon deposits on piston crown	Disassemble and decarbonize
Fuel octane rating too low	Use higher quality fuel

ENGINE BACKFIRES OR KICK-STARTER KICKS BACK

Possible Causes	Remedy
Incorrect ignition timing	Adjust ignition timing
Automatic advance unit sticking	Lubricate the breaker cam and advance unit

ENGINE USES TOO MUCH OIL

Possible Causes	Remedy
Breather valve obstructed	Clean as necessary
Piston rings worn or frozen	Replace as necessary
Chain oiler incorrectly adjusted	Readjust
Engine oil leak to outside	Replace gasket or seal
Oil grade too light	Drain and use a heavier grade oil

OIL DOES NOT RETURN TO TANK

Possible Causes	Remedy
Oil tank empty	Replenish oil supply
Scavenger pump gear sheared	Replace as necessary
Oil feed pump gear sheared	Replace as necessary
Oil return line clogged	Clear out the lines

Engine Troubleshooting

CONTACT POINTS BURN OR PIT RAPIDLY

Possible Causes	Remedy
Defective condenser	Replace
Loose condenser terminals	Secure terminals
Loose or dirty battery terminals	Secure and clean terminals
Dirty contact points	Clean points

RAPID PISTON AND CYLINDER WEAR

Possible Causes	Remedy
Operating in dusty conditions without an air cleaner or with a dirty or clogged air cleaner element	Install air cleaner or replace element

EXCESSIVE VIBRATION

Possible Causes	Remedy
Engine mounting bolts loose	Secure
Broken frame	Consult your dealer
Primary chain badly worn, insufficiently lubricated, or too tight	Consult Chapter 7
Loose axle nuts	Secure
Excessive wheel hub radial play	Replace wheel hub bearings as necessary
Loose spokes	Secure
Rear wheel out of alignment	Align rear axle to path of front wheel
Wheel rims out of true	Consult Chapter 7
Tires unevenly worn	Replace and determine reason why
Tires incorrectly inflated	Correct as specified
Worn steering head bearings	Replace as necessary
Swing arm bearings too tight or too loose	Adjust as necessary

Carburetor Troubleshooting

CARBURETOR FLOODS REPEATEDLY

Possible Causes	Remedy
Float set too high	Position float as described in Chapter 4
Float valve sticking	Free valve and clean seat as necessary
Float valve and/or valve seat worn or damaged	Replace as necessary

Carburetor Troubleshooting

CARBURETOR FLOODS REPEATEDLY

Possible Causes	Remedy
Dirt or other foreign matter between valve and its seat	Disassemble and clean thoroughly
Carburetor float sticking due to improper alignment in bowl	Position float correctly

IDLE MIXTURE TOO RICH

Possible Causes	Remedy
Dirt or other foreign matter in idle passage	Disassemble and clean thoroughly

LEAN MIXTURE AT SUSTAINED MID-RANGE SPEEDS

Possible Causes	Remedy
Jet needle set too lean	Reset clip position and consult Tune-Up Analysis
Needle jet or main jet clogged	Disassemble and clean carburetor
Intake manifold leaking	Replace manifold gaskets as necessary

LEAN MIXTURE AT SUSTAINED HIGH SPEEDS

Possible Causes	Remedy
Dirt or other foreign matter in jet system	Disassemble and clean thoroughly
Main jet too small, damaged, or blocked	Remove and replace or clean as necessary
Main jet plug screw not secured	Secure as necessary

LEAN MIXTURE DURING ACCELERATION

Possible Causes	Remedy
Dirt or other foreign matter in fuel channels	Disassemble and clean thoroughly
Damaged throttle slide	Replace

LEAN MIXTURE THROUGHOUT THROTTLE RANGE

Possible Causes	Remedy
Filter screens plugged or dirty	Clean or replace as necessary
Jet needle set too lean	Reposition needle clip, consult Tune-Up Analysis
Air leak in metering system	Replace or secure all channel plugs, screws, and lead plugs as necessary
Air leak at intake manifold	Secure manifold or replace gasket as necessary
Damaged throttle slide	Replace

Carburetor Troubleshooting

IDLE MIXTURE TOO LEAN

Possible Causes	Remedy
Idle adjustment screw blunt	Replace as necessary
Idle adjustment hole damaged or oversize	Replace carburetor body

RICH MIXTURE AT SUSTAINED MID-RANGE SPEEDS

Possible Causes	Remedy
Jet needle setting too rich	Adjust as directed in Tune-Up Analysis section
Main jet too large, loose, or missing	Replace or secure as necessary
Carburetor flooding	See above

RICH MIXTURE AT SUSTAINED HIGH SPEEDS

Possible Causes	Remedy
Main jet too large, or loose	Replace or secure as necessary
Carburetor flooding	See above

RICH MIXTURE THROUGHOUT THROTTLE RANGE

Possible Causes	Remedy
Carburetor flooding	See above
Choke valve partially closed	Clean and/or adjust as necessary
Jet needle setting too rich	Reposition clip, consult Tune-Up Analysis section

4 · Fuel System Troubleshooting

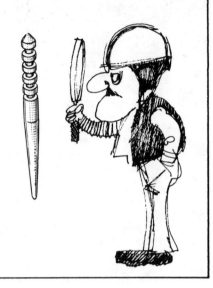

Description and Operation

One basic carburetor design is used on virtually all motorcycles being manufactured today: the slide throttle carburetor, which has been around in various forms for decades. (The one notable exception to this is the pumper or diaphragm type carburetor used on Harley-Davidson V-twins.) The slide type carburetor has many good things going for it: it is quite efficient, it is easy to tune to suit various requirements, it is light and compact, inexpensive to manufacture and easy to work on, and it works better than such a simple fuel metering device has any right to.

Until around 1966 only the direct-control type slide carburetor, in which the throttle cable is connected directly to the slide, was used on motorcycles. The Honda 450 was the first modern bike to use the constant velocity (CV) type slide carburetor, and since then many other models have appeared with them. In addition to most of the other Honda twins (all of which use Keihin CV carburetors), BMW now uses a CV carburetor manufactured by Bing on the R75/5, and Yamaha uses CV carbs on its big four-stroke twins. The different types can be easily identified by the throttle cable connection. In the direct-control type slide carburetor, the throttle cable enters the carburetor top, while in the CV carburetor the throttle cable connects to a lever at the side.

DIRECT-CONTROL TYPE CARBURETOR

These carburetors are quite simple in design, and have been used for years on nearly all motorcycles. British motorcycles use Amal carburetors exclusively, while the Japanese manufacturers rely on Keihin (Honda) and Mikuni (Yamaha, Suzuki, and Kawasaki). Del'Orto is the most commonly used Italian carb, and Bing is the carburetor used on BMW's. All of these carburetors are basically the same, with only detail design differences distinguishing one from the other.

In the direct-control carburetor, the throttle twist-grip is connected to, and directly controls the throttle slide; different slide openings vary the size of the carburetor venturi. After air is drawn into the carburetor and past the slide, it enters a relatively low pressure area and, in doing so, draws fuel up past the jet needle. In this way, due to the relationship between the intake manifold vacuum and air velocity through the carburetor, the proper air/fuel mixture is created. The size of the jet and the taper of the jet needle determine how much fuel is drawn for a given amount of vacuum and air velocity.

It can be seen here that if the throttle is

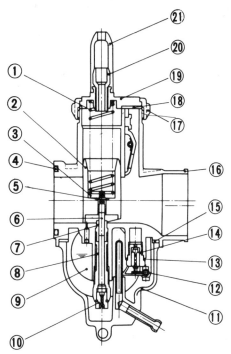

Cross-section of a direct control type carburetor.

1. Coil spring
2. Throttle slide
3. Needle clip plate
4. O-ring
5. Bar clip
6. Jet needle
7. Needle jet
8. Needle jet holder
9. Float
10. Main jet
11. Float chamber body
12. Arm pin
13. Valve seat
14. Slow jet
15. Float chamber washer
16. Body
17. Cap
18. Top washer
19. Top
20. Cable adjuster
21. Rubber cap

opened suddenly (yanking the slide up just as quickly) at low engine rpm, air velocity through the venturi will be low because of the low intake vacuum and large throttle (venturi) opening, and an insufficient amount of fuel will be drawn for the volume of air inducted. This creates a momentary lean mixture condition and causes a hesitation before the engine accelerates cleanly. It can also be seen that lowering or raising the jet needle position relative to the slide or changing the main jet size will have an effect on mixture strength. Changing the position of the needle or changing the needle taper will affect running at mid-range throttle openings (from about $1/4$–$3/4$ throttle), and changing the main jet size will affect full throttle running. This is so because at small throttle openings the needle effectively plugs the jet tube completely and the low-speed system takes over, while at full throttle the needle is withdrawn from the jet tube enough that the main jet is virtually unrestricted.

Low-Speed System

At small throttle openings (approximately $1/4$–$1/8$ throttle), the carburetor low-speed system takes over. Air entering the carburetor is regulated by the air screw, after which it enters the low-speed jet bleed hole. The air then mixes with the fuel entering the low-speed jet and the mixture is discharged from the pilot outlet under the slide. The mixture is then carried into the engine along with the small

UP TO $1/8$ OPEN	FROM $1/8$ TO $1/4$ OPEN	FROM $1/4$ TO $3/4$ OPEN	$3/4$ TO FULL OPEN
PILOT JET	**THROTTLE CUT AWAY**	**NEEDLE–POSITION**	**MAIN JET SIZE**

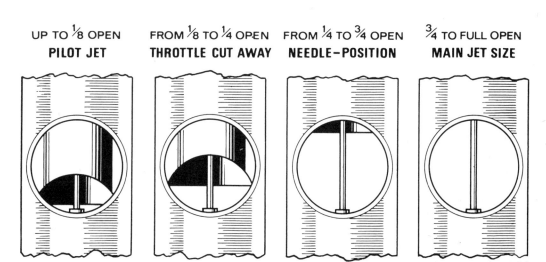

The illustrated throttle openings are controlled mainly by the indicated factors

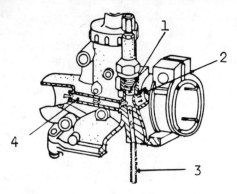

1 Plunger
2 Mixture passage
   (to venturi)
3 Fuel passage
4 Air passage

Starter circuit (two-strokes)

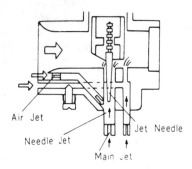

Air Jet
Needle Jet
Jet Needle
Main Jet

Low-speed circuit

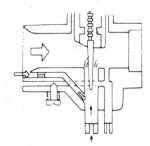

Mid-range circuit

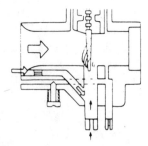

High-speed circuit

amount of air allowed to pass through the slight opening or cutaway of the slide. As the slide is raised past 1/4 throttle opening, the relatively small amount of mixture dis-

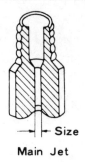

Size

Main Jet

charged by the low-speed jet is overshadowed by the volume of air now being allowed to enter, and, of course, the main jet system is coming into play as the needle is withdrawn from the jet tube. At the same time, increased air flow and vacuum (bypassing the air screw), and increased pressure through the venturi (over the low-speed jet discharge outlet) effectively closes off the low-speed system and the transition to the main system is complete.

Float Chamber

In order to maintain the correct flow of fuel to the carburetor jets at all engine speeds and throttle openings, a sufficient amount of fuel under relatively constant delivery pressure must be available. The float chamber serves to accomplish this. Fuel entering the float chamber from the fuel tank must pass between the float needle and seat valve. As fuel fills the chamber, the float rises with the fuel level and when a preset level is reached, the float shuts off flow by pressing the needle against its seat, closing the valve. As fuel is consumed and the level drops, the float will have followed the level, allowing more fuel to enter so that a constant level will be maintained.

It is very important that the float level be correctly set so that the proper mixture strength is maintained. An adjustable float level gauge, suitable for most motorcycle carburetors, is available from Honda dealers (part number 07144-99998). An improperly set float level can cause poor or erratic performance at both the low- and high-speed ranges.

CONSTANT VELOCITY CARBURETOR

The CV carburetor is basically the same as the direct-control type carburetor, ex-

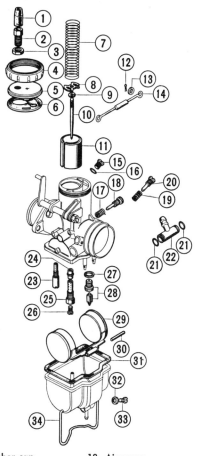

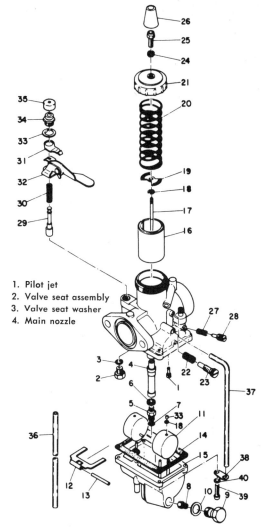

1. Pilot jet
2. Valve seat assembly
3. Valve seat washer
4. Main nozzle

1. Rubber cap	18. Air screw
2. Cable adjuster	19. Throttle stop screw spring
3. Locknut	20. Throttle stop screw
4. Cap	21. O-ring
5. Top	22. T-connector
6. Rubber gasket	23. Low speed jet
7. Slide return spring	24. Main jet tube
8. Needle retaining clip	25. Main jet holder
9. C-clip	26. Main jet
10. Jet needle	27. Flat washer
11. Slide	28. Needle and seat assembly
12. Cotter pin	29. Float
13. Flat washer	30. Float hinge pin
14. Choke linkage rod	31. Float bowl gasket
15. Plug	32. Flat washer
16. Flat washer	33. Drain plug
17. Air screw spring	34. Float bowl clip

Exploded view of a Keihin carburetor

5. Needle jet setter	23. Throttle screw
6. Needle jet washer	24. Wire adjusting nut
7. O-ring	25. Wire adjusting screw
8. Main jet	26. Cap
9. Banjo bolt	27. Air adjusting spring
10. Gasket	28. Air adjusting screw
11. Float	29. Starter plunger
12. Float arm	30. Plunger spring
13. Float pin	31. Starter lever plate
14. Float chamber gasket	32. Starter lever
15. Float chamber body	33. Cap
16. Throttle valve	34. Plunger cap
17. Needle	35. Plunger cap cover
18. Clip	36. Overflow pipe
19. Spring seat	37. Air vent pipe
20. Throttle valve spring	38. Plate
21. Mixing chamber top	39. Pan head screw
22. Throttle stop spring	40. Spring washer

SH type Mikuni carburetor

cept that the throttle twist-grip is not connected directly to the throttle slide. Instead, in the CV carburetor, the throttle grip and cable are connected to a butterfly valve located between the intake manifold and throttle slide. As the throttle butterfly is opened, the manifold vacuum evacuates air from the top of the slide chamber through a passage in the slide. Consequently, on demand from the engine, the slide is raised, more air is admitted, and the tapered jet needle is proportionally lifted out of the jet tube to admit more fuel.

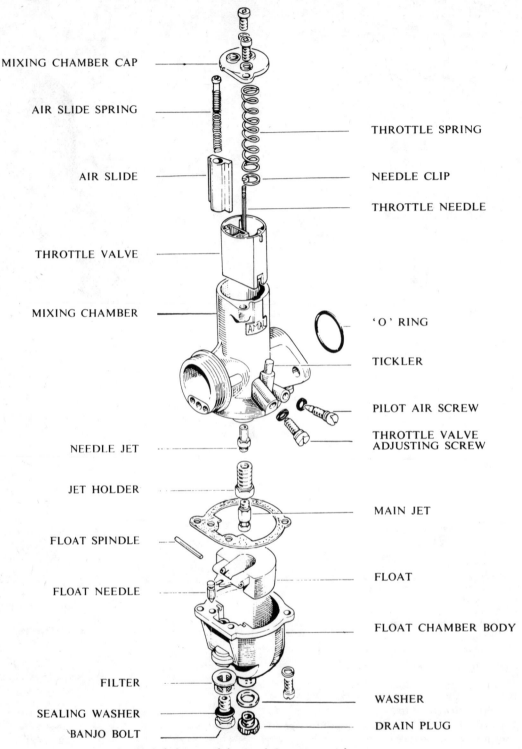

MIXING CHAMBER CAP

AIR SLIDE SPRING

THROTTLE SPRING

AIR SLIDE

NEEDLE CLIP

THROTTLE NEEDLE

THROTTLE VALVE

MIXING CHAMBER

'O' RING

TICKLER

PILOT AIR SCREW

THROTTLE VALVE
ADJUSTING SCREW

NEEDLE JET

JET HOLDER

MAIN JET

FLOAT SPINDLE

FLOAT NEEDLE

FLOAT

FLOAT CHAMBER BODY

FILTER

SEALING WASHER

BANJO BOLT

WASHER

DRAIN PLUG

Exploded view of the Amal Concentric carburetor.

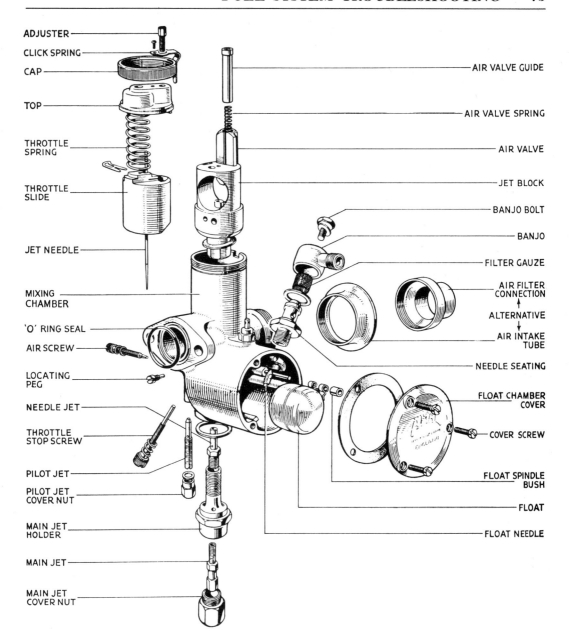

ADJUSTER
CLICK SPRING
CAP
TOP
THROTTLE SPRING
THROTTLE SLIDE
JET NEEDLE
MIXING CHAMBER
'O' RING SEAL
AIR SCREW
LOCATING PEG
NEEDLE JET
THROTTLE STOP SCREW
PILOT JET
PILOT JET COVER NUT
MAIN JET HOLDER
MAIN JET
MAIN JET COVER NUT

AIR VALVE GUIDE
AIR VALVE SPRING
AIR VALVE
JET BLOCK
BANJO BOLT
BANJO
FILTER GAUZE
AIR FILTER CONNECTION
ALTERNATIVE
AIR INTAKE TUBE
NEEDLE SEATING
FLOAT CHAMBER COVER
COVER SCREW
FLOAT SPINDLE BUSH
FLOAT
FLOAT NEEDLE

Amal Monobloc carburetor

The term "constant velocity" (or constant vacuum) refers to the speed of the air passing over the main jet tube and the vacuum in the carburetor throat (between the butterfly and the slide), which remains constant due to the movement of the piston in relation to the vacuum. As the engine demands more air and the manifold vacuum increases, the slide responds by lifting in proportion to the vacuum. Thus the carburetor air speed and vacuum remain constant, because an increase in vac-

uum means an increase in slide lift, which in turn increases the amount of air passing through the carburetor by altering the size of the air passage (venturi), and compensating for the increased engine demands with a larger flow of air. A constant vacuum indicates a constant velocity, and vice versa.

The advantages of the CV carburetor are good fuel economy, smooth throttle response, and steady performance throughout the entire rpm range.

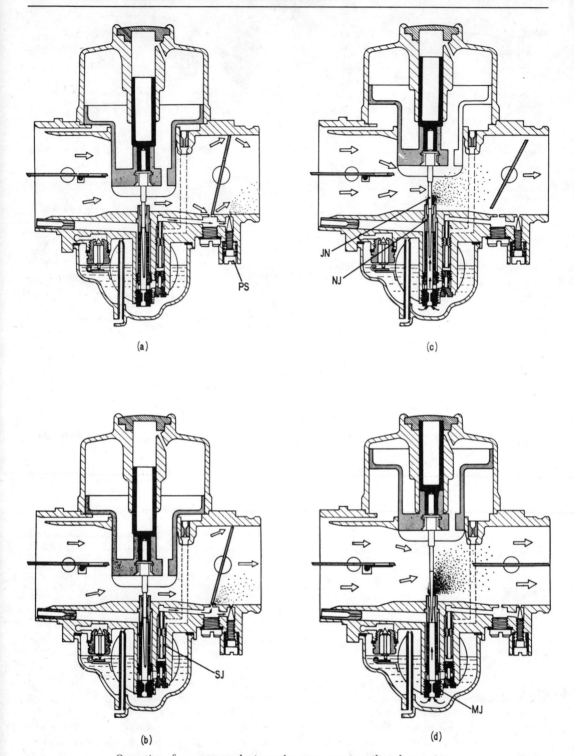

Operation of a constant velocity carburetor at various throttle openings

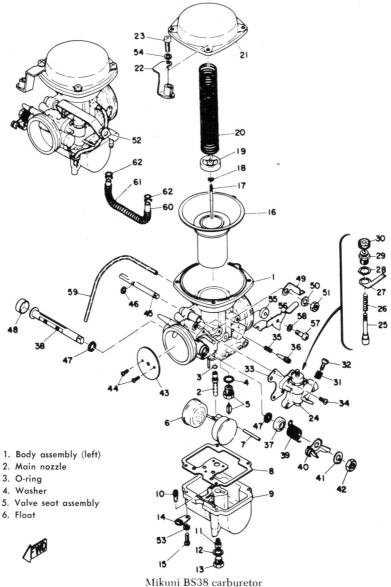

1. Body assembly (left)
2. Main nozzle
3. O-ring
4. Washer
5. Valve seat assembly
6. Float

Mikuni BS38 carburetor

7. Float pin
8. Float chamber packing
9. Float chamber body
10. Pilot jet
11. Main jet
12. Washer
13. Plug screw
14. Plate
15. Pan head screw
16. Diaphragm assembly
17. Needle
18. Clip
19. Set needle plate
20. Diaphragm spring
21. Diaphragm cover
22. Throttle bracket (left)
23. Pan head screw
24. Starter body assembly
25. Starter plunger

26. Plunger spring
27. Set lever starter spring
28. Washer
29. Plunger cap
30. Plunger cap cover
31. Throttle stop spring
32. Throttle stop screw
33. Starter packing
34. Flat head screw
35. Pilot screw spring
36. Pilot screw
37. Cap
38. Throttle assembly shaft
39. Throttle spring
40. Throttle lever
41. Washer
42. Nut
43. Throttle valve
44. Oval head screw

45. Starter shaft
46. Clip
47. Seal
48. Cap
49. Starter lever
50. Washer
51. Nut
52. Connector lever
53. Spring washer
54. Spring washer
55. Ring
56. Lever assembly
57. Pan head screw
58. Spring washer
59. Overflow pipe
60. Fuel pipe
61. Spring
62. Pipe clip

Carburetor Troubleshooting

INDICATIONS OF A RICH MIXTURE

A rich mixture (too much fuel in the fuel/air ratio) can cause any or all of these conditions:

1. Black, sooty spark plug;
2. Banging or popping in exhaust on deceleration;
3. Black (not blue) exhaust smoke;
4. Misfiring at high rpm;
5. Strongest engine performance at something less than full throttle;
6. Heavy, labored running;
7. Increased fuel consumption.

If you find that your engine is running rich, investigate these areas:

1. Float valve not seating properly due to dirt obstruction or wear;
2. Float height incorrectly set;
3. Too large a main jet;
4. Worn needle and jet tube;
5. Clogged air cleaner;
6. Loose main jet.

INDICATIONS OF A LEAN MIXTURE

A lean mixture is much more hazardous to your engine's health than a rich mixture because it can easily cause overheating and internal damage. Look for these signs:

1. Overheating, with the accompanying pre-ignition, loss of performance, and rapid spark plug erosion;
2. Erratic, stumbling low-speed running;
3. Spitting back in the carburetor and/or backfiring;
4. Smoother engine performance when the choke is partially closed.

Lean running can be caused by:

1. An air leak at the intake tube clamps, at the balance tube (if applicable), or in the carburetor;
2. Fuel contamination;
3. Fuel starvation due to line blockage or an improperly set float level;
4. Clogged jets;
5. Too small a main jet, or an improperly positioned jet needle.

EXCESSIVE FUEL CONSUMPTION

In many cases, excessive fuel consumption is caused by something really dumb like a leak around the fuel tap or lines. Even though it can make a big difference in mileage, a fuel leak can be very hard to detect. If you want to be sure that everything is tight, add a little oil to the gas and watch for the appearance of oily areas around the fuel system. Also, some leaded high-test fuels have a dye added to them that leaves a stain anywhere fuel evaporates, and this can be helpful in tracking down leaks.

The only other conditions that can cause excessive fuel consumption are rich running, which was covered earlier, and mechanical wear in the top end, which only an overhaul can remedy. This is assuming, of course, that your engine is in reasonable tune. It would be a little bit ridiculous to complain about lousy mileage if your engine hasn't been serviced in the last 10,000 miles.

BACKFIRING THROUGH THE INTAKE MANIFOLD

Backfiring through the intake manifold is usually an indication of a weak (lean) mixture, probably caused by an air leak. An air leak can easily be detected by spraying a solvent (such as kerosene) around areas that could be leaking, such as the intake manifold flanges, while the engine is running. Be careful not to set your pride and joy alight while performing this trick. If the engine speed changes noticeably, you've found the trouble. For further investigation of a lean mixture, refer to the preceding section that deals with indications and causes of lean running.

BACKFIRING THROUGH THE EXHAUST SYSTEM

Backfiring is not too common a problem with most motorcycles, but if it occurs, here is what to look for:

1. Lean fuel mixture.
2. Burned exhaust valve.
3. Improper ignition timing or a faulty ignition advance unit.
4. A rich fuel mixture coupled with an air leak in the exhaust system (which would cause light pops in the exhaust rather than loud bangs).

CARBURETOR FLOODING

Actual carburetor flooding, in which the flow of gas to the carburetor is obviously excessive, is nearly always attributable to the float needle and seat valve. This little device controls the flow of gas from the fuel tank, and can sometimes be very temperamental. If the slightest piece of dirt or grit is caught between the needle and seat, it will cease to function, and the carburetor will flood. Wear of the valve can also be responsibile for flooding, although in this case it would sneak up on you gradually. If the float valve is under the harsh light of suspicion, simply remove the float bowl from the carburetor and unscrew the valve for examination. If there is any doubt as to its condition, replace it with a new one.

FUEL FEED

Fuel feed problems can only stem from one of three possibilities: an empty fuel tank, clogged fuel filter or line, or a choked tank vent. On most models a fuel filter is located in the fuel tap or inside the gas tank; in either case it is easily accessible by unscrewing the sediment bowl from the tap or unscrewing the tap from the tank. (Try not to dump gas all over everything.) If everything looks OK and the line isn't clogged, try running the engine with the gas cap removed. If that solves the problem, all you have to do is unclog the air vent (either a small hole in the gas cap or a valve on top of the tank) and your worries are over. If you find that your gas tank is dry, or, in other words, empty, then you merely have to fill it to recapture all the thrilling performance that your engine is capable of producing.

CABLE CONTROLS

Since the throttle cable regulates the carburetor, which in turn controls the engine speed, it is a good idea to see to it that the cable(s) are maintained in as splendid a condition as possible. Most complaints stem from binding of the cable, which can be caused by insufficient lubrication, kinking, or pinching.

Most machines are now equipped with nylon or Teflon® lined outer cable sheaths which greatly reduce friction and require much less lubrication. The best way to lubricate a cable, in any case, is to remove the inner cable and coat it with a molybdenum base grease. Moly grease has the desirable characteristics of good retention and excellent pressure resistance, and it doesn't get sticky at low temperatures. If, upon examination of the cable, you find

any worn or frayed spots, don't hesitate to replace it.

A kinked or pinched cable is generally caused by improper routing. To remedy this, remove the gas tank and check the path of the cable from the twistgrip all the way to the carburetor. Make sure that the outer cable hasn't slipped out of the junction block under the tank, and that it isn't being pinched by the tank. After reinstalling the tank, make sure that there is enough cable free-play so that the cable isn't pulled and engine speed inadvertently increased as the handlebar is swung from side to side. If your machine is equipped with a handlebar mounted choke or starter jet control, all of the above holds true for this control cable as well.

EFFECT OF ALTITUDE ON CARBURETION

Increased altitude tends to produce a rich mixture; the greater the altitude, the smaller the main jet required. Most standard jetting is suitable for use in altitudes up to approximately 3,000 feet. If you use your machine constantly in altitudes between 3,000 and 6,000 feet, the main jet size should be reduced about 5 percent. A further reduction of 4 percent should be made for every 3,000 feet in excess of 6,000 feet altitude. No adjustment can be made to compensate for the loss of power due to rarefied air.

CARBURETOR TUNING

Refer to Chapters 2 and 3 for information on carburetor tuning, which should be carried out in conjunction with a complete tune-up. It should not be necessary for a carburetor to receive any more attention than the other components serviced in a tune-up.

AIR FILTERS

Proper servicing of the air filter is essential to good engine performance, as a clogged filter can cause hard starting, a loss of performance, increased fuel consumption, etc. Do not be tempted to run your machine without the filter, for as well as the greatly increased cylinder bore wear due to the lack of filtration, removing the filter can upset carburetion and cause lean running. If you insist on running without a filter, be sure to run a spark plug check and increase the main jet size if necessary.

5 · Electrical System Troubleshooting

Operational Descriptions

MAGNETO GENERATOR

The magneto generator, mounted in the flywheel, is one of the simplest types of charging systems and is commonly used on two-strokes that do not require much electrical power. The magneto base is usually mounted on the left side crankcase and is surrounded by a flywheel with symmetrical, cast-in magnets. The flywheel rotates around the ignition coils in the magneto base and, as the coils pass in and out of the magnetic field of the flywheel magnets, electricity is created. A cam on the flywheel opens and closes the contact breaker points as it turns. The alternating current (AC) generated by the magneto is used to power the ignition, headlight, and taillight directly on most machines. On bikes equipped with a battery, horn, and turn signals, a rectifier is used to convert the alternating current to direct current (DC).

When the contact breaker points are closed, the induced current in the magneto coils reaches approximately 3–5 amps, a relatively low figure. When the contact breaker is opened by the action of the flywheel cam, the current generated by the magneto coils passes through the primary ignition coil, which produces about

200–300 volts, and then through the secondary coil, where the voltage is greatly stepped up to fire the spark plug. A condenser is used in conjunction with the contact breaker to prevent premature spark discharge and to protect the breaker points from burning.

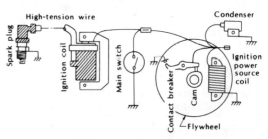

Magneto ignition circuit

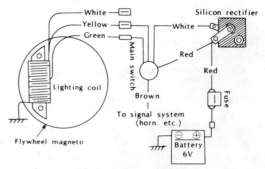

Magneto lighting circuit

In order to supply the greatly varying needs of the charging and lighting system, two separate electrical supply wires are normally tapped from the magneto. The

78

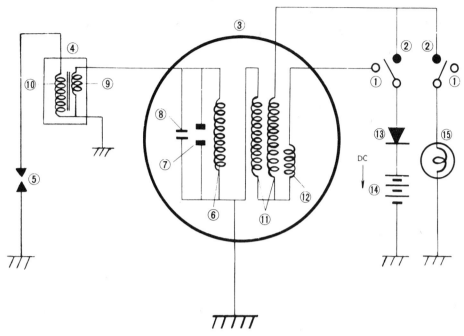

Flywheel magneto wiring diagram

1. Daytime running	6. Magneto coil	11. Lighting coil
2. Nighttime running	7. Contact breaker	12. Differential winding coil
3. Flywheel magneto	8. Capacitor	13. Rectifier
4. Ignition coil	9. Ignition primary coil	14. Battery
5. Spark plug	10. Ignition secondary coil	15. AC lamp load (head lamp and tail lamp)

light-load wire supplies the lesser needs of day (lights off) riding, while the heavy-load wire supplies a greater amount of current to meet the demands of night riding. On a few models, a voltage regulator is used instead of the double supply system, and in this way the regulator, which senses battery voltage, automatically and efficiently controls voltage output of the magneto.

In most old-time machines an independent engine-driven magneto was used simply to supply engine ignition, and dry-cell batteries were used to power the lights. As can be seen, this left much to be desired as far as reliability and maintenance are concerned, and no machine has been equipped with this type of system for many years.

DC GENERATOR

The DC generator produces current in the same manner as an automobile generator. An armature made up of many looped wires around an iron core revolves within

an electromagnet. The strong magnetic field of the magnet induces a voltage in the armature which is then picked up by carbon brushes that contact the commutator (where the looped armature wires meet). The current picked up by the brushes then passes through a voltage regulator and to the condenser, points, ignition coil, spark plug, and the lighting system. Very few machines today use the DC generator system, which is more complicated and less reliable than the alternator systems now used.

STARTER GENERATOR

The starter generator operates similarly to the DC generator except that it usually has an additional electromagnet and an extra pair of brushes, which serve to convert the generator to a starter when necessary. Current from the battery is sent to the windings of the electromagnet and to the armature via the carbon brushes. This current flow sets up a magnetic field in the armature and another surrounding the ar-

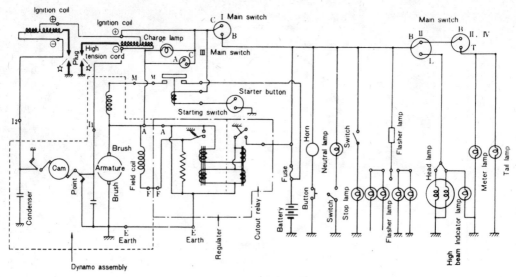

DC generator schematic

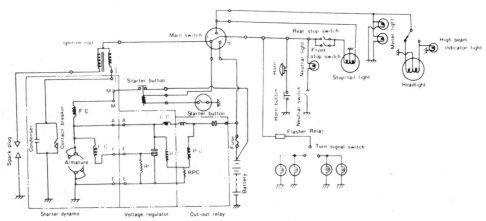

Starter generator schematic

mature. The position of the north and south poles of these fields are contrasting, however, and since like poles repel and unlike poles attract, the armature (secured to the crankshaft), spins around and turns the engine.

ALTERNATOR

The alternator (AC) system consists of the alternator, battery, rectifier, and, on some models, a voltage regulator or zener diode type regulator. The AC charging system is the most common system on to-day's machines.

The alternator consists basically of a stator and rotor, which is bolted to the end of the crankshaft. Electrical current is induced in the stator as the rotor cuts across the magnetic field of the stator magnets.

The advantages of an alternator over a DC generator are that it is less bulky and has fewer moving parts, and it produces a larger voltage at low speeds.

Since an alternator produces alternating current and the battery requires direct current for recharging, it is necessary to employ some means of converting the AC to DC. The selenium rectifier accomplishes this by allowing the alternating current produced by the alternator to pass through it in one direction only, thus converting it before it reaches the battery.

On most smaller displacement machines, alternator output is balanced against the normal electrical needs of the bike, and a voltage regulator is not used. The alternator is matched to the electrical system so that during day running (lights off) the

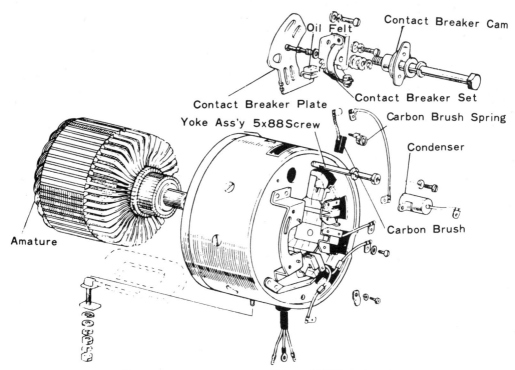

Contact Breaker Cam

Oil Felt

Contact Breaker Set

Contact Breaker Plate

Carbon Brush Spring

Yoke Ass'y 5x88 Screw

Condenser

Carbon Brush

Amature

Starter/generator components (Kawasaki B1L-A shown)

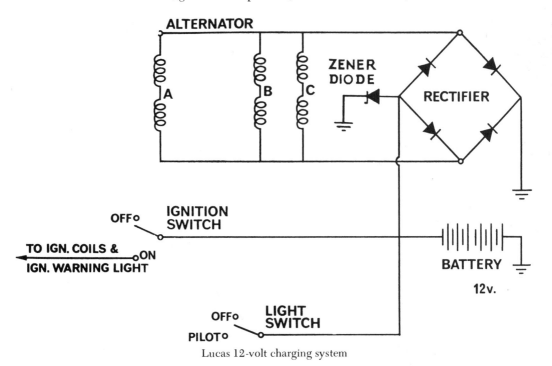

ALTERNATOR

ZENER DIODE

RECTIFIER

A   B   C

OFF

IGNITION SWITCH

TO IGN. COILS &
IGN. WARNING LIGHT

ON

BATTERY

12v.

OFF

LIGHT SWITCH

PILOT

Lucas 12-volt charging system

battery will be receiving a normal charge, and during night running, the battery, with the additional load, will (hopefully) be receiving enough current to keep it from discharging. Frequent battery main-tenance may be necessary if your bike is used almost exclusively for either day or night riding, or other abnormal conditions.

Most larger displacement Japanese machines (350 and up) are equipped with a

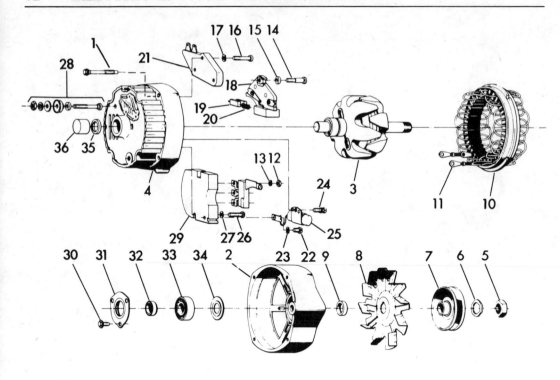

1. Thru bolt (4)	13. Washer (3)	25. Condenser & bracket
2. Drive end frame	14. Screw	26. Screw
3. Rotor	15. Insulator	27. Washer
4. Stator	16. Screw (2)	28. Battery terminal parts
5. Shaft nut	17. Washer (2)	29. Rectifier bridge
6. Shaft nut washer	18. Brush holder	30. Retainer screw (3)
7. Pulley (sheave)	19. Brush (2)	31. Ball brg. retainer
8. Fan	20. Spring (2)	32. Ball brg. seal spacer
9. Fan spacer washer	21. Regulator	33. Ball bearing
10. Stator coil	22. Screw	34. Ball brg. shield
11. Stator coil terminal	23. Washer	35. Needle brg. spacer
12. Nut (3)	24. Screw & lockwasher	36. Needle bearing

Alternator components (late model Harley-Davidson shown)

silicon type voltage regulator which is non-mechanical and cannot be adjusted. With the addition of the regulator, a higher capacity alternator, which is capable of supplying a strong charge at full electrical load, is also used. As long as battery voltage is within the normal range, the regulator does not function, and alternator supplies its total output to the battery. When the normal battery voltage is exceeded and the battery is being overcharged, the regulator functions to ground the excessive current and maintain a normal charging rate.

On most British bikes, a zener diode serves the function of a voltage regulator, tapping off excess alternator current output and rerouting it to a heat sink, where it is grounded to the frame. A zener diode is very efficient as long as it is kept clean,

tight on its mounting, and free from obstruction in the cooling airstream at all times.

On Honda fours, an automotive type three phase excited field alternator is used in conjunction with a mechanical regula-

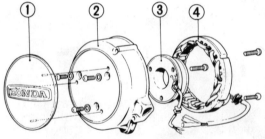

| 1. Side cover | 3. Field coil |
| 2. Alternator cover | 4. Stator coil |

Alternator components (Honda Fours)

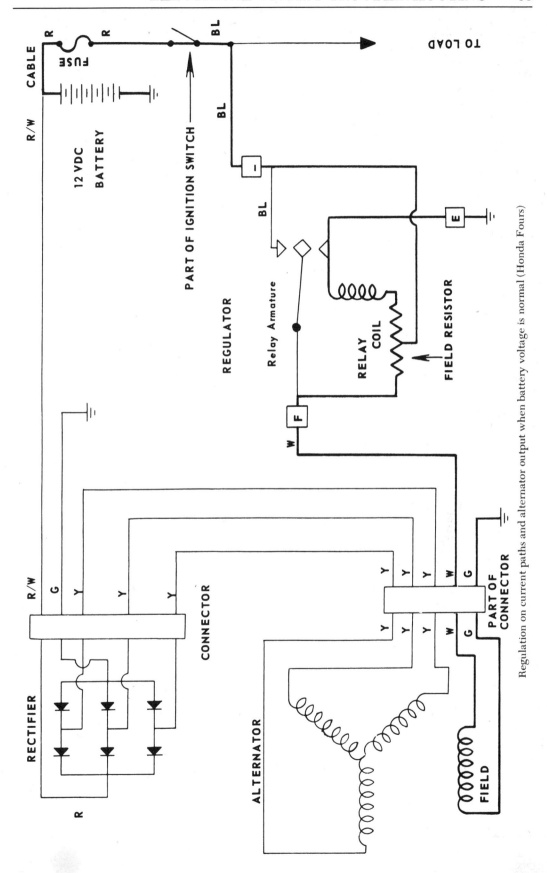

Regulation on current paths and alternator output when battery voltage is normal (Honda Fours)

tor. The advantage of this type of alternator is that the amount of current output can be precisely controlled to suit the needs of the machine. The alternator supplies the battery with the amount of charge it requires, which is monitored by the regulator. When the battery voltage drops below 13.5 volts, the upper regulator contact closes and battery voltage is routed directly to the alternator field coil. Since the field coil is excited in proportion to the amount of voltage fed into it, alternator output increases and the battery recieves a stronger charge. When battery voltage is within the normal range, current through the regulator coil is great enough to open the upper point set, but not great enough to close the lower points. Battery voltage is then routed through a 10 ohm resistor which lowers voltage input to the alternator field coil, consequently lowering alternator output. When battery voltage exceeds about 14.5 volts, the lower regulator contact closes, routing the battery voltage through a 10 ohm resistor and then to ground. This eliminates voltage input to the field coil, which consequently eliminates alternator output. In this way, the alternator supplies just the right amount of current needed for each situation, and is capable of handling any accessory demands that might be made on the bike.

CAPACITOR DISCHARGE IGNITION (CDI)

The capacitor discharge ignition system is basically a modification of the magneto system. In the CDI system, the primary winding of the ignition coil is supplied with current from the capacitor, in response to a timed signal at the time of ignition. Because the capacitor discharges current to the primary windings instantly, high voltage is induced in the secondary windings of the coil and a very strong spark is produced at the spark plug. Self induction in the primary winding occurs faster in the CD ignition system and this short-rise time is why a good spark can be produced across even a fouled spark plug.

Contact breaker points are not used with the CDI system. Instead, an electronic timing detector and electric switch are used to fire the spark plug at the right moment. The signal coil (timing detector) generates a small amount of voltage at every crankshaft revolution and sends it to the electric switch (silicon controlled rectifier, or SCR), which triggers the capacitor.

Capacitor discharge ignition is used on some of the high performance two-strokes currently being produced (notably Kawasaki). Its advantages are that it produces a very hot spark at any rpm, greatly reduces plug fouling, and because it doesn't use contact breaker points, maintenance is cut down and ignition timing (extremely critical on a two-stroke) tends to stay where it is set.

CONSTANT LOSS IGNITION

The constant loss ignition system is basically an alternator system minus the battery. Instead of the battery a capacitor is used, which results in a significant weight reduction for machines used in competition. In operation, the capacitor stores the current from the alternator and releases it at the moment of contact breaker opening. This produces an adequate spark for start-

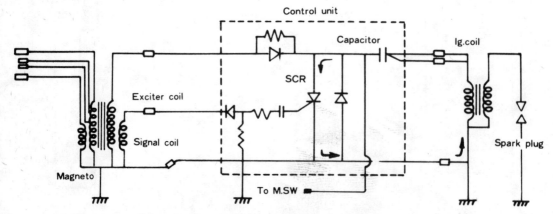

Schematic diagram of the capacitor discharge ignition system

ing, although not as healthy a spark as is produced by the battery. When running, the capacitor also helps to reduce DC voltage ripple. The lighting system will also operate normally, except that the lights will not function when the engine is not running.

In addition to the obvious advantage of not requiring a battery, this system has several other points in its favor: alternator timing is not nearly as critical as on battery powered machines; cold weather does not affect the capacitor, and the system requires less maintenance. However, no street machines are currently being produced with the constant loss system because in most states it is illegal to license a bike that cannot operate its lights with the engine off for a specified interval of time.

Troubleshooting the Charging System

If a charging system fault is suspected, the first thing to do is check the overload fuse, usually located near the battery. If it is not burned out, inspect the charging system wires and connectors. Make sure that the rectifier (if applicable) is securely mounted to the frame. If no obvious fault can be found, refer to the following sections for test procedures applicable to your machine.

BSA

Alternator Output Test

SINGLES

1. Disconnect the alternator output leads.
NOTE: *Earlier machines have three leads; later machines have two.*
2. Start and run the engine at 3000 rpm.
3. Connect a 0–15 volt AC voltmeter with a 1-ohm load resistor in parallel with each of the alternator leads as described below.
4. Three-lead-type stator:
   a. White/green and green/black leads—minimum voltmeter reading 4.0 volts.
   b. White/green and green/yellow leads—minimum voltmeter reading 6.5 volts.

c. White/green and green/black with green/yellow leads—minimum voltmeter reading 8.5 volts.
5. Two-lead-type stator:
   a. White/green and green/yellow leads—minimum voltmeter reading 8.5 volts.
6. If low or no readings are obtained, inspect the leads for damage and make sure that they have tight connections. Check the alternator output again, and if the same results are obtained, the difficulty lies in the alternator itself and must be referred to a qualified repair shop.
7. To check for grounded coils within the stator, connect the voltmeter to each terminal and ground. If a reading is obtained, the coil connected to the lead being tested is grounded.

TWINS

Test the alternator output as described for the single-cylinder models. Correct output. Readings are given in the chart.

Stator Number	System Voltage	Alternator Output Minimum AC Volts @ 3000 rpm		
		A	B	C
47162	6V	4.0	6.5	8.5
	12V			
47164	6V	4.5	7.0	9.5
47167	6V	7.7	11.6	13.2
47188	6V	5.0	1.5	3.5
47204	12V	N.A.	N.A.	8.5
47205	12V	N.A.	N.A.	9.0

A—Green/White and Green/Black
B—Green/White and Green/Yellow
C—Green/White and {Green/Black / Green/Yellow} connected
NOTE: On machines fitted with two-lead-stator, only test C is applicable.

TRIPLES

Check alternator output for the triple in the same manner as described for the three-lead-stator on single-cylinder models. Correct output readings are on the following page.

Alternator Output Minimum AC Volts @ 3000 rpm			
RM20 stator 47209 (12 volt)	green/white and green/black connected 5.0	green/white and green/yellow connected 8.0	green/white green/black and green/yellow connected 10.0

HARLEY-DAVIDSON

Generator Output Test

1. Remove the wire from the generator "F" terminal and connect a jumper wire from the "F" terminal to ground.

2. Remove wire(s) from "A" terminal and connect the positive lead to a 0–30 amp ammeter.

3. Run the engine at 2,000 rpm (40 mph in fourth gear) and briefly connect the negative lead of the ammeter to the positive battery terminal.

NOTE: *Avoid running the engine for long periods with the generator field grounded, and always disconnect the ammeter lead from the battery before stopping the engine so the battery doesn't discharge through the generator.*

CAUTION: *Disconnect the wires from the regulator before grounding the regulator "F" (XLH) or "BT" (XLCH) terminals to check output, or regulator will be damaged.*

4. If the ammeter reads 15 or more amps for a 6 volt generator or 10 amps for a 12 volt generator, the generator is good and the trouble is in the voltage regulator or wiring circuit.

5. When installing generators or batteries and whenever the generator or regulator wires have been disconnected, flash the field coils to make sure the generator has correct polarity. Do this by briefly touching a jumper wire between "BAT" and "GEN" terminals on the regulator before starting the engine and after connecting all of the wires. The momentary surge of current from the battery to the generator will correctly polarize the generator.

Alternator Output Check

Consult the Alternator Check Chart for test specifications and connect the test equipment as shown in the illustration. Make sure that the negative battery terminal is grounded to the frame.

Alternator Check Chart

Component	Connection	Reading	Result
Rotor	Ohmmeter from slip ring to shaft	Very low	Grounded
	110 volt test lamp from slip ring to shaft	Lamp lights	Grounded
	Ohmmeter across slip rings	Very high	Open
	110 volt test lamp across slip rings	Lamp fails to light	Open
	Battery and ammeter to slip rings	Observe ammeter reading	1.9 to 2.3 amp
Stator	Ohmmeter from lead to frame	Very low	Grounded
	110 volt test lamp from lead to frame	Lamp lights	Grounded
	Ohmmeter across each pair of leads	Any reading very high	Open
	110 volt test light across each pair of leads	Fails to light	Open
Diodes	12 volt (or less) test lamp across diode, then reverse connections	Lamp fails to light in both checks	Open
		Lamp lights in both checks	Shorted
1970 and earlier Output	Run under load, adjust rheostat across battery to 14 volts and read ammeter	Ammeter	Rated @ 32 amp 18 amp @ 2000, 28 amp @ 5000 (minimum)
1971 and later Output	Run under load, ground field, adjust rheostat across battery to 14 volts and read ammeter	Ammeter	Rated @ 37 amp 22 amp @ 2000 32 amp @ 5000

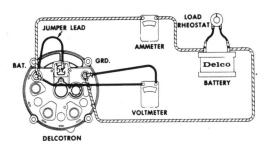

Wiring for testing output

Magneto Spark Check

1. Hold the end of the spark plug lead, with the plug cap removed, about ⅛ in. from the spark plug terminal. When the engine is running a blue spark should appear twice in every 360° rotation of the engine between the end of the lead and the plug terminal. If the spark is constant, the engine should not misfire. Do this on both plugs.

2. To test for spark with the engine off but the ignition on, hold the lead not more than ¼ in. from the plug terminal while kicking the engine over. Perform this on both plugs.

3. An easier test method is to remove the plug, reconnect the wire, and ground the plug tip against the cylinder head. Rotate the engine and watch for a blue spark at the plug tip.

4. If no spark is present, the kill button should be checked for a grounded condition before the magneto is removed for service.

HONDA

Alternator Output Test

125 AND 175

1. Check the state of charge of the battery. If necessary, recharge the battery before proceeding with the test.

2. Connect an ammeter between the positive (+) battery terminal and the input (alternator) side of the rectifier. Start the engine and compare the readings obtained with those in the table.

3. If alternator output is insufficient, the fault lies either in the wiring between the alternator and rectifier or in the alternator itself. If the alternator is producing a sufficient amount of current, it can be assumed that either the rectifier or the wiring between the rectifier and battery is at fault.

NOTE: *Remember that these models do not have a regulator, and running constantly with the lights on or under other heavy electrical load can cause slow battery discharge, which should be considered normal.*

350 AND 450

1. Check the state of charge of the battery. If necessary, recharge the battery before proceeding with the test.

2. Connect the positive lead of an ammeter to the yellow alternator lead and ground the negative lead on the engine. Start the engine and run it at a steady 5,000 rpm. The ammeter should read 1.5–2.5 amps (350) or 4.0–5.0 amps (450). Exces-

Alternator Output Table, 125 and 175

Model	Item	Charging Start	Charging Current /3,000 rpm	Charging Current /5,000 rpm	Charging Current /10,000 rpm
CB 175	Daytime	Max 2,400 rpm	——	Min 0.5 A	Max 3.0 A
	Nighttime	Max 2,800 rpm	——	Min 0.5 A	Max 3.0 A
	Battery voltage	12.3 V	——	13 V	16.5 V
CL 175	Daytime	Max 2,400 rpm	——	Min 0.5 A	Max 3.0 A
	Nighttime	Max 2,800 rpm	——	Min 0.5 A	Max 3.0 A
	Battery voltage	13.2 V	——	14 V	16.5 V
CB 125	Daytime	Max 1,300 rpm	Min 2.0 A	Min 2.7 A	Max 4.5 A
	Nighttime	Max 1,900 rpm	Min 1.2 A	Min 2.0 A	Max 4.0 A
	Battery voltage	6.3 V	6.7 V	7 V	8.3 V
CL 125	Daytime	Max 1,300 rpm	——	Min 1.7 A	Max 3.0 A
	Nighttime	Max 2,000 rpm	——	Min 1.7 A	Max 3.5 A
	Battery voltage	6.3 V	——	7 V	8.3 V
CD 175	Daytime	Max 1,300 rpm	Min 3.0 A	Min 4.0 A	Max 6.0 A
	Nighttime	Max 1,800 rpm	Min 1.2 A	Min 2.0 A	Max 4.0 A
	Battery voltage	6.3 V	7 V	7 V	8.3 V
SS 125	Daytime	Max 1,300 rpm	Min 2.0 A	Min 2.5 A	Max 4.5 A
	Nighttime	Max 2,100 rpm	Min 1.2 A	Min 1.5 A	Max 4.0 A
	Battery voltage	6.4 V	6.7 V	7.5 V	8.3 V

sive amperage indicates a bad regulator.

3. Next, switch the ammeter lead from the yellow wire to the white alternator wire. Start the engine, turn the headlight on (high beam), and run it at 5,000 rpm. The ammeter should read approximately the same as before, 1.5–2.5 amps (350) or 4.0–5.0 amps (450). Battery voltage at 5,000 rpm in either case should be 14.8 volts.

4. If output in steps two and three is sufficient, chances are that the rectifier or wiring between the rectifier and battery is at fault.

5. If alternator output in steps two and three is insufficient, disconnect the yellow wire from the regulator, making sure it does not touch ground, and check the output again at 5,000 rpm with the lights on. If a good reading is obtained, the regulator is at fault (assuming there are no breaks in the wiring). If output is still insufficient, the problem lies in the alternator itself.

500 AND 750 FOURS

1. Check the state of charge of the battery. If battery voltage is less than 12 volts, or if specific gravity is less than 1.26, recharge the battery before proceeding with the test.

2. The test is performed using an ammeter and a voltmeter. Connect the ammeter as follows: Disconnect the positive (+) battery cable and connect it to the positive

side of the ammeter. Connect the negative side of the ammeter to the positive battery terminal. Connect the voltmeter as follows: connect the positive side of the voltmeter to the positive battery cable, and ground the negative voltmeter lead on the engine.

3. Start the engine and check the amperage and voltage output of the alternator under both day riding (lights off) and night riding (lights on) conditions. If the readings obtained are noticeably greater or smaller than those in the accompanying table, adjust the regulator. Slight variation is acceptable due to the effect of the state of charge of the battery on alternator output. If alternator output is satisfactory, refer to the section on testing the rectifier.

KAWASAKI

Flywheel Magneto Component Tests

G SERIES, F6, AND F8

Magneto Ignition Coil

Place a strip of paper between the breaker points to insulate them. Perform the following resistance tests using an ohmmeter.

1. Coil resistance:
a. Measure the resistance between the black lead and ground. The coil is good if the ohmmeter reading is approximately 0.5 ohm.

2. Insulation resistance:
a. Disconnect the ground wire from the coil to the magneto base.
b. Measure the insulation resistance between the iron core and the coil. The reading should be over 5.0 megohms.

Condenser

1. Capacity:
a. The condenser capacity should be between 0.18–0.25 microfarads.

2. Spark quality:
a. Connect the positive and negative wires of the condenser to a 6 volt DC power source for a few seconds to charge it.
b. Disconnect the power source and

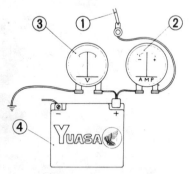

1. Red/white lead   3. Voltmeter
2. Ammeter   4. Battery

Test connections

Engine RPM Charging current	1,000	2,000	3,000	4,000	5,000	6,000	7,000	8,000
Day riding	6.5	0	2.4	1.3	1.0	1.0	0.8	0.6
Night riding	2–3	1	1	1	1	1	1	1
Battery terminal voltage (v)	12	12.4	13.2	14.5	14.5	14.5	14.5	14.5

Alternator output rate, Honda Fours

Flywheel Magneto Specifications (G Series, BIL-A, and F Series)

Model	Type	Manufacturer	Cut-in rpm		Battery
			Day time	Night time	
GA1-A GA2-A	FE101	KOKUSAN	1400	1600	6V 4AH
G3SS-A G3TR-A	FE109	KOKUSAN	s.t.d. 1800 spare 2700	2100	6V 4AH
G4TR	FE109	KOKUSAN	s.t.d. 1800 spare 2700	2100	6V 2AH
G31M-A	NJ101	KOKUSAN	—	—	—
F6	F6079BL	MITSUBISHI	s.t.d. 2000 spare 3000	3000	6V 4AH
F7	HM-01	KOKUSAN	s.t.d. 2000 spare 3000	1800	6V 4AH
F8	FP6309	KOKUSAN	s.t.d. 1600 spare 3000	2000	6V 2AH
F81M	X016	KOKUSAN	—	—	—
F5	HM-01	KOKUSAN	1000	1800	6V 2AH

touch the two wires together. If a spark is produced, the condenser is good.

3. Insulation resistance:

a. Disconnect the ground wire of the condenser.

b. Measure the insulation resistance between the outer case and the positive terminal. The reading should be above 5.0 megohms.

Lighting and Charging Coils

1. Coil resistance:

a. Measure the resistance of each coil with an ohmmeter and compare the readings with the specifications in the accompanying chart.

NOTE: *The lighting coil for the GA1-A and GA2-A models also serves as a charging coil when the headlight is turned on.*

2. Insulation resistance:

a. Disconnect the ground wire.

b. Check insulation resistance between the iron core and the coil. The coil is good if the reading is above 5.0 megohms.

Lighting and Charging Coil Specifications (G Series and F Series)

Model	Lighting coil		Charging coil	
	Yellow	Pink	Blue	Yellow/Green
GA1-A GA2-A	0.41 Ω ± 10%	—	0.36 Ω ± 10%	—
G3SS-A G3TR-A G4TR	0.55 Ω ± 10%	0.55 Ω ± 10%	1.20 Ω ± 10%	0.29 Ω ± 10%
F6	0.48 Ω ± 10%	0.48 Ω ± 10%	0.60 Ω ± 10%	0.54 Ω ± 10%
F8	0.30 Ω ± 10%	0.30 Ω ± 10%	0.58 Ω ± 10%	0.57 Ω ± 10%

Starter / DC Generator Fault Diagnosis

1. Starter does not turn engine over:

a. Check battery terminal connections and state of charge.

b. Switch on the headlight and press the starter button. If the headlight goes dim, it is likely that current is getting to the starter and the starter itself is faulty. If the light does not dim and a click can be heard at the regulator as the button is pressed, then the starter brushes or contact points of the starter switch are at fault. If a click is not heard at the regulator and normal voltage is available at the starter switch, it is probable that the starter switch coil is bad and the switch will have to be replaced.

2. Undercharging, as indicated by the charge light staying on, or overcharging:

a. Disconnect the D and F wires from the engine and start the engine.

b. Ground the F wire on the frame and measure the voltage between the D wire and ground. If the reading is above 13 volts at 2,200 rpm, the voltage regulator is probably at fault. Refer to the preceding section for regulator tests and adjustments.

c. If a low reading is obtained, it is likely that the field coil of the starter/dc generator is broken off or short-circuited.

3. Charge light dimly lit:

a. Regulator cutout points fail to close fully due to break-off of the coil, grounding of the regulator, or short-circuiting. It is also possible that the cutout points are damaged or out of adjustment.

4. Charge light flickers:

a. Most often due to the imminent destruction or short-circuiting of the generator or regulator coil.

SUZUKI

Testing the Magneto

1. The magneto lamp coil can be tested with a continuity tester in the same way as the magneto primary coil is tested. The resistance of the lamp coil is so low that testing it requires a sensitive ohmmeter. Between the yellow/green and red/green wires, resistance should be 1.9Ω; between the yellow/green and green/white, 0.45Ω. No reading should be attainable between the wires and stator housing.

2. The best way to test the lamp coil output is using the voltmeter and ammeter (or milliammeter). First, check out the battery voltage using the voltmeter, hooked up as per the magneto test schematic. It is important that the battery be fully charged before testing output, otherwise the results will not be accurate.

3. If the battery is fully charged, hook up the milliammeter, or better yet 0–5 DC ammeter if your tester has this range, as illustrated.

4. Start the bike and allow it to idle. No current will be shown at idle as a rule.

5. Speed the engine up to 2,000 rpm. At this speed, the output should be about 0.15 ampere, or 150 milliamperes, DC. If you don't have a 0–5 scale, you will have to stop here, otherwise the sensitive milliammeter will be damaged.

6. If you have this scale, speed up the engine to maximum rpm (about 8,000 rpm). The output should be 2.5–3.5 amperes DC.

7. Now, turn on the headlight high beam, or place the ignition switch in the headlight or night position. If all is well, output should be 100 milliamperes at about 2,500 rpm.

8. To check the light coil output, hook up an AC voltmeter as illustrated. Place the electrical system in the night mode, with all lights on. At 2,000 rpm, output should be at least 6.0 volts, and at 8,000 rpm should be not more than 9.0 volts. If these figures are not attainable, check out the wiring, connectors, rectifier, and coils in that order. Sometimes the ignition switch itself is corroded or not making proper contact, so don't overlook it.

Testing the Alternator

1. Hook up a 0–5 ammeter between the positive battery terminal and the wire removed from that terminal.

2. With the lights off, start the engine and gradually run it up to 2,000 rpm while watching the meter. The meter should begin to show a slight charge at this speed.

3. Run the engine up to 5,000 rpm and observe the meter. Charging current should be 1–2 amperes.

4. Turn on the lights and again observe the meter at 2,000 rpm and 5,000 rpm. Readings should be 100 milliamperes and 1.5–2.5 amperes respectively.

5. If the charging current is not to speci-

fications, check the battery, rectifiers, and no-load voltage.

6. To measure no-load voltage, disconnect the wires from the alternator green/white, red/green and yellow/green wires. Connect an AC voltmeter of at least 0–100 volts between the alternator red/green and yellow/green wires.

7. Start the engine and check the output. With the rectifier out of the circuit, some idea of its condition can be ascertained.

Engine rpm	Normal	Minimum	Maximum
2,000	23	17	33
5,000	49	40	60
8,000	82	70	95

These figures may vary for different bikes, but the ratio between them should be approximately the same or the alternator could be defective.

TRIUMPH

Refer to the BSA section. Test procedures and specifications are the same.

YAMAHA

DC Generator Voltage Output

1. Disconnect the generator wiring from the other components.

2. Connect a voltmeter to the armature terminal A (red) and ground field terminal F (black).

3. Run the engine up to about 2500 rpm and check the voltmeter reading. If within reasonable bounds of the necessary output (6 or 12 volts), the generator is not likely to be the source of your problem. If the output is minimal, the cause will likely be found in either the carbon brushes or the field winding insulation.

Troubleshooting the Ignition System

BATTERY AND COIL IGNITION MODELS

The ignition system consists of the contact breaker assembly and one, two, or three ignition coils. The coils are comprised of primary and secondary windings around a laminated, soft iron core—the secondary being closest to the core. When voltage is supplied to the primary winding, it sets up a magnetic field around its turns (approximately 300). This magnetic field induces a voltage in the turns (approximately 20,000) of the secondary winding, resulting in a voltage step-up.

To determine whether an electrical problem is located in the high-tension circuit (secondary winding to the spark plug) or the low-tension circuit (contact breaker to primary coil winding) perform the following check:

NOTE: *On multi-cylinder engines, this test should be performed individually at each coil.*

1. Make sure that the contact points, battery terminals, and main wiring harness fuse are all in good condition.

2. Connect the negative lead of a 0–15 volt DC voltmeter to the "CB" or "+" terminal of the coil, and connect the positive lead to ground.

3. Turn the ignition on and turn the engine until the points open. The voltmeter should read battery voltage.

4. No reading indicates a fault in the low-tension circuit. If the points are suspected of being at fault, you can quickly confirm this by disconnecting the points (CB) wire at the coil. If the voltmeter then reads battery voltage, the points are shorted out (usually caused by incorrect assembly of the insulating washers).

Low-Tension Circuit Test

If the above test shows that the fault exists somewhere in the low-tension circuit, isolate the problem source in the following manner:

NOTE: *Disconnect the zener diode center terminal (12 volt BSAs, Triumphs, and Nortons) or the regulator input terminal.*

1. Place a piece of nonconducting material, such as a strip of rubber between the contact breaker points. Turn the ignition switch on.

2. Using a 0–15 volt DC voltmeter (0–10 volts for 6v machines), make point-to-point checks as described below.

3. Check the battery by connecting the voltmeter between the negative terminal of the battery and ground (frame). No reading indicates a blown main fuse, or a

faulty battery lead; a low reading indicates a poor ground.

4. Connect the voltmeter between the ignition coil negative terminal and ground (one at a time on multis). No reading indicates a faulty lead between the battery and coil terminal, or a faulty switch connection.

5. Connect the voltmeter between ground and one ammeter terminal at a time (if applicable). No reading at the "load" terminal indicates either a faulty ammeter or a break in the lead from the battery; no reading on the battery side indicates a faulty ammeter.

6. Connect the voltmeter between the ignition switch input terminal and ground. No reading indicates a break or faulty terminal along the ignition switch input lead. Check for voltage readings between ground and the input lead terminals at the rectifier, ammeter, and lighting switch (if applicable).

7. Connect the voltmeter between the ignition switch "load" terminal and ground. No reading indicates a faulty switch. A positive reading at this point, but not in step 4, indicates a break or faulty connection along the lead.

8. Disconnect the ignition coil lead from the positive terminal and connect one voltmeter lead in its place. Connect the other voltmeter lead to ground. No reading indicates a faulty primary coil winding.

9. Reconnect the ignition coil lead(s) and connect the voltmeter across the contact breaker points one set at a time. No reading indicates a faulty connection, faulty insulation, or a faulty condenser.

10. Reconnect the zener diode center terminal or regulator input terminal and connect the voltmeter to this terminal and ground. The meter should read battery output voltage.

High-Tension Circuit Tests

If the preliminary ignition system checks showed that the problem lay in the high-tension circuit, check the following:

1. Test the ignition coil(s) as described in component tests. If the coils are in satisfactory condition, either the high-tension cables or spark plug cap(s) are at fault.

2. Remove the spark plug cap(s) from the cable(s) and turn the ignition switch on. Hold the cable $\frac{1}{8}$ in. away from the cylinder cooling fins and kick the engine over. A bright blue spark should jump across the gap; if not, the cable is defective. If the spark does appear, the spark plug cap is faulty.

CAUTION: *High-tension cables are so called because they carry very high voltage. If you aren't careful when handling them, you might find yourself as the shortest path to ground for the coil current.*

Troubleshooting the Starting System

The starting system consists of the starter motor and clutch, the solenoid, and the handlebar-mounted starter switch (except for starter/generator systems, covered in a preceding section). When the button is pressed, the electrical circuit to the solenoid is closed and the solenoid is activated, sending the battery current directly to the

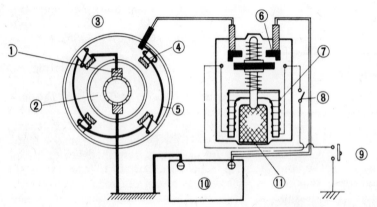

1. Brush
2. Armature
3. Starter motor
4. Pole
5. Field coil
6. Solenoid switch
7. Solenoid electromagnet
8. Ignition switch
9. Starter button
10. Battery
11. Solenoid plunger

Starting system diagram.

starter motor. The starting system is quite reliable and it is unlikely that you will experience any major problems.

Testing

If the starter will not operate, switch on the headlight and observe its intensity. If it is dim when the starter is not being operated, check the battery connections and recharge the battery. If the headlight doesn't light, check the fuse, the battery connections, the ignition switch and its connections, and check the continuity of the wire between the ignition switch and the battery.

If the headlight is bright, press the starter button momentarily and watch the light. If it remains bright, touch a screwdriver blade between the two starter solenoid terminals. If the starter operates, connect a test light between the small wire on the solenoid and ground. If the test light comes on as the button is pushed, the solenoid is faulty. If it does not light, look for defective wiring between the starter button and solenoid or between the starter button and ignition switch, or simply a burned out starter button switch. If the starter does not operate and the headlight dims as the main solenoid terminals are bridged, the starter motor is faulty. If the headlight does not dim, look for a bad connection at the starter. If the starter motor operates freely but will not turn the engine over, the starter drive is not functioning (a rare occurrence).

STARTER SOLENOID

The solenoid is an electromagnetic switch that closes and completes the circuit between the starter and battery when activated by the starter button. The solenoid is a necessary addition to the starting circuit because the starter button switch is not capable of handling the amperage load required to operate the starter and mounting a heavy-duty switch on the handlebar, with the large cable needed to handle the load, is quite impractical.

If the solenoid does not work, check the continuity of the primary coil by connecting a multi-tester or test light and battery to the two small solenoid leads. Lack of continuity indicates an open circuit, and the solenoid must be replaced. If the primary coil winding is continuous, disassemble the solenoid and clean the contact

points with emery paper or a small file. The points, after long use, have a tendency to become pitted or burned due to the large current passing across them.

NOTE: *Be sure to disconnect the battery before disconnecting the cables from the solenoid when it is to be removed.*

Replace the solenoid if cleaning the points fails to repair it.

Component Testing

JAPANESE MACHINES

Rectifiers

If alternator output is satisfactory but the battery discharges as the engine is running, it is quite possible that the rectifier is not functioning properly. (This is assuming, of course, that the battery is not old and tired or has one or more bad cells.) Before removing and testing the rectifier, make sure that it is solidly mounted on the frame. The rectifier is grounded through its mounting and will not operate without a good ground.

CAUTION: *Do not loosen or tighten the nut that holds the rectifier unit together, as this will adversely affect operation of the rectifier.*

To test the rectifier, pull off the connectors, unscrew the nut, and remove the rectifier unit. Inside the rectifier are a number of diodes which, if functioning properly, will allow the electricity to pass only in one direction. To check the diodes, you can use either a multi-meter or test light and the motorcycle battery. If the test light and battery are to be used, simply

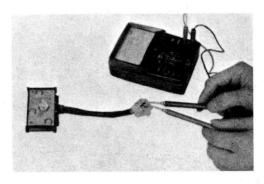

Checking the diodes with a multi-tester.

run a length of wire off one of the battery terminals and connect one of the test light leads to the other terminal. The two free wire ends will be used to check electrical continuity of the diodes.

Connect one of the test leads to one of the diode wires at either end of the pack, and touch the other test lead to each of the other diode wires (except for the one at the other end), in turn. Now, reverse the leads and repeat the procedure. The test light should light (or the gauge needle respond) in one test direction only. If all is well so far, connect one of the test leads to the diode wire at the other end of the pack, and repeat the test as outlined above. Continuity in both directions (when reversing the test leads) indicates a defective diode, in which case the rectifier unit must be replaced.

The diodes are quite susceptible to failure from excessive heat and electrical overload. Observe the following precautions:

1. Do not reverse battery polarity.

2. Do not use high-voltage test equipment to test the rectifier diodes.

3. Do not run the engine with the rectifier disconnected.

4. Do not quick-charge the battery (high output charging equipment) without first disconnecting one of the battery cables.

BRITISH MACHINES

Rectifiers

1. Disconnect and remove the rectifier. Observe these precautions:

Removing and installing the rectifier

a. When removing or installing the rectifier, hold the wrenches as shown in the accompanying illustration. This is to prevent any possibility of twisting the rectifier plates, which could result in broken internal wiring.

b. Never disturb the nuts that secure the rectifier plates together.

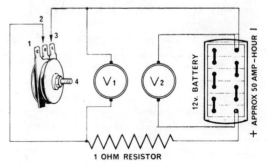

Rectifier bench test set-up

2. Connect the rectifier to a 12V battery and a 1-ohm load resistor.

3. Connect a DC voltmeter in the V_1 position as shown in the accompanying illustration. The meter should read 12 volts.

4. Disconnect the voltmeter and, using the accompanying illustrations for guidance, test each of the diodes with the voltmeter leads. Keep the testing time as short as possible so that the rectifier does not overheat. No reading should be greater than 2.5 volts in Test 1, and no reading should be more than 1.5 volts less than the battery voltage in Test 2 (i.e., 10.5 volts minimum).

5. If the rectifier does not meet specifications, it should be replaced.

Zener Diodes

The zener diode serves the function of a voltage regulator, tapping off excess alternator current output and rerouting it to a heat sink. It is very important that the diode be kept clean and free from obstruction in the cooling airstream at all times. Other than this, if you make sure that the base of the diode and heat sink have firm metal-to-metal contact, the diode is a maintenance free item.

NOTE: *Before making any of the following tests, make sure the battery is in a full state of charge.*

1. Disconnect the zener diode cable and connect a 0–5 amp (minimum) ammeter in series between the diode connector and

TEST 1 CHECKING FORWARD RESISTANCE

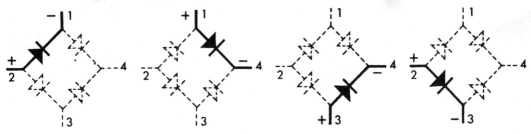

TEST 2 CHECKING BACK LEAKAGE

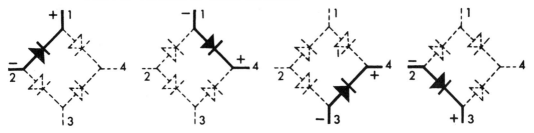

Rectifier diode test sequence

the disconnected cable. The ammeter positive lead must be connected to the diode terminal.

2. Connect a DC voltmeter between the zener diode and the heat sink. The red or positive lead of the voltmeter must be connected to the heat sink, which is grounded to the frame.

3. Make sure all lights are off, then start the engine and slowly increase its speed while observing both meters.

4. Until the voltmeter reaches 12.75 volts, the ammeter should read zero.

Heat sink assembly.

5. Continue increasing the engine speed until the ammeter reads 2.0 amps, at which time the voltmeter should be reading 13.5 to 15.3 volts.

6. If the ammeter registers before the voltmeter reaches 12.75 volts in step 4, or if the voltage is higher than stated in step 5 when the ammeter reads 2.0 amps, the zener diode should be replaced.

Zener diode.

Contact Breaker Condensers

A faulty condenser is usually indicated by burning or arcing of the points. To check the condenser(s), first turn the ignition switch on, then take readings across the contact breaker(s) (open position) with a voltmeter. No reading indicates that the condenser insulation has broken down, and the unit should be replaced.

Capacitors (Constant Loss Ignition)

The capacitor has a limited storage life of approximately 18 months at 68° F, or 9 to 12 months at 86° F. Therefore, it would be wise to check its condition regularly if it is not in use.

1. Connect the capacitor to a 12 volt battery for approximately 5 seconds. Make sure the terminal polarity is correct or the capacitor will be ruined.

2. Let the capacitor stand for at least 5 minutes, then connect a DC voltmeter to the terminals. Note the *steady,* not instantaneous, reading of the meter. A good capacitor will register at least 9 volts.

H1 AND A SERIES KAWASAKIS

CDI Components

Contact breaker points are not used with the CD ignition system. Ignition timing is detected electrically and converted into a pulsing voltage, which is transmitted to an amplifier. It is then routed through a trigger amplifier, which adjusts the voltage pulse to a suitable signal wave. The signal is then passed through a semiconductor switch (thyristor) which acts as a one-way gate to the capacitor. Since the capacitor discharges current to the primary coil windings instantly, high voltage is induced in the secondary windings and a very strong spark is produced at the spark plug. Self-induction in the primary winding occurs extremely rapidly in the CD ignition system, and this short-rise time, along with the amplified timing signal, is why a good spark can be produced across even a fouled spark plug.

SERVICE PRECAUTIONS

1. Do not reverse battery polarity.
2. Do not run the engine with the battery disconnected.
3. Take care to connect any wiring correctly. Improperly connected wiring can damage the CDI components.

4. The battery and ignition coil are matched to the CDI system. When replacement is necessary, use identical parts.

5. Make sure to install any rubber insulators correctly when a component has been removed and reinstalled.

6. The igniters (amplifiers) are sealed with epoxy and cannot be disassembled. Disassembly will invalidate a warranty claim if the ignition system is defective.

H2 SERIES KAWASAKI

The H2 model is equipped with an electrical system different from any of the other models. What Kawasaki has done is combine the best features of both magneto ignition and pointless capacitor discharge ignition to provide a simple, reliable circuit.

Whereas conventional CDI takes a low battery voltage and raises it to 370–500 volts with a converter, magneto CDI taps its high voltage directly from a special generator winding and then rectifies it. Another advantage is that magneto CDI can use the signal generator voltage directly, without amplification.

Magneto CDI also differs from conventional magneto ignition in that two primary ignition coils are used: one contains a high number of windings so that high voltage can be tapped at relatively low rpm, the other contains a low number of windings so that, as rpm rises, voltage can be produced quickly enough to fire the plugs properly.

In addition to the above, magneto CDI differs from the CDI used on other Kawasaki models in that 3 separate CDI units, one for each cylinder, are used.

The system is quite simple and very reliable, so it is highly unlikely that you'll ever run into trouble. If a problem does develop, however, it is best to refer it to a qualified Kawasaki mechanic.

Use the following chart for determining specific areas of fault if you are experiencing trouble with a CDI system.

COILS

1. Check the coil in the machine by removing the spark plug cap and holding the high-tension cable end about 1/8 in. away from the cylinder cooling fins. Turn the ignition on and kick the engine over.

CDI Troubleshooting

No Start

Possible Causes	*Inspection and/or Remedy*
1. No high frequency sound from Unit B	
a. Damaged ignitor Unit B	Replace.
b. Insufficient battery voltage	Charge battery.
2. Strong spark at plugs	
a. Reversely connected high-tension leads	Switch.
b. Insufficient battery voltage	Charge battery.
c. Loose battery terminals	Clean and tighten.
3. Weak spark at plugs	
a. Leaking high-tension leads	Check high-tension circuit and repair as neccessary.
b. Faulty ignition coil	Test and replace if necessary.
c. Faulty ignitor Unit B	Replace.
d. Faulty wiring harness	Test continuity and repair as necessary.
4. No spark at plugs	
a. Faulty ignition coil	Test and replace if necessary.
b. Faulty ignitor Unit A or B	Replace.
c. Faulty signal generator	Replace.
5. Spark without kick-starting	
a. Faulty ignitor Unit A	Replace.

Hard Starting

1. Strong spark at plugs	
a. Incorrect ignition timing	Readjust.
b. Insufficient battery voltage	Charge battery.
c. Loose terminal connections	Clean and tighten.
2. Weak spark at plugs	
a. Leaking high-tension leads	Check high-tension circuit and repair as necessary.
b. Faulty ignition coil	Test and replace if necessary.
c. Faulty ignitor Unit B	Replace.
d. Faulty wiring harness	Test continuity and repair as necessary.
3. No spark at plugs	
a. Faulty ignition coil	Test and replace if necessary.
b. Faulty ignitor Unit A	Replace.
c. Faulty signal generator	Replace.

Poor Running Performance

1. Incorrect ignition timing	Readjust.
2. Faulty spark plugs	Replace.
3. Faulty ignitor Unit A	Replace.
4. Faulty ignitor Unit B	Replace.

Observe the caution given in "High Tension Circuit Tests."

2. Check primary winding resistance by removing the coil and connecting an ohmmeter to the low tension terminals. The readings obtained should be:

6 volt coils—1.8–2.4 ohms
12 volt coils—3.0–3.8 ohms

BATTERY

The battery is located beneath the flip-up seat or behind the side panel on most models. Electrolyte level can be checked through the clear battery case. If necessary, add distilled water to raise the electrolyte level to a position between the upper and lower marks. *Do not overfill.*

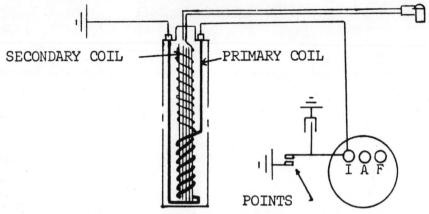

SECONDARY COIL

PRIMARY COIL

POINTS

Ignition coil construction

Maintain electrolyte level between the upper mark (1) and the lower mark (2). CB 500 shown.

Using a hydrometer (1) to determine specific gravity of the battery (2).

CAUTION: *Exercise extreme care in handling the battery. Electrolyte can remove paint and chrome in seconds, as well as cause skin burns. Baking soda can be used, if necessary, as a neutralizer.*

Check the condition of the battery breather tube. It must extend to a point below the frame where relatively little damage can be done if the battery spills or boils over. Make sure that the tube is not pinched or closed off, or the battery may build up enough pressure to explode.

Battery charge should be checked periodically with a hydrometer. If the specific gravity reading on any cell is below 1.200 (at 68° F), the battery should be recharged. Do not use a high-output battery charger unless absolutely necessary. If the battery must be charged quickly, observe these precautions:

1. Do not charge the battery at an amperage rate greater than its rated amp/hr capacity.

2. Never allow electrolyte temperature to exceed 110° F while charging.

3. Do not quick-charge a fully discharged battery.

4. Do not charge the battery in a confined room or near heat, as hydrogen gas is released during charging.

5. Do not quick-charge a battery in which the specific gravity of one or more cells is noticeably lower than the others.

6. Disconnect a cable if the battery is to be charged while on the motorcycle.

7. Thirty minutes is usually adequate charging time at maximum charging rate.

An alternative to the high-output charger is an adjustable low-output charger, available at most automotive supply stores at reasonable cost. A battery that is charged at a low rate will take and retain a fuller charge, and plate damage due to high current input is less likely to occur. When charging a battery at a low rate, observe item 6 above, and do not exceed the following charging rates:

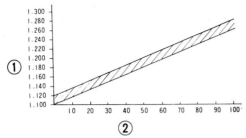

The relationship between specific gravity level (1) and percent of battery charge (2).

6 AH battery—2.0 amps
9 AH battery—2.7–3.0 amps
12 AH battery—3.6–4.0 amps

Do not charge a battery for an extended period of time at a rate of charge greater than $\frac{1}{10}$ its amp/hr (AH) rating.

When rechecking specific gravity of the cells after charging, allow sufficient time for the gas bubbles to be released or a false (low) reading will be obtained. A good battery should have a specific gravity reading in all cells of between 1.260–1.280 at 68° F. The battery should be replaced if one or more cells is excessively low. If charging system fault is suspected, refer to Chapter 7.

Do not neglect to keep the battery case and terminals clean. A solution of baking soda and water works well to remove corrosion. Be careful not to let it enter the cells or the electrolyte will be neutralized. Petroleum jelly can be used as a corrosion inhibitor on the terminals after they have been cleaned.

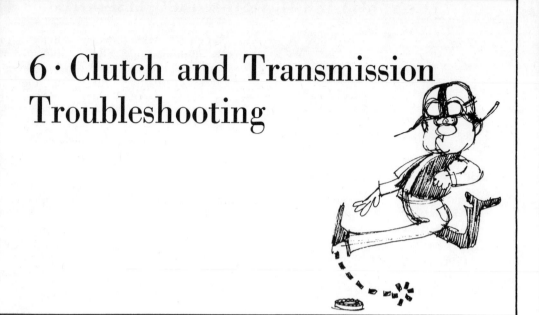

6 · Clutch and Transmission Troubleshooting

If you've got bottom end problems, with the possible exception of a slipping or dragging clutch, it's going to be disassembly time at the old ranchero. There's no reason to assume that you can't set things straight yourself, but some special tools will probably be necessary. The first thing you should do is talk to a mechanic or check out a shop manual so you know what to expect. If your machine has a transmission made up of gears pressed onto the shafts for example, you'll be out of luck unless there's an arbor press somewhere in your life, or if you are strictly a backyard hack with a few rusty tools and a hatchet, maybe it's time to get out the bank book and call the local shop. In any case this chapter will give you an idea of what to look for so all those gears and things don't blow you away when you split the cases.

Automatic Centrifugal Clutch

Most of the small capacity Japanese bikes, such as the famous Honda 50 that you met the nicest people on, utilize an automatic centrifugal clutch. We'll use this Honda clutch, illustrated here, as an example to describe their operation.

The clutch functions according to engine speed, so you can sit at a light with

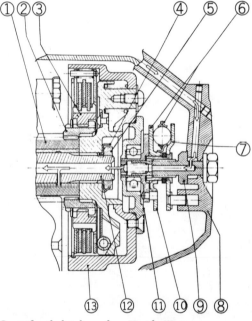

Centrifugal clutch used on Honda 50s

1. Primary drive gear
2. Drive outer
3. Clutch center
4. Lock washer
5. Lock nut
6. Ball retainer complete
7. Clutch lifter plate
8. Right crankcase cover
9. Clutch adjusting bolt
10. Clutch complete
11. Clutch outer cover
12. Crankshaft
13. Clutch outer

the transmission in first gear without moving, and then as the engine picks up speed the clutch engages and away you go. The clutch is tied in with the shifter mechanism so it disengages when the shifter

100

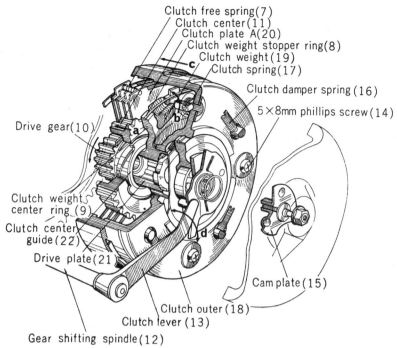

Clutch free spring(7)
Clutch center(11)
Clutch plate A(20)
Clutch weight stopper ring(8)
Clutch weight(19)
Clutch spring(17)

Clutch damper spring(16)

5×8mm phillips screw(14)

Drive gear(10)

Clutch weight
center ring(9)
Clutch center
guide(22)
Drive plate(21)

Cam plate(15)

Clutch outer(18)
Clutch lever(13)
Gear shifting spindle(12)

Centrifugal clutch used on Honda CT-200s. Instead of the rollers used on many models, this clutch uses four weights to operate the unit

pedal is depressed, thereby allowing gear changes to be smooth and quiet. It is for this reason that great wheelies can be accomplished by keeping the pedal depressed, revving it up, and then letting go of the pedal.

The clutch is mounted, in this case, directly to the crankshaft, and the transmission is then gear driven from the primary drive gear. As engine speed increases the small rollers are forced outward by centrifugal force. They press against the clutch plates and cause them to engage; this in turn allows the power produced at the crankshaft to be transmitted through the clutch to the transmission, and then to the rear wheel. As engine speed decreases, the rollers move back in toward the clutch center, and the force they were exerting on the clutch plates is relieved and the clutch disengages.

Manual Clutch

There are several clutch variations used on motorcycles. Most of them are multi-disc wet or dry clutches known as the countershaft type because they are mounted on the transmission countershaft which runs at somewhere between one half and one third engine speed. In most cases the clutch is chain or gear driven from the crankshaft. The advantage offered by this configuration is that its low operating speed is conducive to smooth high speed shifting. Its greatest disadvantage is its relatively large mass and frictional area which necessitates the use of stiff springs which demand a lot of lever pressure.

A few machines, notably BMW, use an automotive type single plate clutch known as a flywheel clutch. These clutches are mounted on the crankshaft and spin at engine speed. This, in some cases, makes high rpm shifting a little rougher than on the countershaft type, but the single plate construction makes the lever light to the touch.

All manual clutches operate in pretty much the same manner, be they wet or dry, single or multi-plated. When the clutch lever is actuated the release worm moves in toward the clutch hub and presses the clutch push rod against the pressure (spring) plate. The force exerted by the push rod(s) compresses the clutch springs while moving the pressure plate

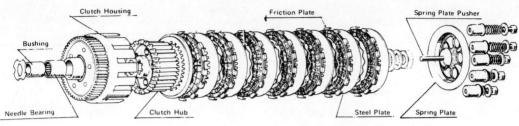

Clutch assembly from a Mach III Kawasaki

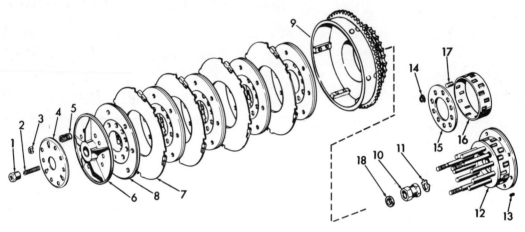

Clutch assembly from a H-D Glide model. Note that the plates on this clutch ride on studs rather than on a splined hub as on the Kawasaki

1. Push rod adjusting screw lock nut
2. Adjusting screw
3. Spring tension adjusting nut (3)
4. Spring collar
5. Springs (10)
6. Outer disc (pressure plate)

7. Steel disc (4)
8. Friction disc (5)
9. Clutch shell
10. Clutch hub nut
11. Hub nut lock washer
12. Clutch hub

13. Clutch hub key
14. Bearing plate spring (3)
15. Bearing plate
16. Bearing retainer
17. Bearing roller
18. Hub nut seal

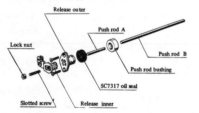

Release mechanism used on the Kawasaki H series model

away from the clutch plates, thereby allowing the plates to disengage and spin freely. When the hand lever is released, a return spring moves the release worm back into its original position and the push rod(s) is pushed back against its seat by the pressure plate which again presses against the clutch plates causing the clutch to engage.

Constant Mesh Transmissions

Constant mesh transmissions enjoy a distinct advantage over their predecessors, the sliding gear type of gearbox, as the latter often suffered tooth decay caused by missed shifts while the former will merely grind itself to death.

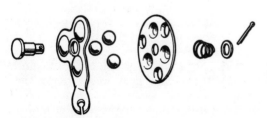

Release mechanism used on 650 Triumphs

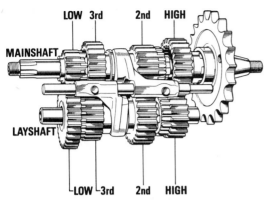

Transmission cluster from a Triumph Trident

Instead of having the gear teeth come into mesh as the gears slide along a shaft, the gears of the constant mesh transmission always stay smoothly meshed and are engaged by sliding dog gears. What you have are a bunch of idler gears that spin freely on their shaft while being meshed with driven gears which are affixed to their shaft—usually the main shaft. On the countershaft, called the layshaft on British bikes, with the idler gears are sliding dog gears, which are splined to the countershaft, with dogs designed to neatly fit into the holes provided in the idler gears. When you shift, the shifter fork moves the appropriate dog gear into mesh with the appropriate idler gear, and this causes the countershaft to spin because the idler gear is in mesh with a driven gear which is splined to the mainshaft. On most machines, such as Hondas, the clutch is affixed to the countershaft at one end, and the countershaft sprocket is at the other end. The clutch serves to disengage the coun-

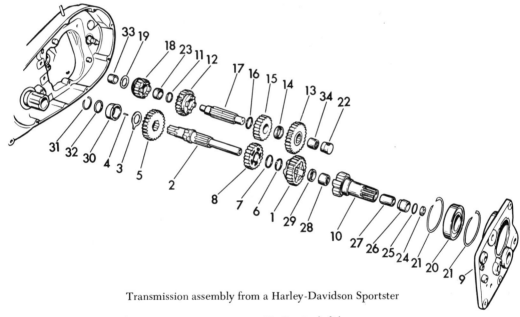

Transmission assembly from a Harley-Davidson Sportster

1. Mainshaft second gear
2. Transmission mainshaft
3. Mainshaft thrust washer (variable thickness)
4. Transmission mainshaft roller (23)
5. Mainshaft low gear
6. Mainshaft third gear retainer ring
7. Mainshaft third gear washer
8. Mainshaft third gear
9. Access cover
10. Clutch gear
11. Countershaft low gear washer
12. Countershaft third gear
13. Countershaft drive gear
14. Countershaft gear spacer
15. Countershaft second gear
16. Countershaft second gear thrust washer
17. Transmission countershaft
18. Countershaft low gear
19. Countershaft low gear washer (variable thickness)
20. Mainshaft ball bearing
21. Mainshaft ball bearing snap ring (2)
22. Countershaft oiler plug
23. Countershaft low gear bushing
24. Clutch gear oil seal (1970 only)
25. Clutch hub nut O-ring (1970 only)
26. Clutch gear oil seal extension (1970 only)
27. Clutch gear bushing
28. Clutch gear needle roller bearing
29. Mainshaft thrust washer
30. Mainshaft roller bearing race
31. Mainshaft roller bearing retainer ring
32. Mainshaft roller bearing washer
33. Countershaft bearing—closed end
34. Countershaft bearing—open end

tershaft, so when you pull in the clutch the countershaft spins but doesn't put out any torque to the rear wheel. There have been, and are, numerous variations in the construction of constant mesh boxes, but the basic principle remains the same.

SHIFTER MECHANISM

There are two basic shifter mechanism configurations in popular use today. The type found on most Japanese machines uses a shifter drum to guide the selector forks; the type in use on most British bikes, and some Harley-Davidsons, uses a camplate and a shift quadrant.

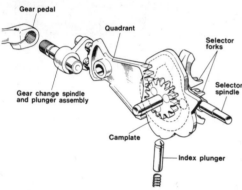

Camplate type shifter mechanism from a Triumph Trident

To better understand the workings of a shifter mechanism consider the following diagrams (the gearbox is from a 650 cc BSA):

Neutral—Neutral is the only position in which the engine may be started on this particular model. The large (index) plunger, which operates at the large end of the camplate to select the gear position, is in the camplate's neutral position, and the selector quadrant plungers are compressed and ready to be moved into either First or Second gear.

First—As the shifter pedal is moved down to select First gear, the large plunger enters the camplate and moves it into the First gear position. This causes the countershaft (layshaft) First gear selector fork to slide the countershaft First gear dog gear into engagement with the countershaft First gear. At the same time the selector (quadrant) plunger moves into the second window of the camplate, ready to move it to Second gear.

Second—The shift to Second gear is performed in the same manner, only this time in the opposite direction. When the shift is completed, two selector plungers will be in the camplate windows making the transmission ready to shift into either Neutral or First and back again.

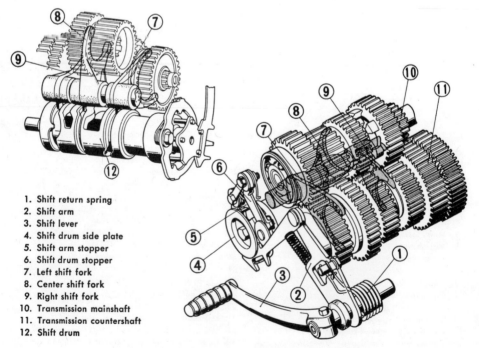

1. Shift return spring
2. Shift arm
3. Shift lever
4. Shift drum side plate
5. Shift arm stopper
6. Shift drum stopper
7. Left shift fork
8. Center shift fork
9. Right shift fork
10. Transmission mainshaft
11. Transmission countershaft
12. Shift drum

Drum type shifter mechanism used on Honda 750

NEUTRAL

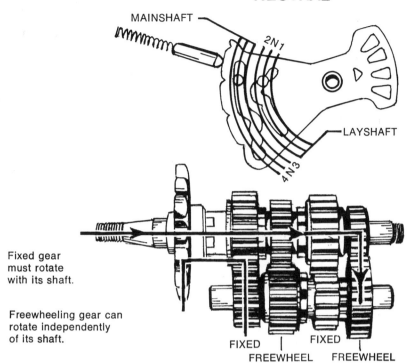

Fixed gear
must rotate
with its shaft.

Freewheeling gear can
rotate independently
of its shaft.

Neutral

FIRST

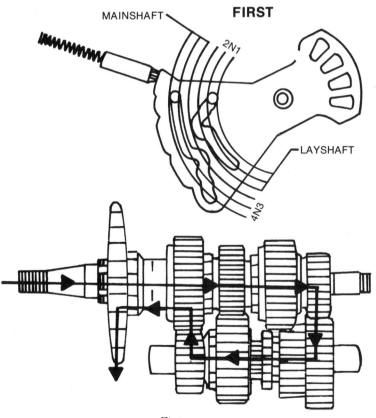

First gear

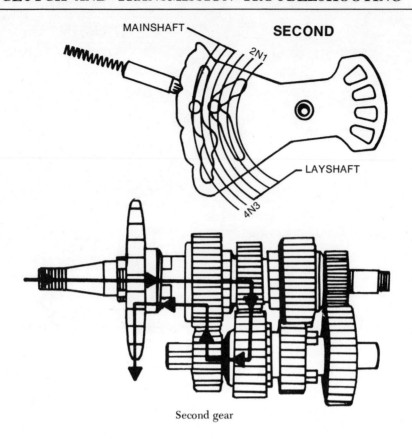

Second gear

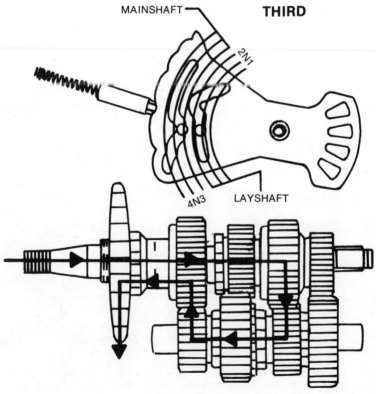

Third gear

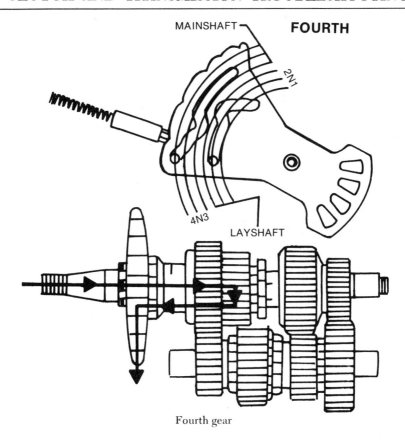

Fourth gear

Third—Shifting into Third brings both selector forks into play; one fork slides the countershaft dog gear out of mesh, and the other brings the mainshaft dog gear into mesh with the mainshaft Third gear. Once again the selector plungers are ready to shift in either direction.

Fourth—Fourth is the top gear on this particular box, so when the shift is completed, the large and selector plungers are so positioned that they can only shift down to a lower gear. Shifting causes the mainshaft selector fork to slide the mainshaft dog gear into mesh with the mainshaft Fourth gear.

The principle is the same on the drum type of shifter except instead of moving the camplate the drum is rotated. The shifter forks ride in the drum at one end, and on the sliding dog gears at the other end. As the drum rotates, the forks ride in their grooves, and the shape of the grooves causes the forks to move the dog gears.

KICKSTARTERS

Kickstarters, like all of the component systems in this chapter, vary in construction from marque to marque, and even from model to model within the same company. Some, such as the starter found on the big British twins, are only operable when in Neutral with the clutch engaged, and others, such as the starter used on the Yamaha Enduro models can be used in any gear as long as the clutch is disengaged.

To give you an idea of how a kickstarter with a kick gear system functions, let's examine the operation of a Kawasaki Mach III starter system.

When the kick lever is depressed the kick shaft is rotated, and therefore the worm gear which is part of the shaft is also rotated. This rotation sets up a centrifugal force which moves the kick gear along the worm until it meshes with the countershaft First gear. The force of the kick is transmitted through the kick shaft to the kick gear and from the kick gear to the countershaft First gear. Then it goes to the mainshaft First gear which causes the mainshaft to spin; then through the clutch to the crankshaft primary gear (which is in mesh with the clutch hub gear) which causes the crankshaft to spin.

As soon as the engine starts, the motion of the countershaft First gear in conjunc-

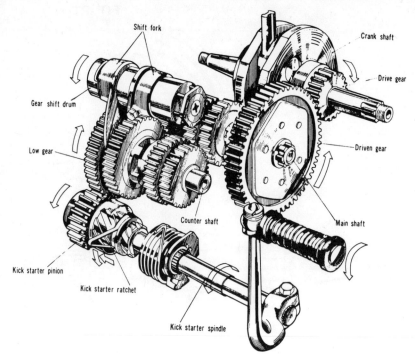

A Honda kickstarter assembly

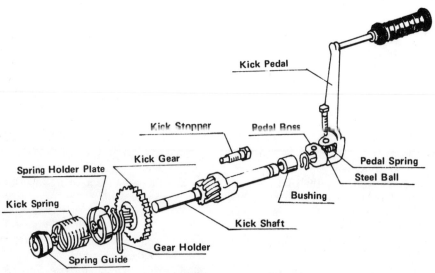

A Kawasaki kickstarter assembly

tion with the pressure provided by the gear holder, causes the kick gear to slide back along its worm gear to its original position. When the kick lever is released the return spring brings the lever back to its rest position which is determined by the location of the kick stopper on the crankcase.

The other type of kickstarter system in general use, and this is the type which most British machines come with, is the ratchet method. As an example of this let's take a look at the kickstarter used on Harley-Davidson Sportsters.

The ratchet mechanism is in two parts and will only mesh in one direction. One half is on the starter clutch (18), and the other half is on the side of the starter clutch gear (6). The starter clutch is riveted to the clutch hub, and the clutch gear

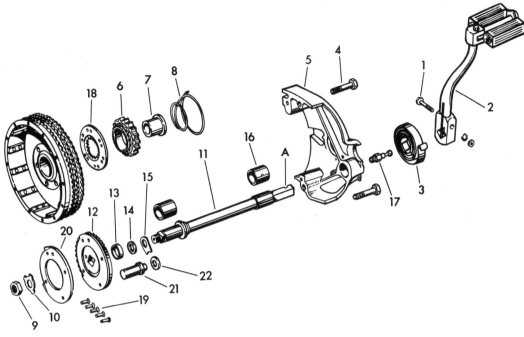

Harley-Davidson Sportster Kickstarter

1. Crank clamp bolt, lock washer and nut	8. Clutch spring	16. Shaft bushing (2)
2. Crank and pedal assembly	9. Shaft nut	17. Spring stud
3. Crank spring	10. Crank gear lock washer	18. Starter clutch
4. Sprocket cover bolt (2)	11. Crankshaft	19. Crank gear cam plate rivet (5)
5. Sprocket cover	12. Crank gear	20. Crank gear cam plate
6. Starter clutch gear	13. Crank oil seal	21. Crank gear stop pin
7. Clutch sprocket spacer	14. Crankshaft shim	22. Crank gear stop pin washer
	15. Shaft thrust plate	

Figure following name of part indicates quantity necessary for one complete assembly.

is spring loaded (8) and free wheeling on the clutch sprocket spacer (7). The ratchet teeth are designed so that when the gears are turned in one direction they will mesh, and when they turn in the other direction they will ratchet or slide over each other without meshing.

The starter shaft has a crank gear, which is in mesh with the clutch gear (12), splined to it and a camplate (20) riveted to the gear. There is also a return spring (3) which brings the pedal assembly (2) back to its original position, and a stop pin (21) which limits how far the shaft can spin by stopping the camplate.

When you step on the pedal the crank gear rotates with the shaft until the camplate is stopped by the stop pin. The crank gear turns the starter clutch gear which is held in mesh with the starter clutch by the pressure exerted by the clutch spring; this causes the clutch to spin and turn the engine over. When the engine starts, the clutch begins to spin faster and the return spring causes the pedal to return to its original position where the stop pin acts against the opposite end of the camplate. This is made possible by the ratcheting action of the ratchet teeth, and because the spring allows the clutch gear to move back against the lip of the sprocket spacer.

Troubleshooting the Clutch

Clutches are amazingly simple to adjust or repair, and once you've taken one apart you'll find that they've forever lost that air of mystery that enshrouds them.

CLUTCH DRAGS

A dragging clutch will cause your bike to creep or stall at stop lights when in gear, shift hard, and overheat. The reason is that the clutch plates never fully release when the hand lever is pulled in, and the end result is a burned out clutch or a wasted gearbox.

First, excessive heat is generated because the clutch plates and discs are unable to separate enough which creates a situation similar to running an engine without enough oil. All this friction will quickly glaze and then wear out the clutch friction disc material, and the heat will scorch and distort the discs and plates, weaken the clutch springs, and may fry the clutch hub bearings (if applicable). One good overheating is enough to sufficiently weaken the springs so the clutch will begin to slip; this will end your dragging problems but will bring on a whole new set of troubles.

The next thing that will happen is the pressure plate will become distorted, and the push rods may be damaged due to the inordinate amount of pressure placed on them. In some cases when people have installed oversize springs in order to get a more positive grab during high speed shifts, or when the spring pressure has been too great due to improper adjustment, push rods have been known to be poked right through the pressure plate causing extensive damage to the entire assembly.

Make sure the correct clutch springs are in use

Finally, after the clutch has been dragging for a while, the dogs on the dog gears will be rounded off so much that the gears no longer will engage smoothly. Chances are that you'll damage the gearbox before the clutch becomes completely burned out, but in any case all that rough shifting is going to do some damage to at least the dogs, and maybe even the shifter mechanism.

The most common cause of clutch drag is incorrect adjustment. Insufficient clearance at the hand lever, an incorrect adjustment of the pushrod at the release mechanism, a worn throwout bearing or release worm or an uneven or too tight adjustment of the clutch springs will cause a clutch to drag. The first thing to check is the adjustment at the lever, and then at the release mechanism. Make sure nothing is obstructing the motion of the release lever and preventing full disengagement. If this isn't the problem check the springs. On many British machines the springs are adjusted by screws which may come out of adjustment if the locking hubs are worn away. This would cause the pressure plate to move unevenly, resulting in only a partial release and eventual distortion of the plate. This may also be caused by one or more collapsed springs or by an already distorted pressure plate or clutch plate. If upon inspection you find that some damage has occured, the damaged parts should be replaced as necessary, preferably as a set in the case of plates, discs, and springs. It is possible that a piece of friction material or some other foreign object has gotten between the plates and taken up the necessary clearance. When securing the clutch springs do so in opposite pairs, making sure than an equal pressure is maintained, as tightening down the springs unevenly may cause an immediate distortion of the pressure plate.

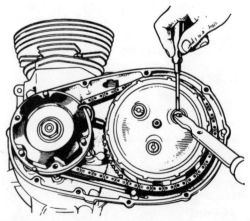

Checking the clutch spring adjustment on a 500 cc Triumph

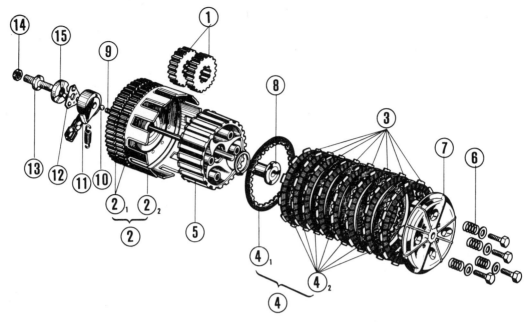

Exploded view of the clutch assembly (350 Honda)

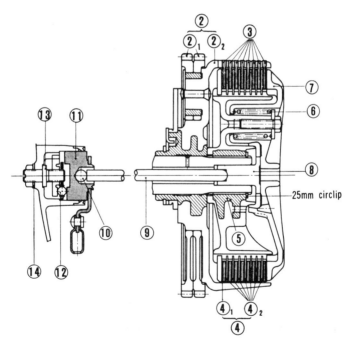

Sectional view of the clutch assembly (350 Honda)

1. Primary drive gear
2. Clutch housing complete
2_1. Primary driven gear
2_2. Clutch housing
3. Clutch friction disc (8 ea.)
4. Clutch plate
4_1. Clutch plate A

4_2. Clutch plate B
5. Clutch center
6. Clutch spring
7. Clutch pressure plate
8. Clutch lifter joint piece
9. Clutch lifter rod
10. No. 10 steel ball

11. Clutch lever
12. Steel ball (clutch ball retainer)
13. Clutch adjuster
14. Clutch adjuster locknut
15. Clutch adjusting cam

CLUTCH SLIPS

A slipping clutch will prevent the power being fed into the clutch from ever reaching the rear wheel. The earliest symptoms are usually slippage during high speed shifts, or under power in the lower gears. It will sound like the clutch is being feathered, and the engine will continue to wind without accelerating. You can feel the engine putting out, but somehow the bike never gets it on like it should. When it begins to slip in the higher gears the time for a clutch job is very near.

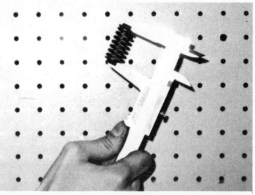

Measuring the spring free length is one way of determining whether or not the springs are up to the job

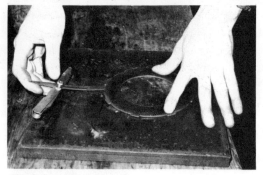

Checking a clutch plate for warpage

The causes of slippage are improper adjustment, weak springs, warped or distorted plates, discs, or pressure plate, oil impregnated, glazed, or worn friction material, a kinked or rusted cable, or anything that could interfere with the motion of the release lever.

The first thing to check is the adjustment at the hand lever and release mechanism. Too much play will cause slippage, and if the motion of the release mechanism is impaired by a hung up cable or something like that, the clutch may not be able to engage fully. Make sure the springs are adjusted correctly (if applicable), as insufficient tension can be responsible also.

If the problem is mechanical it should become immediately evident as soon as the clutch is taken down. The first thing to check here is the springs as they may be weakened even though they aren't obviously collapsed or damaged. Your dealer may have a device for measuring spring tension, or perhaps he will be able to determine their value by comparing them with new springs. Springs must be replaced as a set in order to assure equal tension.

A distorted pressure plate or warped discs and plates should be pretty obvious,

Measuring the thickness of the friction material

and must be replaced if the warpage is greater than the limits specified by the manufacturer. Plates and discs, like the springs, should be replaced as full sets to ensure efficient operation. If you are hard up at the time and the friction discs are oil impregnated they may be cleaned up by soaking them in gasoline and then blowing them dry. Glazed discs may be roughed up in a tight spot, but this is definitely not the best setup and should only be considered a temporary measure. A quick way of determining whether or not the friction material has any life left in it, other than by measuring it with a micrometer or caliper, is to press a thumbnail into the material. If this leaves an impression the disc is OK to reuse. When you reassemble the clutch, make sure you install the plates and discs in the correct order. Try to keep everything as clean as possible, and go easy on it for about a hundred miles; if you do this you can be pretty sure the clutch will last a while.

CLUTCH CHATTERS

A talkative clutch may or may not be a problem, but in any case it's annoying. If the problem is excessive play in the gears or chain that drives the clutch it won't sound too cool, but it probably won't hurt anything and isn't worth repairing if that's all that's wrong. A lot of 750 Hondas, for instance, make a lot of noise when the clutch is out, but as soon as you pull it in and put it in gear, the noise stops. This occurs because the chain(s) from the crankshaft to the clutch hub stretches a little and gets loud. Don't worry, that chain will probably last longer than the bottom end; it will just always be noisy.

If the chatter is caused by a flattened pressure plate, a bad bearing, loose or damaged clutch hub rivets, or wornout hub dampers you may have problems. A flattened pressure plate won't cause any serious damage that a clutch job won't

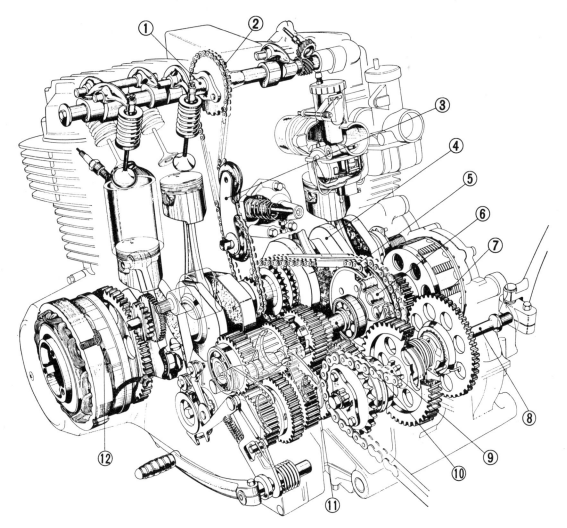

1. Camshaft
2. Camchain
3. Camchain tensioner
4. Crankshaft
5. Primary chain
6. Primary driven sprocket
7. Clutch
8. Kick starter spindle
9. Final driven shaft
10. Mainshaft
11. Countershaft
12. A.C. generator

750 cc Honda primary chains often chatter

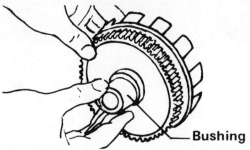

Noise can stem from a wornout clutch hub bushing

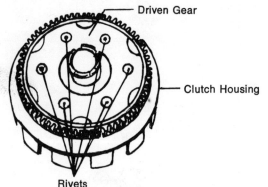

Loose rivets make a lot of noise until they give out. Then they make a mess

Check the hub dampers for a wornout condition that could cause noisy operation

cure, but if the bearing or the rivets go, it'll get messy for sure. Take a look and show it to a mechanic if you can't figure it out. A bad bearing won't rotate smoothly and may even make perceptible noise when spun by hand. Loose or damaged rivets should be obvious.

Troubleshooting the Gearbox

Determining what's wrong inside a gearbox can be pretty tricky if you aren't fa-

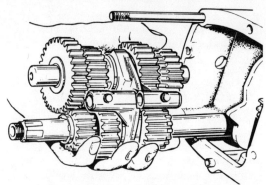

You can't tell anything until it's taken down. The cluster shown is from a BSA Rocket 3

miliar with the way things are when they're right. If you have the opportunity to examine a new shifter mechanism and gear cluster do so because it sometimes is difficult to determine if a contour has been worn that way or if it was designed like that. Look for the little things like worn gear dogs, worn or warped shifter forks, worn grooves in the shifter drum or camplate, fatigued springs, bad bearings, etc. In effect, check out everything as thoroughly as possible, and measure all tolerances carefully as directed by the manufacturer.

When it comes to replacing components keep long-range economy in mind. Replace gear systems rather than just the gears that are obviously worn, or the new parts will soon be damaged by their contact with other used parts. This means that if you have a dog gear with a chipped dog you should replace at least the gears it meshes with, the gear that gear meshes with, and maybe the shifter fork which engages it. Worn parts cause accelerated wear to new parts; the best way is to use all new stuff so it will have a chance to wear in smoothly together. Also, if you replace just the obviously damaged parts, it probably won't be long before it becomes necessary to take down the engine again, and you already know what a hassle that is.

One last thing: change the oil in a new or rebuilt gearbox every 500 miles for at least the first 1,500 miles, and go easy for a couple hundred miles. New parts wear and this causes a certain amount of metal dust to be picked up and circulated in the oil. This isn't the best of situations so it is important to flush out the system often in the beginning.

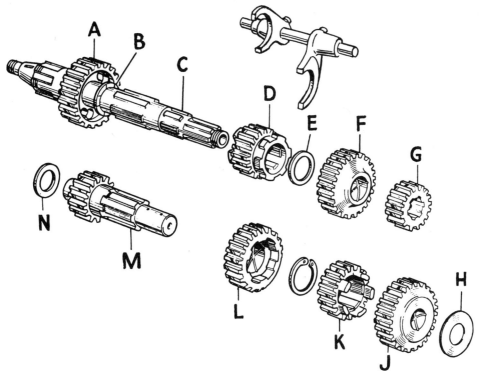

The weakest part of this BSA gearbox are the mainshaft fourth gear and the countershaft gear, neither of which can be replaced without their shaft

A. Mainshaft fourth gear	F. Mainshaft third gear	L. Countershaft second gear
B. Thrust washer	G. Mainshaft first gear	M. Countershaft
C. Mainshaft	H. Countershaft first gear shim	N. Thrust washer
D. Mainshaft second gear	J. Countershaft first gear	
E. Thrust washer	K. Countershaft third gear	

GEARS GRIND WHEN SHIFTING

If the gears grind most notably when putting the bike in First the reason is probably a dragging clutch. On some models there will always be an audible clunk when it goes into First, but the rest of the gears should shift relatively smoothly. Very few boxes are butter smooth, but loud aggravated grinding is definitely not cool.

Grinding can also be caused by worn or damaged gear dogs that aren't engaging smoothly. This will result in the eventual failure of at least that particular gear system, and maybe in the whole transmission if a dog breaks off and is eaten. If this is the case, carefully examining the grit left in the bottom of the drip pan after an oil change will let you know. A little bit of metal is not altogether uncommon, but a lot of metal shreds is a bad sign.

A wornout shifter mechanism can cause

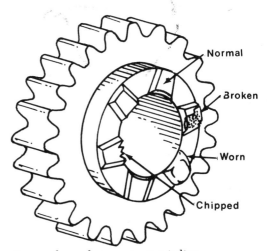

Damaged gear dogs can cause grinding

grinding because it may prevent the gears from meshing as intended. Distorted shifter forks, worn camplate or drum contours, bad linkage, etc. can cause the gears to

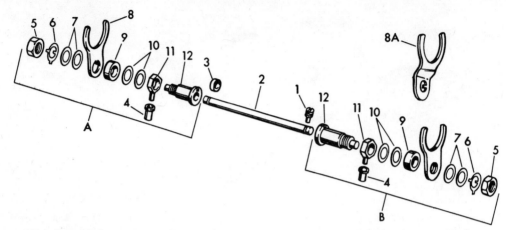

The shifter forks on this Harley-Davidson 74 shifter mechanism are adjusted through the use of variable thickness spacer shims

1. Lock screw
2. Shifter fork shaft
3. Rubber oil seal
4. Shifter finger rollers (2)
5. Nut (2)
6. Lock washer (2)
7. Spacing shim (variable number) (0.007 in.) (0.014 in.)

8. Shifter fork (1 or 2)
8A. Shifter fork (3-speed, reverse only)
9. Standard spacing shim (2)
10. Spacing shim (variable number) (0.007 in.) (0.014 in.)
11. Shifting finger (2)
12. Shifter fork bushing (2)

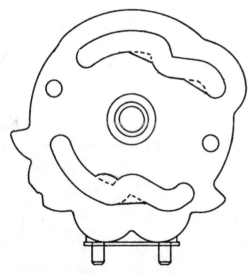

Worn contours can cause funny shifting

mesh only partially or intermittently. Check the alignment of the shifter forks (if applicable) as this is critical in most cases, and take your time during reassembly to make sure everything is just right.

Bad transmission shaft bearings can cause some really horrendous grinding since it causes eccentric rotation of the shafts. This in turn prevents the gears from

meshing smoothly as they may be misaligned. Chances are that if this occurs, the damage to the gearbox will be extensive.

Worn or warped shafts can also cause grinding for the same reasons that bad bearings can. If this is the case it is best to pull out the whole assembly and start over with new parts.

If you are lucky, the noises may stem from contaminated, diluted, or insufficient oil. This is no great prize either because any of these situations will score, gouge, wear, and generally mess up the gears but at least you'll still be able to ride for awhile.

SHIFTER POPS OUT
OF GEAR

By this we mean the bike pops out of gear under power and of its own volition . . . not because there's an inherent defect in the machine such as on some of the early 500 cc Hondas that simply couldn't stay in Third gear, and not because you're feeling lazy and shifting sloppily.

Probably the most common cause of this situation is worn dogs and shifters caused by stomping on the shift lever, speed shifting without the clutch, and just general abuse of a relatively delicate mechanism. If this is the case it will probably be quite obvious once you've taken the gearbox

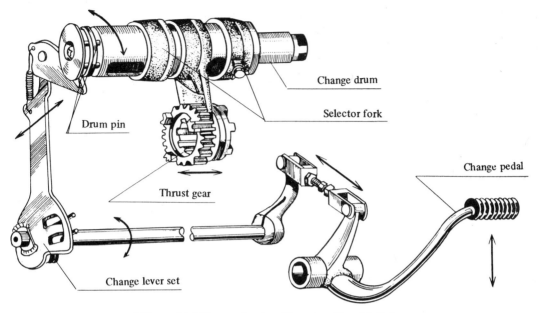

Change drum

Selector fork

Change pedal

Drum pin

Thrust gear

Change lever set

A Kawasaki shifter mechanism. Note the adjustable linkage

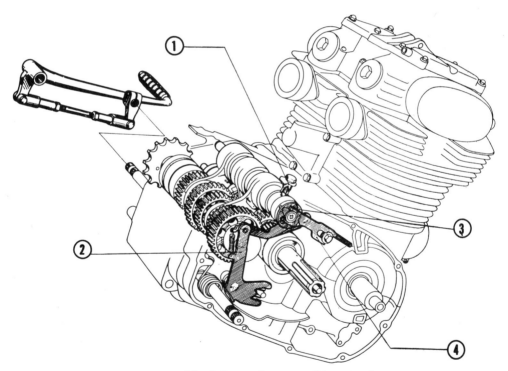

Location of the shifter mechanism on 350 cc Hondas

1. Neutral stopper   3. Drum limit plate
2. Shift arm   4. Shift drum limit arm

down and the situation can be remedied by replacing the necessary components.

Once again the possibility of bad transmission shaft bearings or worn shafts comes up. This might only allow a partial engagement of the gears which could cause the gears to disengage when stressed or when in a certain position. Again, replacement is the only solution.

A final possibility which shouldn't be

overlooked is the shift linkage which may be improperly adjusted, inherently poor, or which may have been damaged in an accident. Some bikes, such as CB/CL 350 cc Hondas, just have linkage that is difficult to set up right. If this is the case, it is sometimes possible to modify the existing system and get good results. If your bike is one of these problem Hondas, a solution may be found in the form of a 500 cc Honda shift lever.

SHIFTER DOES NOT RETURN

In this case the shifter remains in the position you last moved it to, but does not return to the ready position. You still can shift the gears but you'll have to do it by hand, probably because the return spring has broken or is really worn out. Unless the spring gets involved with some other mechanism there won't be any noise, the shifter just won't work.

Another possibility is a bent shifter shaft, especially with bikes like Yamaha Enduros where the shifter shaft runs all the way through the crankcases. If this shaft is damaged or becomes warped it can easily become jammed and fail to return. The solution is replacement of course, but don't overlook the rest of the

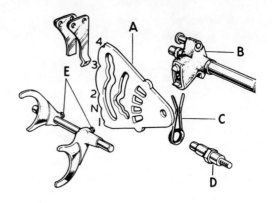

A. Camplate
B. Plunger quadrant
C. Return spring
D. Pivot
E. Shift forks, showing the camplate engagem rollers

BSA shifter mechanism

shifter mechanism as this too may have been damaged.

Check the bearing surfaces of the shifting mechanism for a galled, pitted, gritty, worn, or damaged condition and replace them as necessary. A situation such as this could conceivably cause the mechanism to hang up and therefore not return as it should. Don't overlook the possibility of

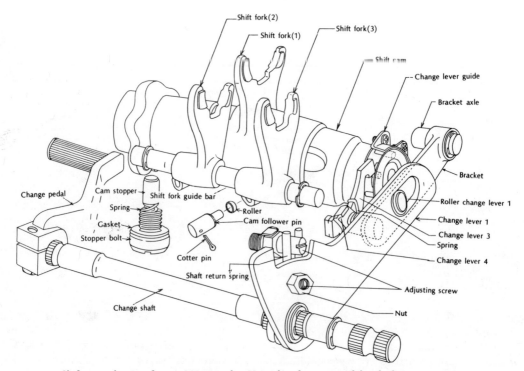

Shifter mechanism from a 360 Yamaha. Note the placement of the shaft return spring

grit in other places also, such as in the drum slots, joints, etc.

Finally there's the matter of the shifter itself. If the linkage is out of adjustment, or if the pedal has been bent by a chance meeting with the asphalt, it may rub against the cases or in some way be prevented from returning properly. This should be pretty obvious but don't write it off without taking a close look.

KICKSTARTER JAMS

If a kickstarter lever becomes jammed, not just temporarily stuck at the bottom of the stroke as some do pretty often without causing any damage, something's bound to be broken inside, and since these mechanisms are so simple you'll probably see what it is right away.

The most common failure is a broken worm, kick gear, or ratchet mechanism. As with the gearbox, the same rules apply about replacing broken parts. If the kick gear is damaged you should also consider replacing the gear it meshes with. If the worm splines on the starter shaft are dam-

Kickstarter return spring from a 650 Triumph. The arrow indicates where the spring is to be seated

aged it would be unwise to reuse the kick gear.

The second most common failure is a broken return spring. Consult an appropriate manual for instructions on pre-loading

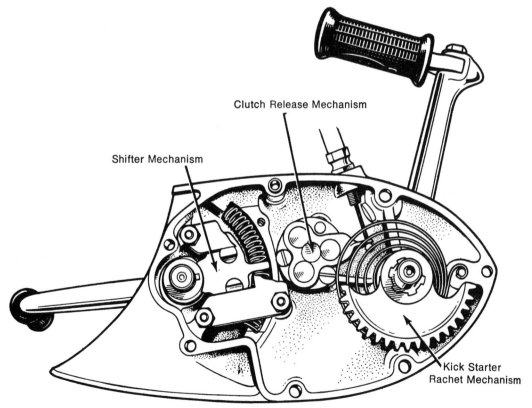

Kickstarter assembly from a 650 Triumph

the spring if necessary, but you probably won't hurt anything if you figure it out by trial and error.

Other possibilities are improperly meshing gear teeth caused by damaged teeth, a weak or damaged clutch spring, warped shafts, grit in the ratchet mechanism or in the kick gear worm, damage to the kick gear worm, or damage to the kick lever which could cause it to jam against the side of the engine case. Remedies for all of the above conditions can be obtained from your local dealer's friendly parts man.

KICKSTARTER SLIPS

A slipping kickstarter may indicate broken or worn gear teeth or a damaged ratchet mechanism that causes the starter lever to slip the length of the damage. If there are still teeth remaining, the starter may grab and operate normally after the point at which the slipping stops. If this is the case, you can get some more life out of the unit by depressing the lever until the

slipping stops and then kick the engine over. Although this may work as a temporary measure, the kickstarter should be looked into before one of those broken gear teeth jam something.

Stripped splines between the gear pedal and the kickstarter shaft, or a bent starter shaft, could also cause slipping. This probably won't wreck too much that isn't already damaged but should be attended to as soon as possible. Like any of the other kickstarter problems you won't really know what's going on unless you take it apart and have a look.

Finally, it should be mentioned that a badly slipping clutch or insufficient cranking compression can cause a kickstarter to slip. You'd probably be aware of such situations long before they'd become so bad that the starter would slip, but if the machine hasn't been run lately these may be the reasons. Also, if your machine has a compression release, check its operation carefully as this may be the source of a no compression problem.

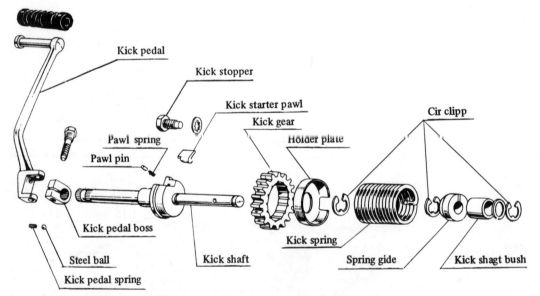

Kickstarter mechanism from an A series Kawasaki

Clutch and Transmission Troubleshooting

CLUTCH SLIPS

Possible Causes	Remedy
Release mechanism improperly adjusted	Readjust
Release worm and lever sticking	Check cable for binding, and lever spring for damage
Clutch spring tension too loose	Readjust progressively, and evenly, until proper operation is achieved
Worn or damaged clutch spring(s)	Replace as necessary
Friction discs or steel plates worn, warped, or oil impregnated	Replace as necessary
Distorted pressure plate	Replace as necessary

CLUTCH DRAGS

Possible Causes	Remedy
Release mechanism incorrectly adjusted	Readjust
Release worm and lever, or throwout bearing, excessively worn or damaged	Replace as necessary
Clutch spring tension too tight	Readjust
Friction discs gummy and sticking	Replace as necessary
Steel plates or pressure plate warped or damaged	Replace as necessary
Clutch sprocket keys excessively worn or damaged	Replace as necessary

CLUTCH CHATTERS

Possible Causes	Remedy
Clutch disc rivets loose	Replace as necessary
Pressure plate excessively flattened	Replace as necessary
Excessive play in the clutch drive chain	Forget about it until time for a bottom end job
Bad clutch hub bearing	Replace as necessary

GRINDING WHEN SHIFTING (ESPECIALLY FIRST GEAR)

Possible Causes	Remedy
Clutch drags	Consult the Clutch Drags section
Worn gear dogs	Replace as necessary
Worn shifter mechanism (ie. distorted selector forks or worn shift drum or cam)	Replace as necessary
Bad transmission shaft bearings	Replace as necessary
Worn transmission shafts	Replace as necessary
Foreign objects in the gearbox	Flush out gearbox

Clutch and Transmission Troubleshooting

GRINDING WHEN SHIFTING (ESPECIALLY FIRST GEAR)

Possible Causes	Remedy
Excessive oil level in the primary case	Drain and refill according to specifications
Transmission oil too heavy for conditions	Drain and refill with lighter oil
Insufficient or diluted gearbox oil	Drain and refill

TRANSMISSION POPS OUT OF GEAR

Possible Causes	Remedy
Shifter rods improperly adjusted or damaged	Readjust or replace as necessary
Shifter forks improperly adjusted or damaged	Readjust or replace as necessary
Insufficient shifter spring tension	Replace as necessary
Worn or damaged gear dogs	Replace as necessary
Worn transmission shaft splines	Replace the shafts as necessary
Worn, damaged, or improperly adjusted shifter mechanism	Replace or adjust as necessary
Improperly adjusted or damaged shift linkage	Readjust or replace as necessary

TRANSMISSION SHIFTS HARD

Possible Causes	Remedy
Clutch drags	Consult the Clutch Drags section
Worn, damaged, or misadjusted shifter mechanism	Readjust or replace as necessary
Worn or damaged gear dogs	Replace as necessary
Worn return spring	Replace as necessary
Improper mainshaft and countershaft alignment	Replace as necessary
Transmission oil too heavy for conditions	Drain and refill with a lighter oil

EXCESSIVE GEAR NOISE

Possible Causes	Remedy
Excessive gear backlash	Replace the worn components as necessary
Worn or damaged transmission shaft bearings	Replace as necessary
Worn or damaged gears	Replace as necessary

FOOT SHIFTER OPERATES POORLY

Possible Causes	Remedy
Worn, damaged, or misadjusted shifter mechanism	Replace or readjust as necessary
Worn or damaged shift lever return spring	Replace as necessary
Galled, gritty, or damaged shifter bearing surface	Repair or replace as necessary

Clutch and Transmission Troubleshooting

FOOT SHIFTER OPERATES POORLY

Possible Causes	Remedy
Gritty shifter mechanism	Thoroughly clean out mechanism
Bent or distorted shifter shaft	Replace as necessary
Bent shifter lever which contacts engine case	Repair or replace as necessary

KICKSTARTER JAMS

Possible Causes	Remedy
First tooth on kick gear badly worn	Replace as necessary
Damaged ratchet pinion teeth	Replace as necessary
Broken, worn, or improperly meshed gear teeth	Replace as necessary
Broken return spring	Replace as necessary
Grit on kick gear worm or in ratchet mechanism	Thoroughly clean out mechanism
Kick lever hung up	Repair or replace as necessary

KICKSTARTER SLIPS

Possible Causes	Remedy
Worn or damaged kick gear or ratchet mechanism	Replace as necessary
Clutch slips	Consult Clutch Slips section
Stripped splines between gear pedal and kick-starter shaft	Replace the shafts as necessary
Bent starter shaft	Replace as necessary
Lack of engine compression	Consult Chapter 2 or 3

7 · Chassis Troubleshooting

Chassis related problems generally make themselves known in one of two ways: suddenly, like just after you smash into a tree because you got your brake linings wet while trying to ford a raging stream, or more gradually over a period of time due to normal wear or negligence. In any case, if any part of the chassis needs attention, or is going to need attention soon, it will let you know by the horrendous noises, vibration, or funny handling characteristics which will develop.

There is no reason for you to assume that you can't repair anything your machine's chassis will throw at you. In most cases it's a matter of replacing worn or damaged parts anyway but some jobs, like straightening bent fork tubes, will definitely require special equipment that you probably won't have, but at least you can beat high dealer prices by doing all the preparation and reassembly work yourself. Again, having a shop manual to work with is not a bad idea, but if you study the assemblies carefully as you take them apart you shouldn't have any trouble.

Operational Descriptions

FRONT FORKS

Before discussing the various fork configurations it is important to understand something about the basic principles of telescopic fork operation; we'll go into the Earle's type forks a little later.

Forks are composed of fork tubes or stanchions, which slide up and down in the fork sliders and are attached to the frame of the motorcycle via the steering stem triple tree assembly which joins the fork tubes to the frame neck. The forks are able to move up and down in the sliders to get over and absorb bumps, and can rotate from side to side because the steering stem rides on bearings in the frame neck. The suspension units themselves consist of the fork springs and the oil damper assemblies which are attached to the fork tubes.

The springs can be wound in two ways, straight or progressively. Straight wound springs provide equal rates of restriction which results in a stiffer ride and more work for the damping system, and are best suited for rigorous use such as on motocross or heavy street machines. Progressively wound springs are the more common of the two and are somewhat more sophisticated in their design since they provide a degree of rebound which is in direct proportion to the degree of compression they are subjected to. They also compress at a progressive rate whereas straight wound springs compress at a uniform rate. By using a smaller spring, known as a booster spring, in conjunction with a straight wound spring, you wind up with a spring action that is similar to that afforded by a progressively wound spring.

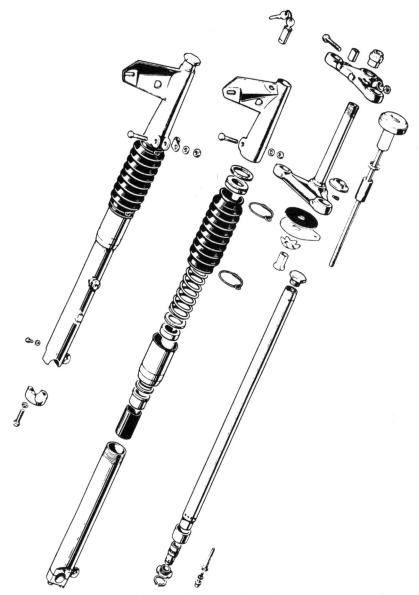

Fork assembly from a BSA Triple

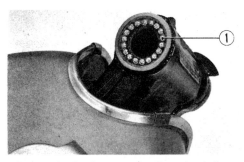

Bearings in the frame neck allow the forks to rotate from side to side

1. Bearings

This is found on some Ceriani type front ends such as the one used on the newer Triumphs and BSAs, and has proven quite effective.

Oil damping systems come in two varieties also, single and double damping. The average single damping system provides about 10 percent hydraulic restriction on the compression stroke (when the fork tubes move down in the sliders) and about 90 percent on the rebound stroke (when the springs push the tubes up and the wheel down). As you can see, the springs take the brunt of it on the compression

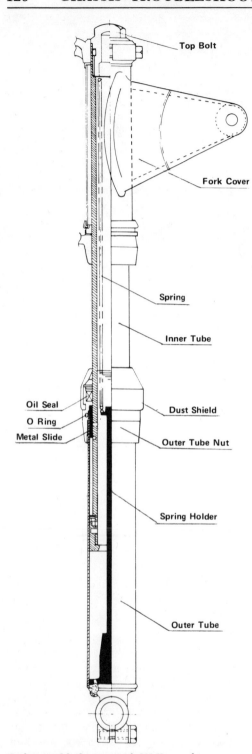

Top Bolt

Fork Cover

Spring

Inner Tube

Oil Seal

O Ring

Metal Slide

Dust Shield

Outer Tube Nut

Spring Holder

Outer Tube

Fork assembly from a Mach III Kawasaki

The spring on the right is straight wound, and the one on the left is progressively wound

stroke while the oil damping does most of the work on the rebound stroke and serves to restrict the expansion of the springs to a smooth, equal rate rather than suddenly as the springs would have it. In most cases

the damping rate is controlled by a number of small holes drilled in the bottom of the tubes or in a piston-like device which is attached to the bottom of the tubes, but on the more sophisticated models there is a series of movable washers which controls the damping rate by restricting the oil flow as desired. As the fork tube or piston comes down in the slider, it displaces the oil from the bottom of the slider by forcing it up in the tube if the tube is hollow or around the tube on models with solid stanchions. The rate at which the compression occurs is determined by the viscosity of the oil, the strength of the spring, and the number or size of the orifices through which the oil must pass. The oil is contained by oil seals attached either to the fork tube or to the slider itself. On the rebound stroke the spring forces the stanchions up, but the rate at which the spring can expand the fork is controlled by the rate at which the oil can return to the bottom of the slider. This of course is determined by the design of the damper assembly. The oil non-return valve remains closed during the extension of the fork and therefore regulates oil flow. At a certain point the orifice will reach the metal slide in the fork slider which stops all oil flow

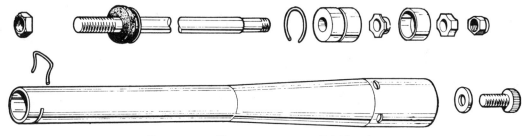

Damper assembly common to many British twins

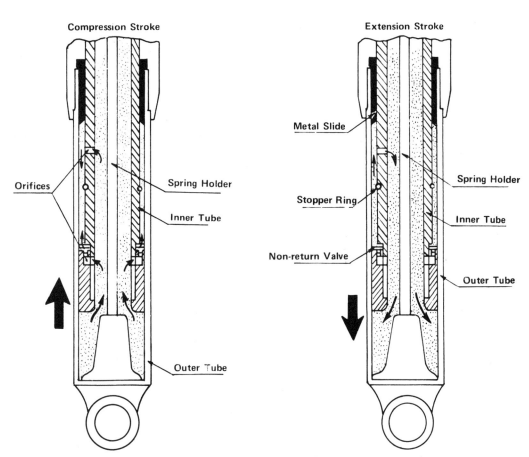

Front fork on the compression stroke

Front fork on the extension stroke

resulting in an oil lock condition which stops the extension of the forks.

Double damped systems work on a ratio of something like 30 percent/70 percent for the compression and rebound strokes, but these figures will vary according to the number of orifices in the damping system and the way in which the spring is wound. The number of holes is calculated to correspond to the spring rate. The stronger straight-wound springs need more oil restriction on the rebound stroke, and the lighter, progressively wound springs require more on the compression stroke. Therefore, while single damped forks are OK for the street and mild trail riding, if you want to really thrash about get yourself a double damped unit.

External Spring Type

As the name implies, this type of fork assembly has its springs on the outside of the fork tubes, and is characterized by the accordion-like rubber dust cover which is used to protect the workings from dirt and water contamination. This has been the most popular telescopic fork configuration and is still used extensively on road bikes and dual-purpose street-scramblers. In most cases these forks are single-damped, although there have been exceptions, and generally use progressively wound springs. One of the main advantages in using this design is that there is ample space within the fork tubes for the damper assembly. Also, the inside diameter of the tubes is not dependent on the size of the springs, and there is room for the use of heavier springs than those found in the Ceriani types.

Internal Spring Type

The internal spring type of forks, also known as the Ceriani type after the innovator of the design, are fast becoming the most popular setup for the street as well as the dirt. The use of an internal spring, which is considerably longer than the spring on a comparable external fork assembly, provides the manufacturer with the opportunity of designing a spring with exactly the correct rebound characteristics for the machine's projected use. Double damping and straight-wound springs result in very accurate fork control and a smooth ride. One of the major disadvantages of this design is that the fork seals are more exposed and this often results in leaky seals and worn parts because most riders neglect their fork oil and allow it to become contaminated.

Leading Link Type

Those strange-looking things that you used to see on little Hondas and big BMWs, and now are seeing a lot of on all

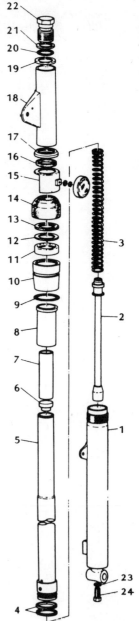

1	Outer tube	13	Oil seal clip
2	Cylinder complete	14	Dust seal
3	Fork spring	15	Outer cover
4	Piston ring	16	Packing (lamp stay)
5	Inner tube	17	Cover under guide
6	Spring upper seat	18	Upper cover
7	Spacer	19	Cover upper guide
8	Slide metal	20	Packing (O-ring)
9	O-ring	21	Cap washer
10	Outer nut	22	Cap bolt
11	Oil seal	23	Packing
12	Oil seal washer	24	Bolt

Fork assembly used on Yamaha Enduros

Earle's forks used on BMWs

sorts of dirt bikes are leading link forks, also known as Earle's forks. This design has been around for about 40 years with-

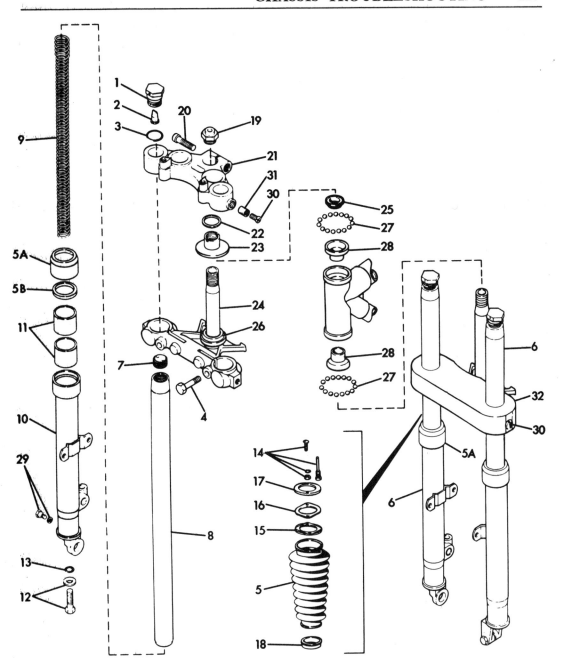

1. Tube cap	10. Fork slider	21. Upper bracket
2. Tube breather valve	11. Fork slider bushing (2)	22. Upper bracket spacer
3. Tube cap seal	12. Tube end bolt and washer	23. Stem sleeve
4. Pinch bolt	13. O-ring	24. Stem and bracket assembly
5. Fork boot (1970)	14. Vent screw and plain screw	25. Upper bearing cone
5A. Fork boot (1971)	(1970)	26. Lower bearing cone
5B. Seal (1971)	15. Boot retainer (upper) (1970)	27. Ball bearings (28)
6. Fork side	16. Boot gasket (1970)	28. Steering head cups (2)
7. Spring retainer	17. Boot retaining disc (1970)	29. Drain plug and washer
8. Fork tube and shock absorber	18. Boot retainer (lower) (1970)	30. Cover screw (2)
assembly	19. Stem sleeve end nut	31. Insert
9. Fork spring	20. Upper bracket pinch bolt	32. Cover

Fork assembly from a Harley-Davidson Sportster

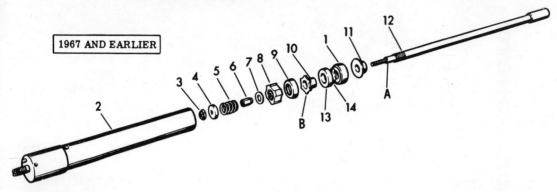

1. Piston stop bushing
2. Shock absorber tube
3. Piston rod nut
4. Recoil valve spring retainer
5. Valve spring

6. Piston spacer
7. Recoil valve washer
8. Piston
9. Piston valve
10. Piston rod stop nut

11. Piston rod guide
12. Piston rod
13. Piston stop collar
14. Piston stop spring

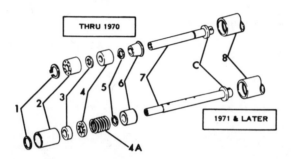

1. Retaining ring
2. Valve body, lower
3. Valve washer
4. Valve body, upper
4A. Spring

5. Piston retaining ring
6. Piston
7. Shock absorber tube
8. Fork tube

Damper assemblies used on Harley-Davidson Sportsters

out going through any radical changes because it is simplicity itself. It is a combination of a telescopic fork, because shock absorbers work telescopically, and a swing arm. Their action is more of a pivoting than a direct vertical motion, and is quite unique in that it lets the wheel swing over objects rather than being forced to bound over it, and maybe even bend back a little in the process as on a telescopic setup. Another nice touch is that while braking, the leading link controls the amount the fork compresses because the brake's backing plate is secured to the swing arm and can pivot with it.

STEERING DAMPER

A steering damper is a device whose purpose is to provide some resistance to the lateral (side to side) movement of the forks. This is especially useful for travel over rough terrain or corrugated road surfaces as the damper will resist rapid deflection of the front wheel and will protect to some extent against lock-to-lock oscillations of the fork.

Dampers are of two types: friction type and hydraulic. Friction type dampers rely upon spring loaded "friction plates" to provide resistance to fork turning. These plates are found on the steering stem (or immediately beneath the stem) and are activated by tightening the damper knob which forces them against the steering stem. The knob can be tightened until the desired degree of damping is reached.

A second type of damper is the hydraulic type. This damper is usually fitted between the fork triple clamp and the

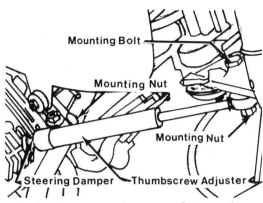

A hydraulic steering damper used on Mach III Kawasakis

draulic unit automatically varies the degree of damping in proportion to the speed at which the forks are turned. For example, if the forks are moved slowly from side to side, little damping will be noticed. But if an attempt is made to yank the forks over quickly, a strong damping action will slow the movement.

REAR SWING ARM

Swing arms, also known as rear forks, provide the mobility necessary for rear suspension. In most cases they are bolted onto the rear of the frame, although some have been bolted onto the rear of the engine, by a long pivot bolt and ride on well-lubricated bushings or bearings. The rear wheel and brake assembly are attached to the swing arm so the wheel is able to go

frame. It functions in much the same manner as the damper unit found on household storm doors, but is, of course, much smaller. Unlike the friction damper, which provides a uniform resistance, the hy-

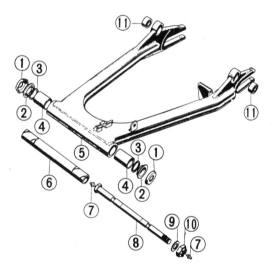

1. Dust seal	7. Grease fitting
2. Thrust bushing	8. Pivot shaft
3. Felt ring	9. Washer
4. Pivot bushing	10. Locknut
5. Swing arm	11. Shock absorber bushing
6. Pivot tube	

Bushed swing arm assembly, with grease fitting, from a 750 Honda

A mechanical steering damper

over bumps instead of having the whole bike bound over any and all road irregularities. Between the swing arm and the frame is the rear shock absorber which functions to keep the swing arm in a reasonable position for keeping the wheel on the ground while the shocks are being absorbed.

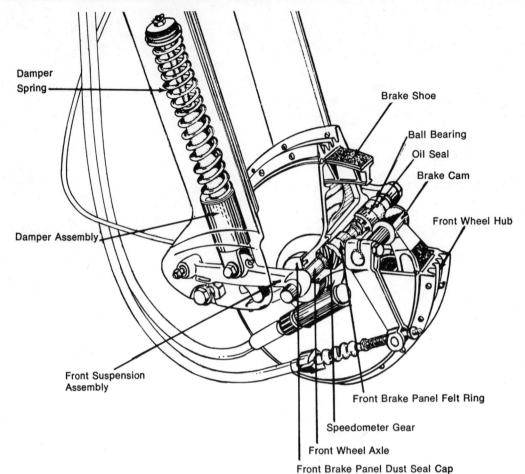

Leading link assembly used on small Hondas

Leading link forks pivot over obstacles

REAR SHOCK ABSORBERS

Rear shocks are similar in operation to telescopic forks with external springs. The spring provides controlled restriction for the downward pressure of the bike or the upward pressure of the wheel, and the shock unit itself controls the rebound rate of the spring, most of which are progres-sively wound, and serves to keep the wheel on the ground while the rest of the bike is bouncing around.

The compression stroke of the rear shock absorber begins when it receives a load compressing both the outer spring and the shock hydraulic unit itself. The cylinder, which contains fluid, rises along

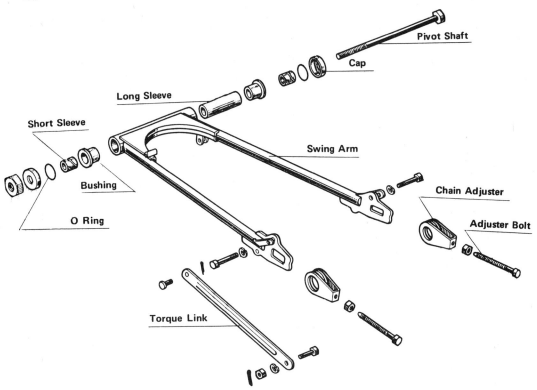

Bushed swing arm assembly from a Mach III Kawasaki

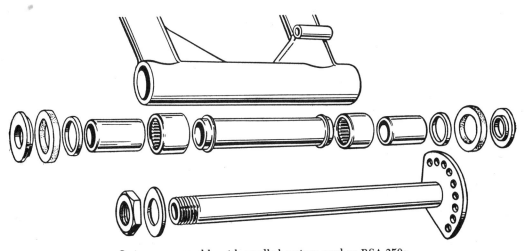

Swing arm assembly with needle bearings used on BSA 250s

the piston rod, causing pressure on the oil beneath the piston. This slows or "damps" the rate of compression. The oil flows through the piston orifice and enters the space above the piston after pushing up the non-return valve held down by valve spring C. At the same time, a small amount of the oil is forced through base valve A, and then base valve B, and enters the chamber between the cylinder and the shock outer shell. When the cylinder, rising along the piston rod, meets the rubber bumper at the top of the rod, the compression ends.

The spring tension caused by compression eventually forces the shock absorber

Girling rear shock used on most British twins

to extend to its normal or static length. The cylinder moves down along the piston rod; the oil which had been forced above the piston returns through the piston orifice and through the piston valve to the space beneath the piston. The oil which had been forced between the cylinder and the outer shell also returns to the reservoir

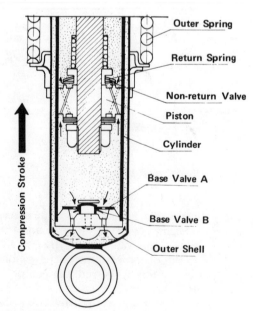

Compression stroke

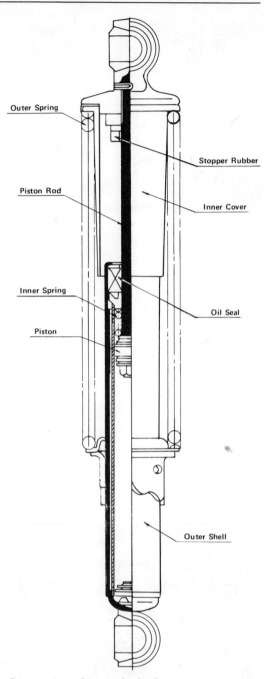

Cross section of Kawasaki shocks

beneath the piston after passing through base valve A. The oil resists the attempt of the outer spring to return suddenly to its normal length. This is known as rebound damping.

Although most rear shocks are hydraulic, some, such as the units found on most Hondas, are filled with gas under pressure. In most cases these gas models

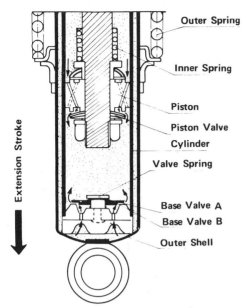

Extension stroke

Outer Spring

Inner Spring

Piston

Piston Valve

Cylinder

Valve Spring

Base Valve A

Base Valve B

Outer Shell

Extension Stroke

DRUM BRAKES

Drum brakes operate on the friction created by the shoes pressing against the drum. There are several variations on the placement and number of the shoes and their actuating cams or hydraulic systems, but without the necessary friction you cannot stop anything.

On mechanical models there are actuating cams which force the shoes against the drum when the brake is applied. The two most common systems are the single leading shoe type which is characterized by, in most cases one cam and one pivot, and the double leading shoe type which has two cams and two pivots. On the single leading type you get less brake shoe area on the drum but the brake will keep the bike from rolling backward down hills when stopped at a light, whereas on the double leading shoe type you get the maximum amount of shoe on the drum and superior stopping power but you will roll backward if you aren't careful.

Traditionally, brakes have two shoes, although in the early days bicycle type stoppers were used on most models and only the very sophisticated machines came equipped with a single-shoe brake, but lately there have been in use some competition style four-shoe brakes, such as on the Suzuki 750.

On some models, notably the Harley-Davidson Glide models, hydraulically assisted drum brakes are used that are very similar to the brakes found on cars. These models have a complete hydraulic system terminating in a pair of pistons which

just aren't up to heavy duty use and the best thing you can do for them is to throw them out and replace them with one of the excellent competition models on the market. In almost all cases the shocks have three external adjustments to compensate for rider weight, passenger weight, and application of the machine. Several of the competition models have more external adjustments in addition to internal adjustments which control the dampening characteristics of the unit. This can serve to extend the life of the shock because you can beef up the dampening to compensate for wear as the shock gets old and tired.

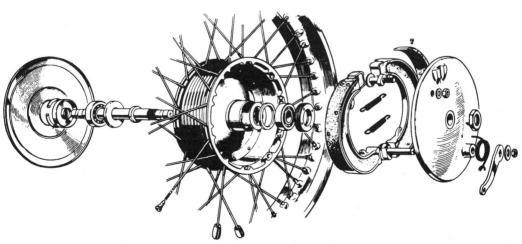

Single leading shoe brake assembly from BSA

Twin leading shoe brake assembly from BSA

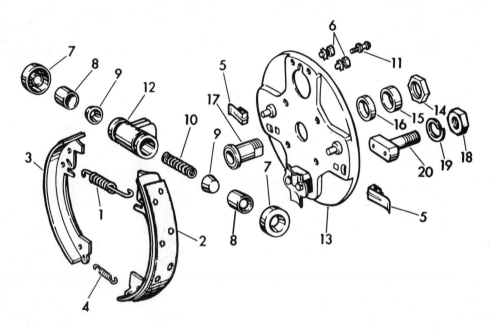

1. Shoe return spring	7. Boot (2)	14. Nut
2. Front brake shoe	8. Piston (2)	15. Spacer
3. Rear brake shoe	9. Cup (2)	16. Collar
4. Brake shoe spring	10. Spring	17. Brake sleeve
5. Hold-down spring (2)	11. Bleeder nipple	18. Nut
6. Cylinder screw and lock washer	12. Wheel cylinder	19. Lockwasher
(2 each)	13. Brake side cover	20. Anchor stud

Hydraulically assisted drum brake used on Harley-Davidson Glide models

press the shoes against the drums. When you step on the brake, as hydraulic drum brakes are found mostly on the rear, the master cylinder forces fluid from the reservoir through the hydraulic line to the wheel cylinder. The fluid exerts pressure on a piston(s) which presses against the shoe. Since the brake lever is connected to the actual brake assembly there is a corresponding increase in fluid pressure with increased pressure on the lever. Most hydraulic systems have rubber boots around the piston to retain the hydraulic fluid and keep it off the brake linings, and there is often a self-adjusting system built into the piston mechanism.

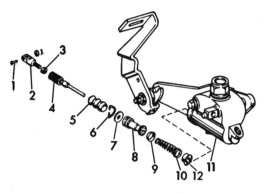

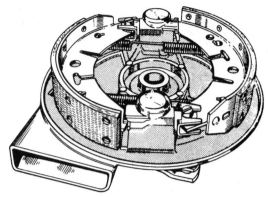

1. Rod clevis pin with washer
   and cotter pin
2. Lever clevis
3. Master cylinder plunger
   lock nut
4. Master cylinder plunger
5. Cylinder boot

6. Stop wire
7. Stop washer
8. Piston assembly
9. Piston cup
10. Piston return spring
11. Master cylinder
12. Valve

Master cylinder assembly for the Glide brake

BSA uses this air scoop to cool their double leading shoe brake

There are some inherent disadvantages in a drum system mainly related to heat buildup and the accessibility of the friction area to water and dirt. Heat causes the brakes to fade, and a combination of heat and foreign matter in the system

causes the shoes to wear, glaze, and distort. Also the internal components are easily damaged by moisture and grit which rusts some parts and gouges others.

DISC BRAKES

Disc brakes are the hot setup for fast, heavy road machines that are difficult to stop with drum brakes. They too have a hydraulic system like drum brakes, but in-

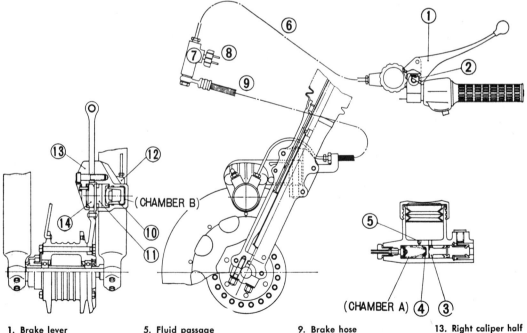

1. Brake lever
2. Lever cam
3. Master cylinder
4. Primary cup

5. Fluid passage
6. Brake hose
7. Brake line junction
8. Brake light switch

9. Brake hose
10. Caliper piston
11. Left brake pad
12. Left caliper half

13. Right caliper half
14. Right brake pad

The Honda disc brake system. Chamber A is in the master cylinder and chamber B is in the brake caliper.

stead of the piston pressing shoes against the drum, it presses brake pads against a disc. This sort of brake stops better than drum types, lasts longer, and requires considerably less attention once it has been set up. Again there are various configurations but the principle remains the same.

FINAL DRIVE

The final drive system consists of the driving sprocket, usually mounted on the countershaft, the drive chain, and the rear wheel sprocket, except in the case of shaft drive machines such as BMW and Moto Guzzi which is an altogether different story. Along the way a few niceties have been added on some models such as chain oilers and rear hub dampers, but you still have to adjust the thing yourself.

The operation of the final drive is quite simple whether it be chain or shaft. The only thing that makes a chain drive system different from a bicycle drive system is the hub dampers which take some of the stress off of the chain. On shaft drive systems, such as on the BMW, there is a steel shaft which rides on bearings in a closed housing. On the transmission end of the shaft is a universal joint and on the rear wheel end is a beveled gear set in dampers which drives the wheel. Lubrication is supplied through the journals and back to the transmission. The use of dampers in the rear wheel hub and around the drive gear, the use of a beveled gear, and the fact that there is no chain to flex and snap as the swing arm moves over bumps, provides the smooth constant power flow these machines are famous for. In addition to this, there is no maintenance necessary, other than changing the gearbox oil periodically, whereas on a chain system you are involved in a constant battle to keep the chain properly lubricated and adjusted.

Troubleshooting the Front Forks

LEAKING FORK SEALS

Probably the most common problem encountered with the forks is leaking fork seals, especially on Ceriani type front ends where the seals are more exposed. The

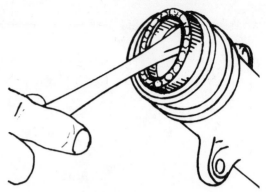

Care must be taken when removing seals to avoid damaging the fork leg as this may result in leaking

main reason that seals begin to leak is because the fork oil is neglected and becomes gritty. This works on the seals until they can no longer provide a tight enough seal. Seals can wear out with age of course, but in most cases something else will get them first.

Other things which can destroy seals are score marks on the fork tubes, bent tubes, using oil of the wrong viscosity, using ATF which can cause rapid deterioration of the seal's rubber, or overfilling the fork with oil. All of the oil-related problems can be rectified by paying more attention to the forks, and such problems as damaged tubes which damage seals can be handled by replacing the offending seal and tube.

If leaking becomes a recurrent problem it may just be due to the use of inferior seals, especially on British machines with Ceriani type front ends. Using a Japanese seal of the same size may provide a solu-

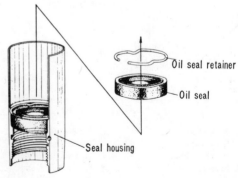

Oil seal retainer

Oil seal

Seal housing

Honda seals may be the answer to your leaking problems

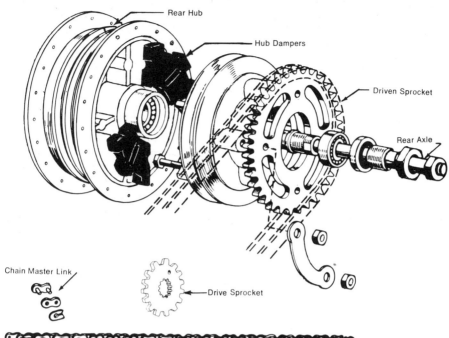

Rear Hub

Hub Dampers

Driven Sprocket

Rear Axle

Chain Master Link

Drive Sprocket

Drive Chain

Chain drive system

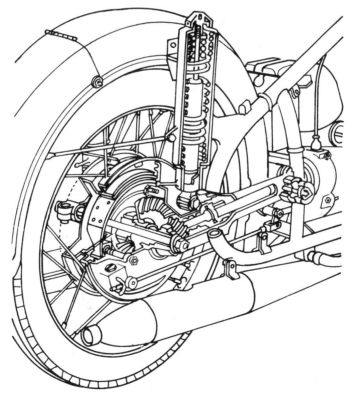

BMW's shaft drive system

tion as they, Honda in particular, make really fine seals that last.

Make sure you aren't damaging the seal during installation as this is amazingly easy to do. The best way is to lubricate the seal before installing it, then tap it into its seat using a suitably sized socket for a drift. Try and find a socket that is just a hair smaller than the seat so it will be able to enter the tube and insure that the seal is firmly seated. If for some reason you have to remove the seal and replace it be very careful how you handle it. Don't pry at it with sharp instruments, and try not to place all the pressure on one side only. The best bet however is never to try and reuse a seal once it has been removed.

This bearing retainer has been scored by dirt and therefore the bearings should be suspected

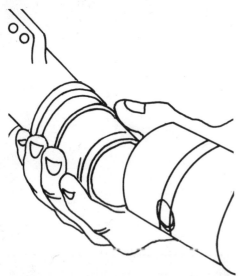

Care must be taken not to damage seals during installation

EXCESSIVE VIBRATION

Most of the things which can cause vibration of the front forks have to do with the associated components rather than with the forks themselves; therefore, before tearing into the front end make sure it's not something else that's the root of your problem.

Start with the front wheel. How are the wheel bearings? Loose, worn, or damaged bearings can cause the front wheel to turn erratically and this may cause vibration which will be transmitted through the forks. Check and make sure that the wheel runout is not excessive, that the spokes are all tightened evenly, that the tire is not worn unevenly, and that the wheel is not

misaligned in the forks. If all this checks out make sure that the fender, instruments, and headlight shell are secured because you may get vibration if these things are moving about. On some models there are rubber vibration dampers that are supposed to absorb the jolts at the handlebars before they get to you. If age has deteriorated the rubber, it will be cracked and the surface will be unusually hard.

Once you've eliminated these possibilities it's time to really check out the forks. The first thing to do, assuming that you haven't found any obviously damaged parts such as a bent fork tube, is drain and refill the fork oil. An unequal amount of oil in the forks, or perhaps diluted oil in one side, may cause some vibration. Loose axle nuts, pinch bolts, filler caps, etc. may also be a source of vibration that you can discover without taking apart the assembly. If you still haven't solved the mystery, it's time to tear it down and take a better look. It is quite possible that the forks are so worn that excessive clearance has developed between the tubes and the sliders and this is causing vibration, or your steering head bearings could be going bad. On leading link type forks, check the swinging arm bushings for excessive play as this is often a source of vibration. Check things out with your dealer or a shop manual and replace any parts which are worn past their serviceable limit.

Finally, if you still haven't found a solution maybe the problem isn't in the front end after all. Bad rear shocks, worn swing arm bushings, loose motor mounts, a bent frame, or any number of other things can cause vibration, and usually this will be most noticeable at the front forks. In any

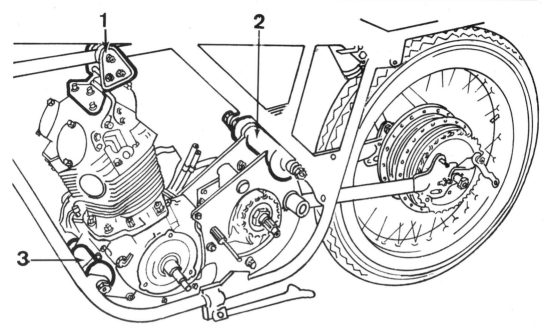

The rubber mounts on Nortons deteriorate with age and then transmit a lot of vibration

case, continue with your troubleshooting until the bike rides like it should.

POOR DAMPENING ACTION

Poor dampening action, characterized by topping or bottoming out of the suspension, can often be rectified without costly repairs or even the need to disassemble anything. In many cases all you need to do is change the fork oil to one of a higher viscosity, or merely replace the oil if it hasn't been changed for a while and has become diluted or has broken down to a point where it isn't serving any useful purpose. If the oil hasn't been changed regularly, it may be full of contaminating particles which can clog the damper orifices preventing the assembly from operating efficiently.

Damage to the fork tubes, damper assembly, or the inertia valve on the tube which, on some models, acts as a piston to force the oil down as the forks compress and then up into the tube, would cause a noticeable decline in the dampening effectiveness of the forks. If none of these things provides a solution, and the problem seems more pronounced on the down stroke rather than on the rebound stroke, look to the fork springs. The springs may be weakened even though they look fine, or they may not even be the right springs for the forks. This last situation often comes up in the case of custom front ends where the spring that best fits may not necessarily do the best job. It may be necessary to replace the springs or add a booster spring or spring spacer to get the performance you are looking for.

POOR REBOUND ACTION

Since this concerns the springs primarily, they are the first things to check. You probably won't have the facilities to check the springs for proper tension, but maybe you can examine and compare them with a new set. Always replace springs in sets for the best performance.

If the rebound action is not smooth, look for something that might cause the assembly to hang up, primarily the fork tubes. Slightly bent tubes can cause the forks to rebound unevenly or more slowly than normal.

EXCESSIVE STEERING HEAD PLAY

Excessive play in the steering head will first become obvious at high speeds where you will feel some flexing in the front end. This is usually caused by loose or worn steering head bearings, but may also be due to a loose steering stem head nut. If it turns out to be bearings, remember to replace both the top and bottom assemblies as a set.

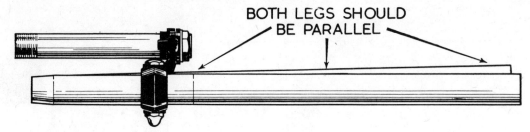

BOTH LEGS SHOULD
BE PARALLEL

Although it would appear that one of these tubes is bent the fact is that the lower triple clamp is the culprit

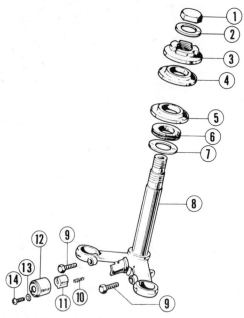

1. Steering head stem nut
2. Steering stem washer
3. Steering head top thread
4. Steering top cone race
5. Steering bottom cone race
6. Steering head dust seal
7. Steering head dust seal washer
8. Steering stem
9. Hex bolt
10. Handle lock spring
11. Handle lock
12. Handle lock case cover
13. 3 mm flat washer
14. Cross screw

The steering stem assembly puts pressure on the steering head bearings

HEAVY OR STIFF STEERING

The first thing to check in a case like this is the steering stem head nut or whatever is used to put tension on the bearings. If it is too tight these symptoms will appear immediately. If an examination shows that this is not the problem, check out the bearings carefully for a worn or damaged condition, insufficient lubrication, or dirt in the bearing races.

If the problem is not related to adjustment, maintenance, or the condition of the bearings, check for damage to the steering stem and frame neck. Deep score marks on the stem or dings in the frame neck can cause enough friction to affect the steering.

Troubleshooting the Shock Absorbers

Usually the first thing to go on a rear shock absorber, and this also applies to the shock units found on Earle's forks, is the oil seal, then the oil leaks out and you are left with a worthless unit that can serve only to support and guide the rear springs. Seals fall prey to dirt, grit, and water which is sucked in through the breathers. The dirt wears away at the seals until they begin to leak, and the water dilutes the oil and therefore reduces the effectiveness of the damping action causing them to feel too soft while in use. Seals also may be damaged if the shock plunger is bent slighty; if the plunger ever gets really bent however, it will most likely prevent the unit from operating smoothly. A note of warning: shock absorbers should be stored in a vertical position to protect the seals. If the seals are left bathed in oil they may warp and begin to leak prematurely. Except for the few rebuildable units available, once a shock goes it must be replaced although the springs may be reused. Springs may fail due to metal fatigue over a period of time but usually they will outlive the shock unit itself. Shocks should be replaced in pairs and the springs should be replaced in this manner also if worn, damaged, or tilted more than

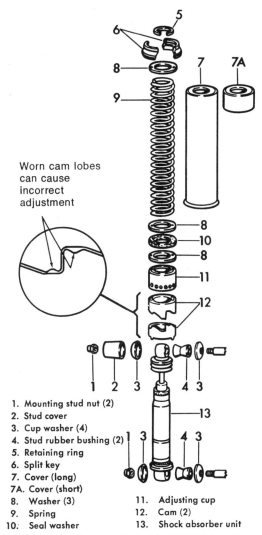

Worn cam lobes
can cause
incorrect
adjustment

1. Mounting stud nut (2)
2. Stud cover
3. Cup washer (4)
4. Stud rubber bushing (2)
5. Retaining ring
6. Split key
7. Cover (long)
7A. Cover (short)
8. Washer (3)
9. Spring
10. Seal washer
11. Adjusting cup
12. Cam (2)
13. Shock absorber unit

A Harley-Davidson shock absorber assembly

Testing a rear shock absorber

ment time. If the shock is not the type that can be disassembled, remove it from the bike and compress it by pressing down with all your weight while the bottom of the shock is on the floor. If the unit is good, it will take twice as long for the plunger to travel the second half of its total distance as it will the first. If you compress the shock and it springs right back up, the only damping action you have is in the spring itself and the unit must be replaced. When you replace shocks buy the best set you can afford. The shocks fitted by the manufacturer often cost as much as a set of really good ones and the difference in handling, especially on big Japanese bikes, between good and mediocre shocks will truly amaze you.

Remember that if you replace a stock shock with a custom unit you may have spring incompatibility problems. Many Japanese manufacturers use too stiff a spring in an attempt to compensate for poor damping characteristics, so it may be necessary to replace the spring also if you want the best possible handling your machine can deliver.

Troubleshooting the Swing Arm and Frame

Except on models such as BMW and Moto Guzzi, in which the final drive system is an integral part of the swing arm assembly, swing arms are straight-forward units made of pressed or tubular steel and there isn't too much that can go wrong with one.

Generally, the greatest amount of attention a swing arm requires is replacement

a couple of degrees, as they may cause damage to the shock itself. Compare the old springs to a new set if possible, or try out the old springs for a while to see if they feel alright. If they do need replacement you can exchange them at any time without too much trouble, but if they are still good you can save yourself some money.

If the shocks haven't lost all their oil it's pretty hard to tell if they are serviceable unless you remove them. Disassemble the shock then pull out the plunger and push it back in. It should take considerably longer for the plunger to go back in than it took for it to come out. If the plunger moves with no resistance, or if it feels the same going in as coming out it's replace-

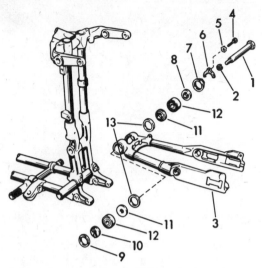

A Sportster swing arm assembly

1. Pivot bolt
2. Bearing lock washer
3. Rear fork
4. Bearing screw
5. Shakeproof washer
6. Lockwasher
7. Bearing lock nut—right
8. Outer spacer
9. Bearing lock nut—left
10. Pivot bolt nut
11. Bearing inner spacer (2)
12. Bearing (2)
13. Bearing shield (2)

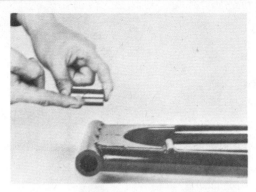

If your swing arm doesn't have a grease nipple this is the way to lubricate the bushings

of the swing arm bushings. These wear out in time, more quickly if not kept well lubricated, and must be replaced in sets. When the bushings begin to go they will affect the handling of the machine even when going in a straight line, and you'll know it by the front end oscillation which will develop. This may be temporarily remedied by putting more tension on the nut which secures the swing arm pivot, or by lubricating the assembly with a heavy grease. On some models, such as the Mach III Kawasaki, the swing arm bushings are made of plastic and simply aren't up to the job. Replacing these with a set of bronze bushings will bring an end to that unnerving feeling which these machines give in

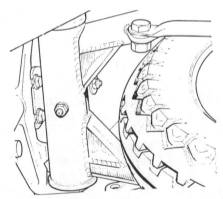

Sometimes, as with this Trident, it takes a little searching to find the grease fitting

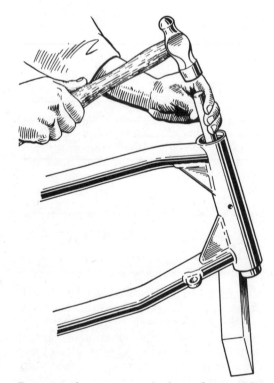

Removing the swing arm bushings from a BSA frame

hard corners. Spacers will probably have to be machined to bring the rear wheel into a more exact alignment, but the trouble will be well worth the effort. Consult your local dealer for more information on setting up your machine's suspension regardless of the make. There are a lot of

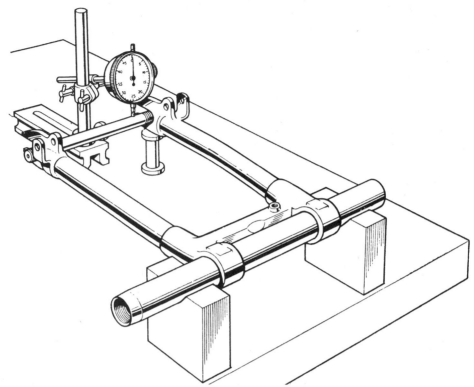

Using a dial indicator to check the alignment of the swing arm

specialty companies bringing out new goodies all the time.

Damage to a swing arm can be determined by removing it, laying it out on a flat surface, and checking carefully for misalignment and twist. Repairs to this part are possible but should be turned over to your dealer or a machinist who knows what he's doing and has the right equipment. This is especially true in the case of a damaged frame which is a very dangerous situation. Don't go in over your head or you may be sorry. Don't trust your life

to any hack with a torch and a hammer because poor quality work is something you definitely don't want here.

Wobbly or uncertain steering, often accompanied by uneven tire and sprocket wear, may be caused by a built-in fault in the swing arm. In many cases the alignment marks, and even the axle groove may be improperly aligned right from the fac-

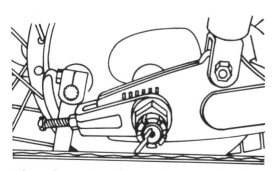

These alignment marks may be wrong when they come from the factory

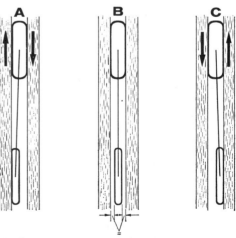

Checking alignment

tory so don't place all your faith in them until you're sure they are right. One of the best ways to do this is by placing boards along the wheels as illustrated so you are sure the wheels are correctly aligned, then see what the adjuster marks say. Scribe your own marks if the alignment is not what it should be. Once you have the wheels pointed in the same direction make sure that the drive sprockets are also correctly aligned and shim them into alignment if necessary.

Troubleshooting the Final Drive

CHAIN DRIVE

Chains and sprockets wear out over a period of time, but their life expectancy can be greatly increased if proper maintenance is applied. The greatest single problem with a drive chain is keeping it properly lubricated. The chain oiler systems incorporated by many manufacturers spray a controlled amount of engine oil onto the chain but this is not usually sufficient as the oil is too thin and most of it is thrown off before it ever penetrates the links to lubricate the rollers. One of the many chain lubricants available commercially should be applied at least once a week under normal road riding conditions, or more often if the machine is used in dirt or water. Grit gets in the chain and wears out rollers and sprockets very quickly so it's important to thoroughly clean and lubricate the chain after doing any offroad riding, especially if you ride in sand. Also, a well-lubricated chain isn't as likely to kink and bind like a dry one will and this can prevent chain failure.

Keeping a chain properly adjusted is also important because a chain will break or be thrown from its sprockets more readily if too tight or too loose. When you adjust the chain, do so with someone sitting on the seat so the swing arm is in the normal riding position, and make sure you are measuring the play at the chain's tightest point. If you raise and then rotate the rear wheel the tightest point should become fairly obvious. You can determine if tight spots are being caused by the chain or the sprocket by marking the chain and sprocket with daubs of paint every time a

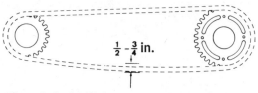

Chain slack should be measured halfway between the two sprockets

tight spot is discovered. If the tight spot is caused by the chain it will be tight at that point every time, but if the tight spot is caused by the sprocket the chain will get tight every time the bad spot is at the back of the sprocket directly behind the swing arm joint. Adjust the chain until there is from $\frac{1}{2}$–$\frac{3}{4}$ in. of slack at a point directly between the two sprockets. Make sure the wheels are aligned before securing the adjusters. This can be accomplished by laying a straightedge alongside the two wheels. Both wheels should touch the board in the same manner. The wheels may be aligned by sight also if the front wheel is sighted from behind the rear wheel.

A chain may be worn out even if it looks serviceable. After a period of time, and this will vary according to the type of machine and how it's driven, the chain stretches beyond the point of adjustment. If this happens, the chain must be immediately replaced. Such measures as removing one or two links should be avoided because although the chain will fit it will be too weak to handle the stress placed on it and may break causing severe damage to the crankcases, wheels, or maybe your leg. Actually the chain should be replaced before it has stretched to the end of its possible adjustment. Whenever you can pull the chain more than $\frac{1}{4}$ in. off of the rear sprocket the chain is ready for replacement. Another way to determine if the chain should be replaced is to stretch it out to its full length and measure it. Then compress the links so the chain is as short as it can be without being bent and measure it again. If the difference is more than $\frac{1}{4}$ in. per foot of chain, or more than 3% of its total length, the chain has had it and should be replaced immediately. For those

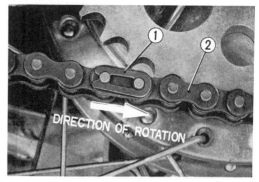

Secure the master link properly

1. Spring clip   2. Drive chain

Checking for excessive wear

of you who demand a more exacting method of determining when wear of the pins and bushings has brought the chain painfully close to the end of its usefulness, try this:

Clean the chain thoroughly, lay it out, and measure its compressed length; then stretch it out and measure it again. Divide the difference by the nominal length of the chain and multiply by 100. The chain's nominal length is the number of links multiplied by the pitch of each link (i.e. either $\frac{1}{2}$ or $\frac{5}{8}$ in.). For example, a $\frac{1}{2}$ in. pitch chain with 100 links is worn out when elongation is $100 \times 0.5 \times 0.3 = 1.5$ in. Therefore the chain must be replaced when the difference between the compressed and stretched length is 1.5 in.

Whenever you remove, adjust, or lubricate the chain you should check it carefully for signs of abnormal wear or damage. Bound links, minute cracks in rollers, excessive play between links, or signs of pitting, rust, or corrosion are the sort of warning signals you have to look out for. In many cases the overflow tube from the battery dumps acid right on the chain causing damage that is almost un-

noticeable unless you are alert for it. Inspect the master link for signs of distortion or fatigue of the spring clip, and replace the master link, or at least the spring clip, each time you remove it because this is the weakest point of the chain. One final word about master links; always install the spring clip so that the closed end is pointing in the direction of normal rotation.

Slapping noises indicate that the chain is too loose (this also applies to primary chains), and a whining noise indicates that the chain is too tight. If the machine seems jerky when pulling away from a stop and you are sure that the clutch is adjusted and functioning correctly, the input pulse dampers are probably in need of replacement. These are rubber units, usually mounted in the rear hub, which take up some of the shock which occurs when the torque produced by the engine reaches the rear wheel.

SHAFT DRIVE

Other than the routine maintenance called for in the owner's manual, there is no other attention which shaft drive units require. Both of the more popular shaft driven models, BMW and Moto Guzzi, have dampers incorporated in the rear hub where the shaft rides, but only the BMW requires periodic attention. If you hear excessive gear noise, if you can hear the bearings making a hollow sort of sound, or if the machine jerks when pulling away from a stop, you've got problems which will necessitate the replacement of parts and your dealer should be consulted or you should pull the assembly apart and see what's wrong. There aren't any adjustments that will rectify the situation; you'll just have to replace the worn or damaged parts.

SPROCKETS

The only thing you can do for your sprockets is to keep the chain properly adjusted and lubricated, and make sure they are always perfectly aligned. Sprockets will wear naturally with time but this process can be minimized through efficient maintenance. Remember that the sprockets and chain are more or less a complete system and that if one is worn it is going to affect the others. Don't bother to replace the chain without replacing the sprockets if they are worn because you'll just be needing a new chain again before you know it.

Sprockets wear in two basic patterns, but break and chip in a multitude of ways. If the sprocket teeth appear to be hooked from the back it's probably due to normal wear or because the chain was kept too tight. The other form of wear is side wear and this is caused by the rear wheel being out of alignment, bad wheel bearings, or by a warped hub or sprocket. In either of the above cases, the sprockets should be replaced along with the chain and the problem solved before a new final drive is mounted.

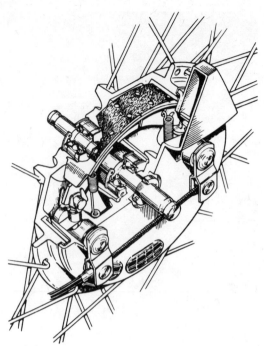

Cross section of a BSA double leading shoe front brake assembly

noisy. Whenever something makes noises which it normally doesn't make, trouble is usually just around the corner, or as in the case of brakes, it may already have arrived.

Squeal is probably the biggest offender and is caused by a high pitched harmonic vibration in the drum which may be caused by glazed linings, dirt on the shoes, a hairline crack in the linings, or because the return springs are weak. The dirt or glazing can be easily remedied by taking off the wheel and cleaning out the brake assembly, but if there is a crack in the lining, probably caused by excessive heat, the

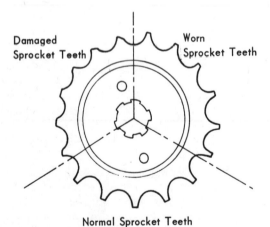

Sprocket wear patterns

Troubleshooting the Brakes

DRUM BRAKES

One of the most often encountered complaints about drum brakes is that they are

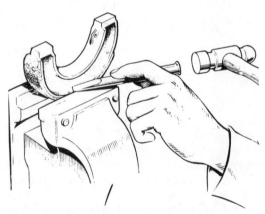

Chiseling off brake rivets

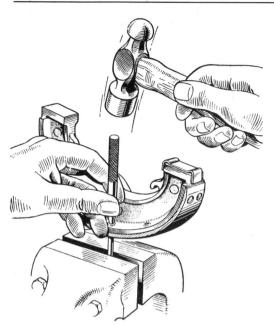

Riveting new linings onto the shoes

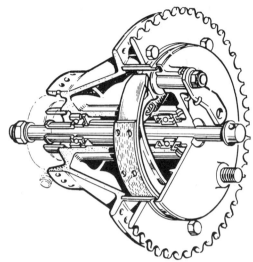

Cross section of a BSA rear brake assembly

shoe must be replaced (unless you wish to replace the lining only, which is not the recommended procedure except on certain British machines). Glazing can be removed with coarse sandpaper or a wire wheel, but if removing the glazing leaves you with less than 2 mm of lining on bonded shoes, or if the rivets are not below the surface of the shoes, it's time to replace the brakes. If the return springs have had it, the shoes may always run on the drum and make noise. Compare the old springs to new ones and replace them, in sets, if necessary. If you need to replace one shoe it's a good idea to replace the other also because since they both operate at the same time, the new shoe lining will contact the drum before the older one and this will cause unnatural wear to the new lining.

Brakes will chatter if the drum is out of true, if there is uneven wear on the shoes, or if there is dirt between the shoes and the drum. If the shoes are worn unevenly they may be sanded down until they are even, provided there is still enough lining left, or the shoes can simply be replaced. Uneven wear is a symptom, the cause of which must be determined before the brake is put back together. If the drum is out of true it can be turned down by a qualified machinist (your dealer can probably recommend a place to go if he cannot do the work himself). If the shoe was worn unevenly due to dirt, this can easily be

taken care of unless the dirt has scored the drum (in which case you should consult your dealer); if the wear was caused by a bent or warped actuating cam, the cam will have to be replaced.

Scraping sounds must not be disregarded for even a day because they are an indication that the linings have worn

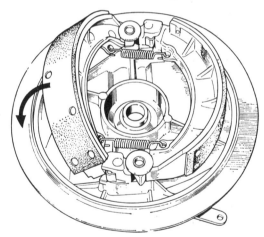

Fold the shoes onto the backing plate to aid in installation

down far enough to expose the rivets and the rivets are contacting the drum, or that something has already broken inside. If you continue to ride under such circumstances you can be fairly sure that you'll ruin the drum by scoring it.

If you apply the brakes and they don't grab, it's probably because there is grease, water, oil, or hydraulic fluid on the linings, the linings are glazed, there is a leak in

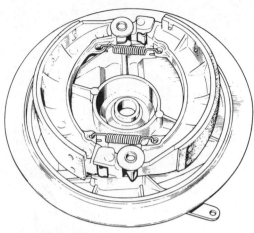

The installed brake shoes

Bleeding the hydraulic system

1. Bleeder nipple   2. Plastic tubing
           3. Container

the master cylinder, or there is air in the hydraulic lines somewhere. It is also possible that the linkage is improperly adjusted or assembled, especially on mechanically actuated brakes, or the linings are shot, so carefully check over the whole system. If the problem is hydraulic fluid on the linings you'll have to replace them, but if it's only grease or oil, the linings can be cleaned with gasoline and then sanded down to raise the abrasion level. If there is a leak in the hydraulic system, you can

probably get a rebuilding kit that will have replacement parts; drain and replace the hydraulic fluid but take care in doing this because hydraulic fluid is notorious for ruining paint jobs. Remember that it is false economy to only use the parts in a re-building kit that replace obviously damaged components. Use the whole kit, fresh fluid, and carefully bleed the system to purge it of all air.

DISC BRAKES

Like drum brakes, one of the most frequent complaints about disc brakes is that they make a lot of noise sometimes. Disc brakes squeal unless everything is just right, and even then they often squeal. Glazed disc pads, a warped disc, an improperly adjusted caliper, or an extremely dusty or dirty front brake assembly are the reasons for this noise. The pads can be lightly sanded with coarse sandpaper to remove glazing but it's generally best to replace them. In either case, you'll have to go easy on the brake for the first hundred miles or so to give the pads a chance to seat properly. If the caliper is out of adjustment, the solution is pretty obvious but is easier said than done since the adjustment must allow the pads to ride just a hair above the disc. If the noise is related to dirt on the pads or disc they may be cleaned with water. Never use a high pressure spray though, as this may damage the assembly. If the brake still squeals but operates efficiently, leave it alone. The noise is more of a nuisance than a problem and may correct itself when the pads wear a little more.

Another problem which is often encountered is a spongy feeling in the hand lever usually accompanied by excessive lever travel and a reduction in braking performance. The first thing to check in this case, especially if the machine has a lot of miles on the pads, is the condition of the pads. Each manufacturer has a method of determining when the pads are in need of replacement so consult your handbook or your local dealer. If the problem isn't in the pads it may be due to air in the hydraulic system or a leak in the master cylinder, caliper, or brake lines. If the problem is mechanical, get a rebuilding kit and use all of the parts in it, not only those which you think need replacement, because not doing so is false economy. After

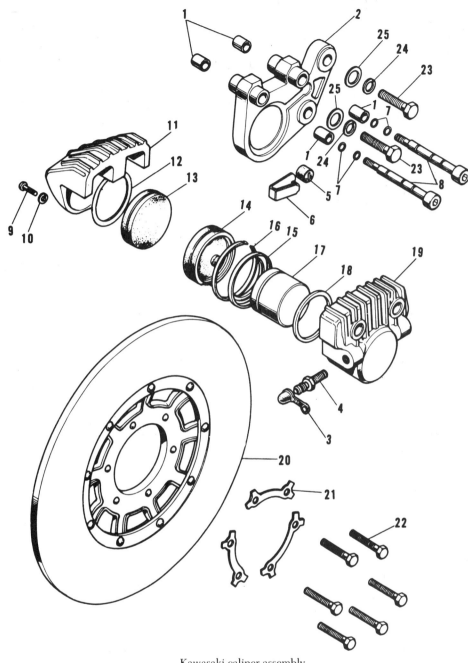

Kawasaki caliper assembly

1. Dust seal
2. Caliper mounting
3. Bleeder valve cap
4. Bleeder valve
5. Bushing
6. Stopper
7. O ring
8. Shaft
9. Screw
10. Lock washer
11. Caliper B
12. Ring
13. Pad B
14. Pad A
15. Dust seal
16. Band
17. Piston
18. Ring
19. Caliper A
20. Disc
21. Lock washer
22. Bolt
23. Bolt
24. Lock washer
25. Washer

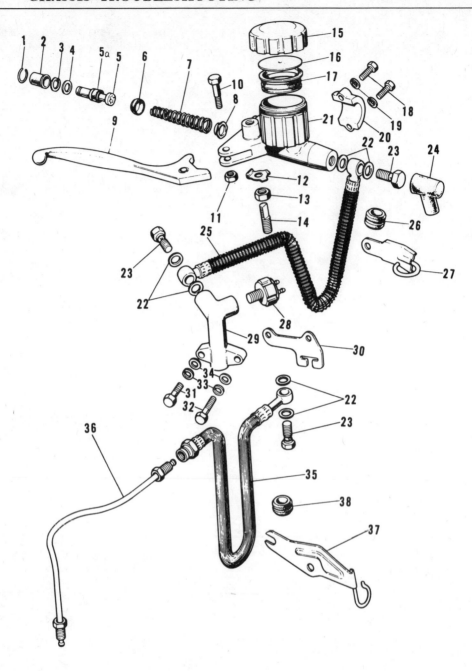

Kawasaki master cylinder assembly

1.	Stopper, dust seal	13.	Nut	26.	Grommet
2.	Dust seal	14.	Bolt	27.	Bracket
3.	Circlip	15.	Cap	28.	Pressure switch
4.	Stopper, piston	16.	Plat	29.	3-way fitting
5.	Piston assembly	17.	Cap seal	30.	Guide
5.a	Secondary cup	18.	Bolt	31.	Bolt
6.	Primary cup	19.	Washer	32.	Bolt
7.	Spring assembly	20.	Master cylinder mounting	33.	Lock washer
8.	Check valve assembly	21.	Master cylinder body	34.	Washer
9.	Brake lever	22.	Washer	35.	Hose
10.	Bolt	23.	Banjo bolt	36.	Pipe
11.	Nut	24.	Dust cover	37.	Bracket
12.	Lock washer	25.	Hose	38.	Grommet

you drain the system, taking care to keep the hydraulic fluid off any painted surface to avoid damaging the finish, bleed the system thoroughly to remove any air. Hydraulic fluid should be changed at regular intervals or whenever necessary. A remote possibility for a symptom such as this is that the lever adjuster, such as the one on pre-K1 750 Hondas, is improperly adjusted, however few hydraulic disc systems have such a device. If this is the case, a careful adjustment is in order.

The last symptom prevalent with disc brakes is brake shudder. This is probably due to a warped disc but may also be due to distorted pads or oil or brake fluid impregnation of the pads. The only way to remedy a situation such as this is to replace the culprit once you decide which part he is.

Troubleshooting the Wheels

Aside from repairing or replacing bent rims, broken spokes, and wornout bearings, the only wheel troubleshooting left is to keep them balanced and trued.

Wheel balancing is done on a jig or a truing stand usually, but may be done on the bike if it is supported off the ground, the chain is disconnected when the rear wheel is done, and the brakes are not dragging although this is not the recommended procedure. Truing stands can easily be constructed out of an old bicycle fork or any other device which would allow the wheel to spin freely on a flat plane. Balancing should be done with balance weights but in a pinch solder can be

Using balance weights to balance the wheels

wrapped around the spoke nipples instead. The way to do it is to spin the wheel and see where it stops, then mark the rim at its lowest point. Do this several times to determine where the heaviest section of the wheel is, and then begin adding weight to the opposite side of the rim as a counter balance. When you've got it right the wheel shouldn't stop at any one spot in particular. If all of that sounds like a hassle try using some of the tire balancing fluid on the market. This stuff is really fine and easy to use. All you have to do is put some of it in the wheel right through the air valve and then spin the wheel. When the stuff settles after a few miles you've got a perfectly balanced wheel that will remain balanced at any speed.

Wheel truing is a little more difficult and must be done with great patience. A truing stand should be used in conjunction

Truing the wheels with a dial indicator

with a dial indicator or a fixed stylus so the amount of runout can be accurately determined. A spoke nipple wrench, and these are so cheap you really should have one, should be used to protect the nipples and the surface of the rim, but a pair of wrapped-up pliers will do. Work slowly, avoid overtightening the nipples, and always maintain an even tension on the spokes. The job should be done with the tire removed so you can be sure that the spokes will not puncture the tube, but you can get away with doing it with the tire mounted if you're too lazy to do it the right way. The following are some pretty basic procedures. You'll have to supply the patience.

1. Install the wheel in a stand so the hub will turn freely on the axle. Make sure the axle is on a parallel plane with the floor.

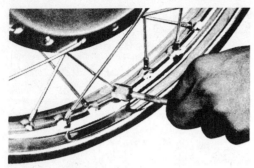

Tightening the spoke nipples

2. Turn each nipple until the spoke threads are just covered. A spoke wrench or pliers should be used but a screwdriver can be used if necessary once the tire and tube have been removed.

3. Working from the valve hole, turn in each nipple three full turns. If the spokes are not taut, turn each nipple one more full turn.

4. Lay a straightedge across the hub and rims on both sides of the wheel to determine if the hub is centered. The object of the following steps is to bring both side measurements into agreement.

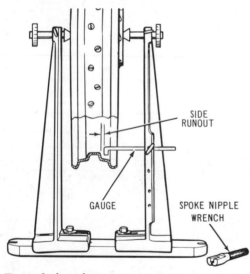

SIDE
RUNOUT

GAUGE   SPOKE NIPPLE
                 WRENCH

Truing for lateral runout

5. Slowly rotate the wheel and set the gauge or stylus to touch the rim at its highest point to correct sideways runout.

6. Loosen the gauge side nipples at their highest point and tighten the opposite nipples an equal amount.

7. Continue to perform the above procedure until the rim passes the gauge at equal distances all around the rim.

8. Correct for excess distance between the rim and gauge by reversing the above procedures until a sideways runout of $\frac{1}{32}$ in. or less is attained.

9. Slowly rotate the wheel and set the gauge to correct for radial runout.

10. Radial runout is corrected by loosening the nipples at those points where the wheel does not run on the gauge and then by tightening the opposite nipples where the rim does run on the gauge.

11. A correctly trued wheel will skim over the gauge with radial variations of $\frac{1}{32}$ in. or less.

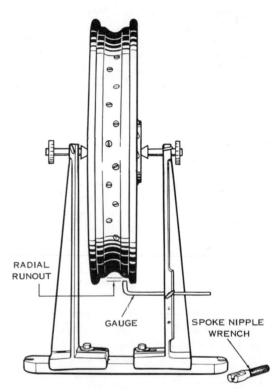

RADIAL
RUNOUT

GAUGE   SPOKE NIPPLE
                 WRENCH

Truing for radial runout

12. Working from the valve hole, tighten the nipples one turn at a time each, all around the rim until the spokes are normally taut. Repeatedly check the rim with a gauge.

13. Seat the spokes into the hub flange by punching them smartly with a flat-nosed punch and hammer.

14. Smooth off the spoke ends at the rim with a file to prevent tube damage.

There isn't too much you can do about straightening rims unless you have the necessary special tools so consult your dealer. As for replacing broken spokes, you shouldn't have any trouble now that you know how to true the wheels so all that remains is the question of bearings.

Check the bearings by grabbing the wheel at points 180° apart along the axle plane and shaking it back and forth. There shouldn't be an appreciable amount of play, but a slight amount is normal. If you have doubts about the bearings, and you should if you've neglected them or sprayed them with a high-powered car wash hose, pull them out. Once again it's nice to have a shop manual around when you're doing this but a little care is probably all you need. Spin the bearings, when lubricated, and check them for rough or erratic motion then replace them as necessary. It's not such a hot idea to reuse dust seals so replace them also.

Installing the bearing retainer on a Triumph 500 rear hub

Chassis Troubleshooting

EXCESSIVE VIBRATION

Possible Causes	Remedy
Loose, broken, or worn motor mounts	Secure, replace, or repair motor mounts
Loose axle nuts	Secure axle nuts
Excessive hub bearing play	Adjust or replace hub bearings
Loose spokes	Secure spokes and true wheel if necessary
Rear wheel out of alignment	Align wheels
Wheel rims out of true or damaged	True or repair wheel rims
Irregular or peaked tire wear	Replace tire and check wheel alignment and trueness
Tires overinflated	Check air pressure with tires cold
Tire and wheel unevenly balanced	Balance wheels
Worn steering head bearings	Adjust or replace bearings as necessary
Worn rear shock bushings or shocks	Replace shocks or bushings as necessary
Swing arm bushings too tight or too loose	Adjust bushings as directed by manufacturer
Excessive front end loading	Remove excessive weight from front end
Cylinder head bracket loose or broken (models on which head and frame are attached)	Secure or repair cylinder head bracket
Broken or bent frame, forks, or swing arm	Repair or replace damaged components
Primary chain badly worn, insufficiently lubricated, or too tight	Replace, lubricate, and/or adjust chain
Incorrectly adjusted ignition timing	Adjust timing to specifications

Chassis Troubleshooting

EXCESSIVE VIBRATION

Possible Causes	Remedy
Incorrectly assembled clutch mechanism	Inspect and repair clutch as necessary
Excessively worn crankshaft	Repair or replace crankshaft assembly

UNCERTAIN OR WOBBLY STEERING

Possible Causes	Remedy
Worn or bad steering head bearings	Adjust or replace bearings
Worn or bad hub bearings	Adjust or replace bearings
Bent forks or swing arm	Repair or replace damaged components
Worn swing arm bushings	Adjust or replace bushings
Bent steering stem or frame neck	Repair or replace damaged components
Wheels improperly aligned	Align wheels
Tires improperly seated on rim	Seat tire so bead is even all around
Tires unevenly worn	Replace tires as necessary
Defective steering damper	Replace as necessary
Loose front wheel	Secure wheel

PULLS TO ONE SIDE

Possible Causes	Remedy
Faulty right or left shock	Replace shocks as a set
Incorrectly adjusted drive chain	Adjust as necessary
Wheels improperly aligned	Align wheels as necessary
Wheels out of true	True wheels as necessary
Incorrectly balanced tires and wheels	Balance wheels as necessary
Defective steering head bearings	Adjust or replace bearings as necessary
Faulty steering head damper	Replace as necessary
Bent or damaged forks, frame, or swing arm	Repair or replace damaged components

HEAVY OR STIFF STEERING

Possible Causes	Remedy
Low front tire pressure	Check tire pressure with tires cold
Bent or damaged steering stem or frame neck	Repair or replace damaged components
Bad steering head bearings and/or races	Replace or adjust bearings as necessary

Chassis Troubleshooting

HEAVY OR STIFF STEERING

Possible Causes	Remedy
Defective steering damper	Replace as necessary
Incorrect damper adjustment	Adjust as necessary

POOR FORK OPERATION

Possible Causes	Remedy
Contaminated fork oil	Drain and replace fork oil
Worn or leaky seals evidenced by dirt or water in the fork oil or by oil on tubes	Replace seals
Weak or damaged fork springs	Replace springs as necessary, preferably as a set
Worn shock absorber assembly (leading link type forks)	Replace as a set as necessary
Worn breather valves	Replace as necessary
Excessive clearance in slider bushings as evidenced by excessive play between the slider and the tube	Replace worn components as necessary
Bent tubes, brackets, dampers, or sliders	Replace damaged components as necessary
Too little fork oil, oil is diluted, or oil is of wrong viscosity	Drain and replace fork oil
Wrong fork springs in use	Replace springs as necessary

STIFF FORK ACTION

Possible Causes	Remedy
Excessive amount of fork oil	Drain and replace fork oil according to specifications
Wrong fork oil viscosity	Drain and replace oil with a lighter grade
Wrong fork springs in use	Replace springs as necessary

WORN REAR SHOCK ABSORBERS

Possible Causes	Remedy
Weak or collapsed springs	Replace springs as a set
Faulty damper unit	Replace shocks as a set
Wrong spring in use	Replace springs as necessary
Shocks adjusted incorrectly	Adjust shocks as necessary

Chassis Troubleshooting

STIFF REAR SHOCK ABSORBERS

Possible Causes	Remedy
Faulty damper valve	Replace shock absorbers as a set
Wrong spring in use	Replace springs as necessary
Shocks incorrectly adjusted	Adjust shocks as necessary

WHEEL ROTATES OUT OF TRUE

Possible Causes	Remedy
Wheel and tire out of balance	Balance wheel as necessary
Excessive hub bearing play	Adjust or replace bearings
Deformed wheel rims	Repair or replace rim as necessary
Loose spokes	Adjust spokes for even tension
Loose swing arm bushings	Adjust as necessary
Drive chain too tight	Adjust chain as necessary
Bent frame or swing arm	Repair or replace damaged components

BRAKES DO NOT HOLD (DRUM BRAKES)

Possible Causes	Remedy
Brake shoes glazed or worn	Repair or replace shoes
Brake shoes oil or grease impregnated	Replace shoes
Brake linings worn away	Replace linings
Brake drum worn or damaged	Replace or have drum turned down
Insufficient hydraulic fluid or air in brake lines	Drain system and refill with fresh fluid, then bleed system
Brake linkage incorrectly adjusted	Adjust linkage as necessary
Brake control cables insufficiently lubricated or binding	Lubricate or replace cable as necessary

BRAKES DRAG (DRUM BRAKES)

Possible Causes	Remedy
Lack of play in the linkage	Adjust linkage as necessary
Weak or damaged return springs	Replace springs as a set
Rusted cam and lever shaft	Replace as necessary

UNADJUSTABLE BRAKES (DRUM BRAKES)

Possible Causes	Remedy
Worn brake shoe linings	Replace shoes or rotate the actuating lever a few degrees on its splined shaft (if applicable)

Chassis Troubleshooting

UNADJUSTABLE BRAKES (DRUM BRAKES)

Possible Causes	Remedy
Worn brake shoe cam	Replace the cam as necessary
Worn or damaged brake drum	Replace the drum or have it turned down

BRAKES MAKE SCRAPING SOUNDS (DRUM BRAKES)

Possible Causes	Remedy
Linings worn down to the rivets	Replace the linings and have the drum turned or replaced as necessary
Broken brake shoe	Replace the shoes and repair or replace the drum as necessary
Dirt in the drum	Blow the assembly out with compressed air and replace or repair the drum as necessary
Scored or out of round brake drum	Repair or replace the drum as necessary
Broken pivot	Replace the pivot

BRAKES SHUDDER (DRUM BRAKES)

Possible Causes	Remedy
Unevenly worn shoes	Replace shoes
Out of round brake drum	Repair or replace drum

EXCESSIVE LEVER TRAVEL WITH A LOSS OF BRAKING POWER (DISC BRAKES)

Possible Causes	Remedy
Air in hydraulic system	Drain and replace fluid, then bleed system
Master cylinder low on fluid	Refill the cylinder and bleed system
Loose lever adjuster bolt	Secure and adjust lever and bolt
Leak in hydraulic system as evidenced by fluid loss	Rebuild system as necessary
Worn disc pads	Replace pads as necessary

BRAKE SQUEAL (DISC BRAKES)

Possible Causes	Remedy
Glazed pads	Clean up or replace pads
Improperly adjusted caliper	Adjust caliper
Extremely dusty brake assembly	Thoroughly blow out assembly

BRAKE SHUDDER (DISC BRAKES)

Possible Causes	Remedy
Warped disc	Replace disc

Chassis Troubleshooting

BRAKE SHUDDER (DISC BRAKES)

Possible Causes	Remedy
Distorted pads	Replace pads
Oil or brake fluid impregnated pads	Replace pads
Loose mounting bolts	Secure assembly

BRAKE PADS REMAIN ON DISC (DISC BRAKES)

Possible Causes	Remedy
Loose adjusting ring	Secure adjusting ring
Piston binding in bore	Rebuild caliper assembly
Relief port blocked by piston in master cylinder	Rebuild caliper assembly

CHAIN WHINE

Possible Causes	Remedy
Chain too tight	Adjust chain correctly
Chain rusted or kinking	Lubricate or replace chain

CHAIN SLAP

Possible Causes	Remedy
Chain too loose	Adjust chain correctly
Bent chain guard	Repair chain guard so chain rotates freely

ACCELERATED CHAIN AND SPROCKET WEAR

Possible Causes	Remedy
Sprockets improperly aligned	Align sprockets
Rear wheel out of alignment	Align wheels
One or both sprockets slightly damaged	Replace sprockets and chain
Chain worn or damaged	Replace chain and sprockets
Chain insufficiently lubricated	Keep chain lubricated thoroughly

Appendix

FRACTIONS TO DECIMALS AND MILLIMETERS

Fractions	Decimals	mm	Fractions	Decimals	mm
1/64	0.015625	0.3969	33/64	0.515625	13.0969
1/32	0.03125	0.7937	17/32	0.53125	13.4937
3/64	0.046875	1.1906	35/64	0.54675	13.8906
1/16	0.0625	1.5875	9/16	0.5625	14.2875
5/64	0.078125	1.9844	37/64	0.578125	14.6844
3/32	0.9375	2.3812	19/32	0.59375	15.0812
7/64	0.109375	2.7781	39/64	0.609375	15.4781
1/8	0.125	3.1750	5/8	0.625	15.8750
9/64	0.140625	3.5719	41/64	0.640625	16.2719
5/32	0.15625	3.9687	21/32	0.65685	16.6687
11/64	0.171875	4.3656	43/64	0.671875	17.0656
3/16	0.1875	4.7625	11/16	0.6375	17.4625
13/64	0.203125	5.1594	45/64	0.703125	17.8594
7/32	0.21875	5.5562	23/32	0.71875	18.2562
15/64	0.234375	5.9531	47/64	0.734375	18.6531
1/4	0.25	6.3500	3/4	0.75	19.0500
17/64	0.265625	6.7469	49/64	0.765625	19.4469
9/32	0.28125	7.1437	25/32	0.78125	19.8437

FRACTIONS TO DECIMALS AND MILLIMETERS

Fractions	Decimals	mm	Fractions	Decimals	mm
19/64	0.296875	7.5406	51/64	0.796875	20.2406
5/16	0.3125	7.9375	13/16	0.8125	20.6375
21/64	0.328125	8.3344	53/64	0.828125	21.0344
11/32	0.34375	8.7312	27/32	0.84375	21.4312
23/64	0.359375	9.1281	55/64	0.859375	21.8281
3/8	0.375	9.5250	7/8	0.875	22.2250
25/64	0.390625	9.9219	57/64	0.890625	22.6219
13/32	0.40625	10.3187	29/32	0.90625	23.0187
27/64	0.421875	10.7156	59/64	0.921875	23.4156
7/16	0.4375	11.1125	15/16	0.9375	23.8125
29/64	0.453125	11.5094	61/64	0.953125	24.2094
15/32	0.46875	11.9062	31/32	0.96875	24.6062
31/64	0.484375	12.3031	63/64	0.984375	25.0031
1/2	0.5	12.7000	1		25.4000

MILLIMETERS TO INCHES

mm	0	10	20	30	40	mm	50	60	70	80	90
0		0.39370	0.78740	1.18110	1.57480	0	1.96851	2.36221	2.75591	3.14961	3.54331
1	0.03937	0.43307	0.82677	1.22047	1.61417	1	2.00788	2.40158	2.79528	3.18891	3.58268
2	0.07874	0.47244	0.86614	1.25984	1.65354	2	2.04725	2.44095	2.83465	3.22835	3.62205
3	0.11811	0.51181	0.90551	1.29921	1.69291	3	2.08662	2.48032	2.87402	3.26772	3.66142
4	0.15748	0.55118	0.94488	1.33858	1.73228	4	2.12599	2.51969	2.91339	3.30709	3.70079
5	0.19685	0.59055	0.98425	1.37795	1.77165	5	2.16536	2.55906	2.95276	3.34646	3.74016
6	0.23622	0.62992	1.02362	1.41732	1.81103	6	2.20473	2.59843	2.99213	3.38583	3.77953
7	0.27559	0.66929	1.06299	1.45669	1.85040	7	2.24410	2.63780	3.03150	3.42520	3.81890
8	0.31496	0.70866	1.10236	1.49606	1.88977	8	2.28347	2.67717	3.07087	3.46457	3.85827
9	0.35433	0.74803	1.14173	1.53543	1.92914	9	2.32284	2.71654	3.11024	3.50394	3.89764

MILLIMETERS TO INCHES—FRACTIONS

1/1000		1/100		1/10	
mm	inches	mm	inches	mm	inches
0.001	0.000039	0.01	0.00039	0.1	0.00394
0.002	0.000079	0.02	0.00079	0.2	0.00787
0.003	0.000118	0.03	0.00118	0.3	0.01181
0.004	0.000157	0.04	0.00157	0.4	0.01575
0.005	0.000197	0.05	0.00197	0.5	0.01969
0.006	0.000236	0.06	0.00236	0.6	0.02362
0.007	0.000276	0.07	0.00276	0.7	0.02756
0.008	0.000315	0.08	0.00315	0.8	0.03150
0.009	0.000354	0.09	0.00354	0.9	0.03543

INCHES TO MILLIMETERS

Inches	0	10	20	30	40
0		254.0	508.0	762.0	1016.0
1	25.4	279.4	533.4	787.4	1041.4
2	50.8	304.8	558.8	812.8	1066.8
3	76.2	330.2	584.2	838.2	1092.2
4	101.6	355.6	609.6	863.6	1117.6
5	127.0	381.0	635.0	839.0	1143.0
6	152.4	406.4	660.4	914.4	1163.4
7	177.3	431.8	685.8	939.8	1193.8
8	203.2	457.2	711.2	965.2	1219.2
9	228.6	482.6	736.6	990.6	1244.6

DECIMALS TO MILLIMETERS—FRACTIONS

1/1000		1/100		1/10	
inches	mm	inches	mm	inches	mm
0.001	0.0254	0.01	0.254	0.1	2.54
0.002	0.0508	0.02	0.508	0.2	5.08
0.003	0.0762	0.03	0.726	0.3	7.62
0.004	0.1016	0.04	1.016	0.4	10.16
0.005	0.1270	0.05	1.270	0.5	12.70
0.006	0.1524	0.06	1.524	0.6	15.24
0.007	0.1778	0.07	1.778	0.7	17.79
0.008	0.2032	0.08	2.032	0.8	20.32
0.009	0.2286	0.09	2.286	0.9	22.86

To change		Multiply	
cc $\longrightarrow$ cu in.	cc $\times$	0.0610	= cubic inches
cc $\longrightarrow$ oz (Imp)	cc $\times$	0.02816	= ounces (Imperial)
cc $\longrightarrow$ oz (U.S.)	cc $\times$	0.03381	= ounces (U.S.)
cu in $\longrightarrow$ cc	cu in. $\times$	16.39	= cubic centimeters
ft-lb $\longrightarrow$ in. lbs	ft-lb $\times$	12	= inch pounds
ft-lb $\longrightarrow$ kg-M	ft-lb $\times$	0.1383	= kilogram-meters
gal (Imp) $\longrightarrow$ liter	Imp gal $\times$	4.546	= liters
gal (U.S.) $\longrightarrow$ liter	U.S. gal $\times$	3.785	= liters
in $\longrightarrow$ mm	in $\times$	25.40	= millimeters
kg $\longrightarrow$ lbs	kg $\times$	2.205	= pounds
kg-M $\longrightarrow$ ft lbs	kg-M $\times$	7.233	= foot-pounds
kg/sq cm $\longrightarrow$ lbs/sq in	kg/sq cm $\times$	14.22	= pounds/square inch
km $\longrightarrow$ mi	km $\times$	0.6214	= miles
lb $\longrightarrow$ kg	lb $\times$	0.4536	= kilograms
lb/sq in $\longrightarrow$ kg/sq cm	lb/sq in. $\times$	0.0703	= kilograms/square centimeter
liter $\longrightarrow$ cc	liter $\times$	1,000	= cc
liter $\longrightarrow$ oz (U.S.)	liter $\times$	33.81	= ounces (U.S.)
liter $\longrightarrow$ qt (Imp)	liter $\times$	0.8799	= quarts (Imperial)
liter $\longrightarrow$ qt (U.S.)	liter $\times$	1.0567	= quarts (U.S.)
mi $\longrightarrow$ km	mi $\times$	1.6093	= kilometers
mm $\longrightarrow$ in	mm $\times$	0.03937	= inches
qt (Imp) $\longrightarrow$ liter	Imp qt $\times$	1.1365	= liters
qt (U.S.) $\longrightarrow$ liter	U.S. qt $\times$	0.9463	= liters

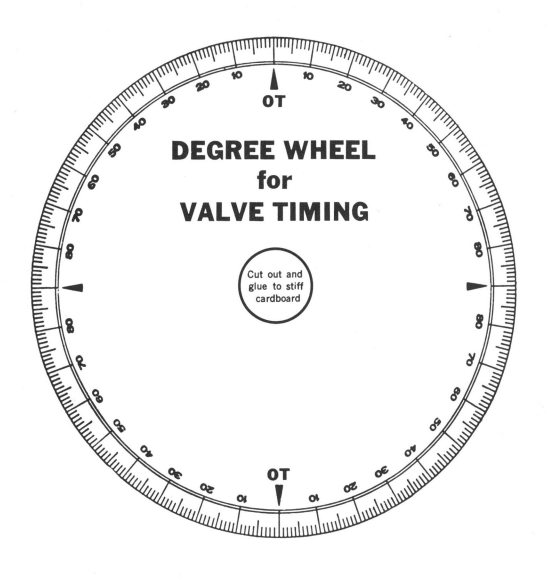

DEGREE WHEEL
for
VALVE TIMING

Cut out and glue to stiff cardboard